British Expeditionary Force - Advance to Victory

British Expeditionary Force - Advance to Victory

July to September 1918

Andrew Rawson

Pen & Sword
MILITARY

AN IMPRINT OF PEN & SWORD BOOKS LTD.
YORKSHIRE – PHILADELPHIA

First published in Great Britain in 2018 by
Pen & Sword Military
An imprint of
Pen & Sword Books Ltd
Yorkshire – Philadelphia

ISBN 978 1 52672 340 6

A CIP catalogue record for this book is
available from the British Library.

Printed and bound in England by TJ International Ltd, Padstow, Cornwall.

Pen & Sword Books Limited incorporates the imprints of Atlas, Archaeology,
Aviation, Discovery, Family History, Fiction, History, Maritime, Military,
Military Classics, Politics, Select, Transport, True Crime, Air World, Frontline
Publishing, Leo Cooper, Remember When, Seaforth Publishing, The Prae-
torian Press, Wharncliffe Local History, Wharncliffe Transport, Wharncliffe
True Crime and White Owl.

For a complete list of Pen & Sword titles please contact

PEN & SWORD BOOKS LIMITED
47 Church Street, Barnsley, South Yorkshire, S70 2AS, England
E-mail: enquiries@pen-and-sword.co.uk
Website: www.pen-and-sword.co.uk

Or
PEN AND SWORD BOOKS
1950 Lawrence Rd, Havertown, PA 19083, USA
E-mail: Uspen-and-sword@casematepublishers.com
Website: www.penandswordbooks.com

Contents

Regiments		vii
Introduction		xi
Chapter 1	A Foot by Foot Defence	1
Chapter 2	Countering Operation Peace Storm	9
Chapter 3	Phantoms of the Imagination	21
Chapter 4	It All Looked a Certain, Confident Success	29
Chapter 5	We have Nearly Reached the Limit of our Powers of Resistance	51
Chapter 6	The Finest Attack in Open Warfare	73
Chapter 7	A Sense we had Reached Success at Last	93
Chapter 8	Keep the Same Attitude and Continue Your Pursuit	115
Chapter 9	Indeed a Magnificent Performance	135
Chapter 10	The Hardest Fighting During the Whole Advance	153
Chapter 11	Germany is Defeated and the Sooner We Recognise it the Better	175
Chapter 12	They Went Over Like a Pack of Hounds	189
Conclusions		195
Index		203

Regiments

Regiments in Alphabetical Order	Abbreviations Used
Argyll & Sutherland Highlanders Regiment	Argylls
Bedfordshire Regiment	Bedfords
Black Watch Regiment	Black Watch
Border Regiment	Borders
Buffs (East Kent) Regiment	Buffs
Cambridgeshire Regiment	Cambridgeshire
Cameron Highlanders Regiment	Camerons
Cameronians (Scottish Rifles) Regiment	Scottish Rifles
Cheshire Regiment	Cheshires
Coldstream Guards	Coldstreamers
Connaught Rangers	Connaughts
Devonshire Regiment	Devons
Dorsetshire Regiment	Dorsets
Duke of Cornwall's Light Infantry	DCLI
Duke of Wellington's (West Riding) Regiment	Duke's
Durham Light Infantry	Durhams
East Lancashire Regiment	East Lancashires
East Surrey Regiment	East Surreys
East Yorkshire Regiment	East Yorkshires
Essex Regiment	Essex
Gloucestershire Regiment	Gloucesters
Gordon Highlanders	Gordons
Green Howards (Yorkshire) Regiment	Green Howards
Grenadier Guards	Grenadiers
Hampshire Regiment	Hampshires
Herefordshire Regiment	Herefords
Hertfordshire Regiment	Hertfords
Highland Light Infantry	HLI
Honourable Artillery Company	HAC
Irish Guards	Irish Guards
King's (Liverpool) Regiment	King's

King's Own (Royal Lancaster) Regiment	King's Own
King's Own Scottish Borderers	KOSBs
King's Own (Yorkshire Light Infantry) Regiment	KOYLIs
King's (Shropshire Light Infantry) Regiment	Shropshires
King's Royal Rifle Corps	KRRC
Lancashire Fusiliers	Lancashire Fusiliers
Leicestershire Regiment	Leicesters
Leinster Regiment	Leinsters
Lincolnshire Regiment	Lincolns
London Regiment	Londoners
Loyal North Lancashire Regiment	Loyals
Manchester Regiment	Manchesters
Middlesex Regiment	Middlesex
Monmouthshire Regiment	Monmouths
Norfolk Regiment	Norfolks
Northamptonshire Regiment	Northants
North Staffordshire Regiment	North Staffords
Northumberland Fusiliers	Northumberland Fusiliers
Oxford and Buckinghamshire Light Infantry	Ox and Bucks
Princess Patricia's Canadian Light Infantry	PPCLI
Queen's (Royal West Surrey) Regiment	Queen's
Queen's Own (Royal West Kent) Regiment	Queen's Own
Rifle Brigade	Rifle Brigade
Royal Berkshire Regiment	Berkshires
Royal Dublin Fusiliers	Dublin Fusiliers
Royal Fusiliers	Royal Fusiliers
Royal Inniskilling Fusiliers	Inniskilling Fusiliers
Royal Irish Fusiliers	Irish Fusiliers
Royal Irish Regiment	Irish Regiment
Royal Irish Rifles	Irish Rifles
Royal Munster Fusiliers	Munsters
Royal Scots Regiment	Royal Scots
Royal Scots Fusiliers	Scots Fusiliers
Royal Sussex Regiment	Sussex
Royal Warwickshire Regiment	Warwicks
Royal Welsh Fusiliers	Welsh Fusiliers
Scots Guards	Scots Guards
Seaforth Highlanders	Seaforths

Sherwood Foresters (Notts and Derbyshire)	Sherwoods
Somerset Light Infantry	Somersets
South Lancashire Regiment	South Lancashires
South Staffordshire Regiment	South Staffords
South Wales Borderers	SWBs or Borderers
Suffolk Regiment	Suffolks
Welsh Regiment	Welsh
Welsh Guards	Welsh Guards
West Yorkshire Regiment	West Yorkshires
Wiltshire Regiment	Wiltshires
Worcestershire Regiment	Worcesters
York and Lancaster Regiment	York and Lancasters

Introduction

This is the penultimate book in my ten part series on the Western Front in the Great War. It covers the first three months (July to September) of the British Expeditionary Force's offensives in the summer of 1918. It starts with the small engagements by British and Australian troops before moving onto the part that four divisions played, the counter-offensive on the Marne during the second half of July. It covers Fourth Army's offensive astride the Somme, starting on 8 August, and then Third Army's follow-up attack, starting on 21 August, between Arras and Albert. The story explains the great advances made across the 1916 Somme battlefield, covering many actions, including the fight for Bapaume, the capture of Mont St Quentin and the breaking of the Drocourt–Quéant Line. It ends on 11 September, as both Third Army and Fourth Army prepared to clear the maze of trenches in front of the Hindenburg Line. The fight for the three old British trenches and the three German trenches merged into one battle which lasted three long weeks in September. I have decided to keep this series of connected engagements together in the next volume.

The backbone of the story comes from the two relevant volumes of the Official History of the Great War. Part one was published in 1939 (just before the Second World War broke out) and it covers the June and July battles, particularly the Allied counter-offensive on the Marne. Brigadier General James Edmonds soon completed the transcript covering the fighting from 8 August into September but paper shortage caused by the war meant that it was 1947 before it could be published. The Committee of Imperial Defence probably felt it had little to learn from the Great War after the huge advances in military tactics and hardware made by 1945.

Record-keeping during these battles was more-or-less complete but Edmond had little incentive to create a detailed account, resulting in a bland account of what was a successful time for the BEF. New combined tactics proved to be successful but the huge numbers of men and material captured were offset by the huge numbers of casualties. Fighting almost continuously along a 40-mile front was a costly business in lives.

Most of the details were discovered in the dozens of divisional and regimental histories published in the interwar years. The standard of these books varies tremendously, and while some draw heavily from the unit war diaries, others give the minimum of information. But they all give far more information than the Official History. Units can be relied on to spell out their successes while blaming others for their failures but they all focus on the brave deeds of the members of their unit.

Many of these divisional and regimental histories can be accessed for a small fee at the militaryarchive.co.uk. You are also able to look at medal rolls, army orders and army lists to locate biographical information, awards and photographs of individuals. Joining the archive has given me annual access to these resources for the same cost as a day in the London archives.

Some information comes from the WO95 series of war diaries held by the National Archives at Kew. They are the original source material of a unit's battle experiences; however, the information about the summer offensives is often sketchy because of the fast-moving nature of the fighting. Some battalion records were destroyed or lost while material was sometimes removed or misplaced after the war. The war diaries can be accessed through ancestry.co.uk and similar websites, again for a reasonable fee.

As with all the volumes in this series, I have had to estimate how much detail to include. There is little to learn if the information is too superficial but the story can become overpowering if there is too much detail. This is not an exhaustive narrative of the Allied attacks on the Marne and across the Somme but it is a comprehensive explanation of the BEF's experiences between June and mid–September 1918.

A detailed account would be twice as long while an exhaustive account would be even longer. The emphasis of the story is (as in all the series) on the experiences of the British and Empire soldiers. There is little information on the liaison between the War Cabinet, the Chief of the Imperial General Staff, the BEF's General Headquarters and the French Grand Quartier Général (GQG). The same applies to the relevant Supreme War Council conference, while meetings between British and French politicians and generals are referred to in brief. There is discussion on the British tactics and the German reaction to them but the detail about German units rarely goes below army level.

Few details of casualties are discussed unless they were exceptionally high or unusual. Casualties were sometimes high in the fast-moving battles and both sides suffered; thousands of prisoners were taken too. This is a time when advances often topped 1 mile in a day and even as far as 8 miles on 8 August, a remarkable achievement considering the style of warfare we usually associate with the Great War. I have chosen quotes which reflect the men's pride in their fighting abilities and their achievements during these often exhilarating days for the BEF. Sometimes their dark humour perfectly proves a point.

So what will you find in the book? The BEF's planning for the attacks is covered, as well as the recovery of the BEF after the German spring offensives. The day by day attacks by each corps are discussed, along with the reasoning behind the accomplishments and occasional failures. Often the men who led the attacks or who stopped the counter-attacks are given a mention; so are all the men who were awarded the Victoria Cross.

The British and Empire soldiers faced many tactical problems during the offensive battles in the open. A large number were young replacements for the casualties suffered during the spring battles and they were in their first battle. But time and again they fought with tanks, machine guns and mortars until their ammunition ran low and then they regrouped to fight another day.

The well-used saying is 'a picture is worth a thousand words' and I believe the same applies to battle maps. I believe many books on the Great War use too few maps, and those they have are of too small a scale to complement the narrative. I think the Official Histories suffer from this problem, as paper shortages reduced the maps to small inserts at the back of the books. I believe this approach is wrong, so sixty tactical maps are included to help the reader understand the campaign. Typically there is one for each corps covering each stage of the battle and 1:40,000 maps (the sort used by the artillery) have been used because the advances made in the summer of 1918 were so long. Plenty of detailed maps has been a feature of the all the books in this series.

My inspiration for this series was Noah Trudeau's A Testing of Courage, which covers the 1863 battle of Gettysburg during the American Civil War. Several books on this three-day engagement had left me confused, but the many maps in Trudeau's book prepared me for a visit to the battlefield. It has been my ambition to do the same for the Western Front.

Even the soldiers complained the Marne maps provided by the French were too large scale, so I have prepared skeleton maps detailing the July battles. But the terrain across the Somme has changed little so the enclosed maps can be used to help visitors.

The symbols indicating movements have been kept the same on all the maps. The front lines at the beginning of the day are marked by solid lines, while ground captured is marked by a line of dots. Rivers are marked by dashed lines and army and corps boundaries are marked by a line of dashes and dots.

Each division is marked with its number, but brigades and battalions moved so quickly that it would be impossible to chart their progress without obscuring the topographical information. It is relatively easy to estimate their movements by checking the text and the maps.

I have also bucked the army convention of describing events from right to left. We read text and look at maps from left to right, so I have written the narrative the same way. This does mean that it follows the action from the north to south, the BEF's left to its right. Occasionally the sequence of events dictates it is best to describe events another way.

I first visited the Somme area in detail in the early 1990s when few took interest in the 1916 campaign and even fewer took notice of the 1918 battle. Sadly, few still do cross the Somme to look at the successful campaign in August 1918. The visitor's book which celebrates the 8 mile advance by the Canadian Corps on 8 August has been at the Le Quesnel memorial for ten years!

My twenty-year interest in the Somme mirrors my friendship with Professor John Bourne, who has guided me through my long research and writing career. Yet again he has given me advice while his extensive knowledge of the generals of the BEF has been particularly useful.

I have enjoyed writing about the battles which included the 'black day for the German Army'. It has increased my understanding about how the British and Empire soldiers struck back after the ordeal of the spring battles. I hope you enjoy reading about their brave deeds as much as I have writing about them.

I stayed at No 56 Bed and Breakfast in La Boisselle while covering the Somme offensive. David and Julie Thomson have looked after me many times at their 'Oasis on the Somme' during my research trips. They even drove me around the Somme area as they shared my exploration of the August and September 1918 battlefield.

I dedicate this book to my great-uncle, Private Farewell Lomas, 47995, 8th West Yorkshire Regiment. He died of wounds on 19 July 1918, at the very beginning of the Advance to Victory, which started in the Aisne region.

Chapter 1

A Foot by Foot Defence

June and early July 1918

After surviving the huge offensives of March and April, the BEF had time to recuperate while the Germans turned their attentions to the French. The front between Ypres and Amiens remained quiet during the offensive on the Aisne at the end of May but several British divisions were caught up in the fighting. The same applied during the attack against the French along the River Matz at the beginning of June.

Time and again the Germans had used short, sharp bombardments to neutralise the French troops, before their *stosstruppen* broke into the defences, but each time the momentum of the offensive waned due to logistic problems after only a few days, often in the face of heroic defences and rapid withdrawals. The relative calm along the BEF's front throughout May and June allowed it to rebuild its weary divisions. The replacements Field Marshal Sir Douglas Haig had been asking for since the beginning of the year arrived, and while many were teenagers, there was time to let them settle into their routines. The Tommies were also pleased to see American troops training in their rear areas. Great Britain's armaments factories were churning out artillery pieces and ammunition but the time was not yet ripe for a counter-offensive on the British front.

Intelligence sources reported plenty of divisions opposite the BEF and Haig believed the German Supreme Army Command (Oberste Heeresleitung or OHL) still wanted to capture the rail centre of Hazebrouck, to destabilise the Flanders front. Crown Prince Rupprecht was preparing such an offensive, codenamed Operation Hagen, but Field Marshal Paul von Hindenburg and General Erich Ludendorff first wanted to drive the French back to the River Marne. That would pull French reserves south and then they could drive the BEF back to the Channel ports.

XI Corps, La Becque in Flanders, 28 June

Even a small advance on First Army's front could bring the German heavy guns in range of Hazebrouck, so General Sir Henry Horne told Lieutenant

General Sir Richard Haking to push his front line away from the Nieppe Forest. Operation Borderland was set for 6 am on 28 June and there would be no bombardment along XI Corp' front.

On 31st Division's front, the 18th Durhams advanced a short distance along the Rue du Bois as Lieutenant Colonel Nutt's 15/17th West Yorkshires captured La Becque Farm, close to Vieux Berquin. Some 93 Brigade men, including veteran Major Traill of the 10th East Yorkshires, were hit by their own creeping barrage as they advanced through waist-high corn. But the 11th East Yorkshires, 11th East Lancashires and the 10th East Yorkshires

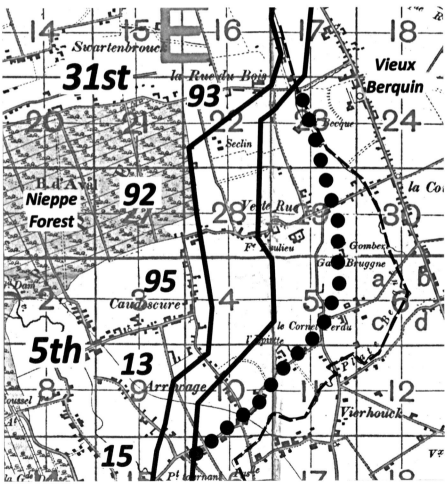

31st and 5th Divisions both pushed the Germans away from the Nieppe Forest on 28 June.

found the Germans had 'stood down when daylight came, as was proved by the boots and sets of equipment which were found in every deserted bivouac'.

On 5th Division's front, Major General Reginald Stephens' 'men displayed the greatest eagerness to get to grips with the enemy' and they were in their trenches the moment the barrage lifted. The 12th Gloucesters captured Le Cornet Perdu while the 1st DCLI got close to the Plate Becque. The 2nd KOSBs suffered casualties clearing the wire around Itchin Farm but 1st Queen's Own had more luck around Boar Farm; the 15th Warwicks advanced along the east bank of the Bourre stream.

The front around the Nieppe forest had been made safe but, while 450 prisoners had been taken, it had cost over 1,900 casualties. It was, however, the first successful British offensive operation of the year and the 'congratulations poured in'.

The Australian Corps, Le Hamel on the Somme, 4 July

General Sir Henry Rawlinson wanted to capture a limited area around Le Hamel, between the River Somme and Villers Bretonneux. He chose 4 July, American Independence Day, because four companies of the 33rd American Division were going to be engaged for the first time on the BEF's front. Australian 'Peaceful Penetration' tactics had discovered that Le Hamel village and the nearby woods were fortified but there were few trenches in between.

Major General Ewen Sinclair-Maclagan was given sixty fighting tanks and twelve supply tanks and Brigadier General Courage's machines would carry the same amount of ammunition and engineer stores that 1,250 men could. Some of Lieutenant Colonel Bingham's Mark IV and Mark V tanks would cut the wire, while the rest cooperated with the infantry. Lieutenant General John Monash's plan was to send patrols through the woods and the village while tanks and machine-gun teams covered the flanks. The rest of the troops would advance past and fan out on the far side.

Batteries took five nights to move into position while the guns either side drew the enemy's attention. Over 625 artillery pieces and nearly 150 machine guns were assembled and targets were registered during the daily bombardments, so the Germans did not notice them. The infantry started moving into the battle zone only two nights before zero hour.

Two RAF squadrons would fly overhead looking for enemy positions for the troops on the ground. One squadron would attempt air supply, dropping ammunition boxes at prearranged points or when a machine-gun team requested them.

Artillery fired a creeping barrage mixed with smoke in front of 5th Australian Division, on the north bank of the River Somme, to draw attention away from Le Hamel. Major General Sir Talbot Hobbs' 15 Brigade was then able to capture the German trenches around Sailly-Laurette.

Opposite Le Hamel, the infantry 'were lined up with bayonets fixed; we all felt nervous but we took our places, lay down and soon forgot we were to go over the top. We were soon asleep.' As zero hour approached, the tanks coasted towards 4th Australian Division's front line as planes flew low overhead, drowning out the engine noise. Then the artillery opened fire at

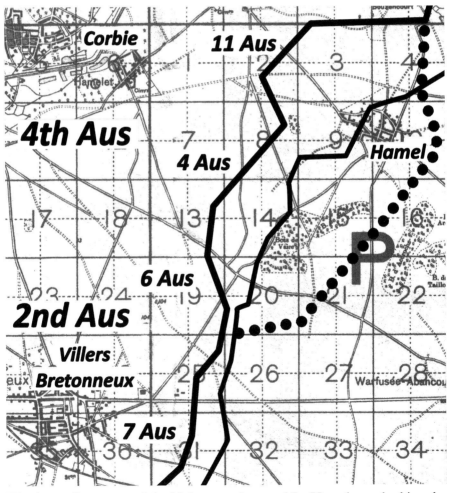

The Australians secured the high ground around Le Hamel, overlooking the Somme on 4 July.

eight minutes before zero so the Germans did not hear the tanks crawling across no man's land.

Monash was confident everything had been thought out and he believed 'the only answer the enemy can make to this plan is to discover it and put down a bombardment.' Every gun fired at zero hour and four waves of infantry advanced as 'the last tank arrived dead on time, roaring like a hundred aeroplanes.' A few of the guns fired short, hitting the advancing troops, but the general opinion was that the barrage was 'glorious'.

Zero had been set for 3.10 am, when it was light enough to identify a uniform at 20 yards, while enough smoke was fired to fool the enemy into putting their gas masks on. However, the dust kicked up by the bombardment meant the infantry and tank crews struggled to keep direction.

Six tanks moved between the enemy machine-gun posts as Lieutenant Colonel Bingham's 42nd Battalion advanced north of Le Hamel. Another six stopped on the trench covering the village, to fire lengthways along it, 'crushing all the spirit that the enemy may have had to fight'. The garrison were trapped in their dugouts as 43rd Battalion passed through the ruins, while twelve tanks escorted 44th Battalion onto the high ground to the east.

A dozen tanks climbed the slope south of Le Hamel but machine-gun fire raked 15th Battalion as Lewis gunners returned fire from the hip. Lieutenant Colonel McSharry's men then cleared the Pear and Vaire Trench. A wounded Private Harry Dalziel shot one team with his pistol and then fired a Lewis gun until he was wounded a second time; he was awarded the Victoria Cross.

Captain Wood was mortally wounded leading 16th Battalion's advance, but Lance Corporal Jack Axford cleared Kidney Trench, throwing the German machine guns over the parapet. The rest of Lieutenant Colonel Drake-Brockman's men then cleared Vaire Wood as six tanks crawled along the central ride. Axford would be awarded the Victoria Cross.

The 13th Battalion bypassed the south side of Vaire Wood before spreading out on the far side, where they took eighty prisoners around one strongpoint. On the right flank, six tanks helped 23rd and 21st Australian Battalions form a flank south of Vaire Wood for 6 Australian Brigade. All along the line the tanks waited until the Australians had consolidated their objective before withdrawing. Only five had been hit and they were all salvaged and repaired. There had been less than 900 Australian and American casualties while over 1,450 prisoners had been taken. Rawlinson wanted to make another attack but Haig refused because he did not want to lengthen Fourth Army's front while the BEF was still short of reserves.

XV Corps, Meteren in Flanders, 19 July

Major General Hugh Tudor's 9th Division had been decimated during the two German spring offensives. He had welcomed many young conscripts but there was little time to train them in before they entered the trenches on 26 May. Lieutenant General Sir Beaurevoir de Lisle wanted Tudor to take the Meteren ridge, to get a good view over the Lys plain. So the artillery

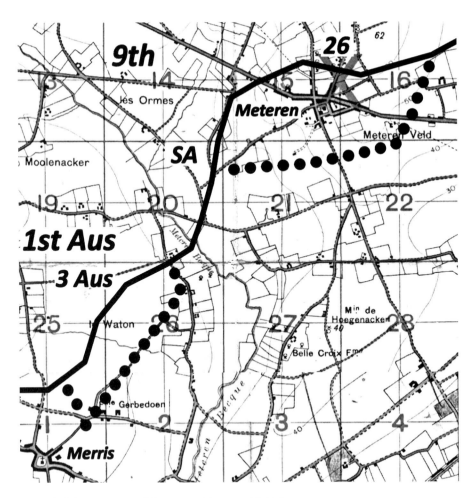

9th Division capture Meteren ridge on 19 July.

targeted Meteren village for two weeks, often using a mixture of smoke and gas shells to trick the Germans into putting their gas masks on every time the guns opened fire.

Shells crashed down at 7.54 am on 18 July and the infantry advanced one minute later. Wind scattered the smoke but 400 barrels of burning oil exploded across the German trench south of Meteren three minutes later. Over 250 of the 8th Black Watch were hit trying to cut through the wire on the left flank, but the 5th Camerons, the 2nd Scots Fusiliers and a composite South African battalion had more luck. The objective was taken in less than an hour and the 350 Germans prisoners were wearing their gas masks when they were taken, making it difficult for them to fight. A company of 9th Australian Battalion had also surprised the garrison of Gerbedoen Farm on the right flank.

Where Would the Next German Attack Fall?

On 1 July Généralissime Ferdinand Foch circulated his ideas on what the Germans might do next. An attack astride the Somme could separate the British and French armies, while an advance beyond the Marne would threaten Paris. Foch wanted Field Marshal Haig and General Philippe Pétain to plan 'a foot by foot defence' while they assembled their reserves.

The Supreme War Council met again in Versailles the following day and the prime ministers of Australia, New Zealand, Canada and Newfoundland attended for the first time. There were discussions about sending troops to Russia and Siberia and talks about the Balkan situation. The transport of American troops across the Atlantic was looked at while the role of the Military Representatives was agreed. The Council did not speak about the Western Front during their three-day meeting.

The BEF's army commanders did when they held their monthly meeting on 5 July. Haig wanted Second Army to stay on the defensive in Flanders while Third Army and Fourth Army were to prepare an offensive across the Somme. Intelligence sources highlighted the Marne threat but there was evidence of a possible attack towards Hazebrouck. Both areas concerned Foch but Haig thought the Marne threat was a diversion. He was right. Ludendorff wanted to draw French reserves south, so the main thrust could be made towards the Channel ports.

Foch and Pétain met Haig's Chief of the General Staff, Lieutenant General Sir Herbert Lawrence, while he was on leave. He agreed to move two divisions south of the Somme while promising to plan an attack north of Béthune, to reduce the threat to the surrounding coalfields. Foch was planning his own attack across the River Aisne and he later increased his request to four divisions. Haig was against the idea and General Jan Smuts found him in a pessimistic mood, saying, 'the War Cabinet and the Generalissimo would take the credit if things went well; if ill, he himself would be the scapegoat.' The extra divisions were sent south, leaving the BEF dangerously short of reserves.

The speculation ended early on 15 July, when four German armies attacked either side of Reims; it was the start of Operation Peace Storm. So while Foch faced a fight to defend Paris, Haig still worried about a new offensive in Flanders.

Chapter 2

Countering Operation Peace Storm

15 July to 6 August

General Philippe Pétain wanted to use new defensive tactics for what would turn out to be the last German offensive of the war. Outposts would disrupt the attack through the First Position and Intermediate Position as the German artillery wasted its ammunition on the lightly manned positions. Unfortunately, Fourth Army did not have enough troops to hold the Second Position in strength, so General Henri Gourard had to concentrate his troops in the Intermediate Position. Meanwhile, General Henri Berthelot's Fifth Army had not completed the required fortifications to the west of Reims.

Pétain's main advantage was that prisoners and deserters had given the time and date of the attack as well as details of the bombardment. They even gave away the codename: Operation Peace Storm (Friedensturm). Aerial observers had also seen columns of troops and transport heading for the front. The French guns opened fire early on 15 July, hitting the enemy infantry and artillery before zero hour, disrupting First German Army's and Third German Army's attack against the Fourth French Army east of Reims. However, Seventh German Army pushed through the Fifth French Army's weak defences west of Reims and even crossed the River Marne across a 15 mile front around Dormans.

Pétain asked permission to call off the attack planned for 18 July but experience made Foch believe that the Germans would be vulnerable after seventy-two hours on the offensive. His hunch was correct and Operation Peace Storm had run out of steam by the time the Allies attacked the flanks of the Marne salient.

Lieutenant General Sir Alexander Godley was concentrating his four divisions in the French Fourth Army's area on 16 July while Foch issued orders to counter-attack the Marne salient. General Pétain directed 15th and 34th Divisions to the French Third Army, west of the salient. He also sent 51st and 62nd Divisions to the French Fifth Army, to the east. The following day Lieutenant General Herbert Lawrence asked Foch to return the four divisions as soon as possible because he was sure the Germans were about to attack the British in Flanders. But they had hard fighting ahead of them first.

The German attack had stalled by 17 July and the French artillery and air force were hitting the bridges over the Marne. General Max von Boehn wanted to withdraw Seventh Army from the vulnerable bridgehead, and while Ludendorff agreed in principle, he did not issue an order. Instead the decision was made when Pétain launched his counter-attack the following day.

General Charles Mangin's Tenth Army attacked the west side of the salient while General Jean Degoutte's Sixth Army struck the German positions on the west bank of the Marne. Nine American Divisions (nearly 300,000 men) and nearly 500 tanks supported the advance. The plan was for Ninth Army to follow up on the east bank of the Marne while the Fifth and Fourth Armies went on the offensive either side of Reims. However, General Henri Berthelot asked for help because he thought the Italian Corps under his command was too weak to make Fifth Army's attack south-west of the city.

Tenth Army and part of Sixth Army advanced another couple of miles towards Buzancy and Oulchy-le-Château on 19 July but Fifth Army was struggling. Lieutenant General Godley was told to move XXII Corps to the area, to stop the Germans shifting their reserves around the salient. Both 51st and 62nd Divisions made a long march to join Fifth Army, ready to advance through the Italian line early on 20 July. Meanwhile, Ninth Army was still waiting for two battalions of light tanks to help it, unaware the Germans were evacuating the Marne bridgehead.

Pétain's plan came to fruition on 20 July with attacks all around the Marne Salient. Tenth Army and Sixth Army made little progress but they had captured over 15,000 men and 400 guns over the past three days. Ninth Army reached the Marne in the centre but Fifth Army faced a tough battle on the east side of the salient.

The failure of Operation Peace Storm had been a severe blow for Ludendorff because he had told the German Foreign Secretary, Admiral Paul von Hintze, that it would 'finally and decisively conquer the enemy'. Instead it was time to tell Crown Prince Rupprecht to call off Operation Hagen in Flanders and instead expect an Allied offensive.

The Eastern Counter-Offensive, 20 to 30 July

Lieutenant General Godley's men faced a nightmare journey through the woods. 'Thick blackness was everywhere excepting a faint illumination showing where the tops of the trees were. On and on we stumbled in single file, colliding with trees and our neighbours while plunging into deep holes full of sticky mud.' No one could understand their Italian guides, and then high explosive and gas shells started exploding in the tree tops (one fatality was my great uncle, Private Farwell Lomas of the 8th West Yorkshires).

There was insufficient time to organise a barrage with the French gunners, so they were told to fire 1,000 yards ahead of the start line, missing many enemy machine-gun posts. The lines of men moved off at 8 am but they faced a daunting advance astride the Ardre stream, where waist-high crops covered the valley floor and woods covered the ridges. To make matters worse, the shells were armed with sensitive fuses and many exploded prematurely in the tree tops.

51st Division, 20 to 30 July, Bois de Courton to Mont de Bligny

Major General George Carter-Campbell's men found the Germans waiting south of the Ardre stream. Lieutenant Colonel M'Corquodale's 1/6th Black Watch cleared the outpost line in Bois de Courton and reached Bois d'Eclisse. The 1/7th Gordons and 1/7th Black Watch were ambushed several times in the 'desperate, tangled undergrowth' en route to Espilly and they were being driven back until Lieutenant Colonel Miller organised a line through the trees.

The 1/4th Seaforths became disorientated in Bois de Courton, mistook Marfaux for Chaumuzy, and were pinned down as they realigned themselves with the Ardre stream. The barrage was lost and Lieutenant Colonel Bickore was mortally wounded as he led the 1/4th Gordons into crossfire from the farms and woods. Brigadier General Buchanan eventually sent the 1/7th Argylls forward to secure the line south of the Ardre and they stopped a counter-attack.

Major General Carter-Campbell was told to attack at 8 am, to cooperate with the French on the left but it left little time to issue orders. The jumping off line turned out to be behind the German machine-gun teams waiting in in Bois de Courton and the 1/6th Gordons 'met with the stoutest opposition from the outset, a storm of bullets greeting them as soon as their advance began'. The French failed to advance, so the 7th Black Watch had to form a defensive flank while the 1/5th Seaforths and 152 Brigade eventually had to shore up the line.

Attempts to 'dribble forward by individual rushes' by the 7th and 6th Black Watch late on 23 July failed to clear Bois de Courton. The supporting barrage fell amongst the 7th Argylls and 4th Gordons the following morning

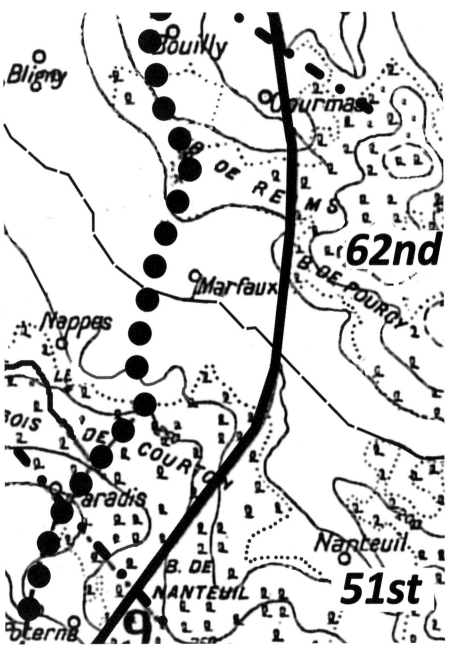

The counter-attack against the east side of the Marne salient between 20 and 23 July.

while the 5th and 6th Seaforths struggled to make progress. Early on 27 July the 6th Black Watch and the 7th Gordons found that Bois de Courton and Bois d'Eclisse had been abandoned while the 5th Seaforths discovered the Germans had abandoned the Chaumuzy area. The corps cavalry were sent forward and they found the new enemy position on Mont de Bligny.

On 28 July, the 1/6th Black Watch entered Chambrecy while the 1/7th Gordons climbed to the top of Mont de Bligny. A counter-attack failed to recapture the summit from the 7th Argylls on the 30 July and 51st Division was able to hand over the hill to the French the following day.

62nd Division, 20 to 28 July, Bois de Reims to Mont de Bligny

Both Major Stewart's 2/5th West Yorkshires and Lieutenant Colonel England's 8th West Yorkshires came under crossfire from the villages along the Ardre and the woods to their right. They 'faced an invisible foe' and hardly 'ever caught sight of the Boche'. The same fate awaited Lieutenant Colonel Bastow's 1/5th Devons and Brigadier General Viscount Hampden soon heard that the survivors were crawling back across the corn fields.

Lieutenant Colonel Peter's 5th KOYLIs struggled to advance through the Bois de Reims, and while the 2/4th York and Lancasters captured Courmas, Lieutenant Colonel Hart's men could not hold on to Commétreuil Chateau or Bouilly despite help from Lieutenant Colonel Chaytor's 2/4th KOYLIs.

Major General Braithwaite's orders to attack arrived late, so his men were not ready to advance until only a few minutes before zero hour. Crossfire from Marfaux and the Bois de Reims then stopped 186 Brigade's patrols advancing up the Ardre valley while the 9th Durhams had been given the wrong start line. They ran out of Bois de Reims to catch the barrage up, only to be met by 'a perfect inferno of fire' from 'hundreds of machine guns'. The 2/4th York and Lancasters again failed to take Commétreuil Chateau on the right flank.

At 12.15 pm 22 July, Lieutenant Colonel Walker's 5th Duke's advanced along the edges of Bois de Reims in a move which was 'probably unequalled for sheer excitement and deadly danger'. The artillery hit the centre of the wood as the two columns formed cordons which shot into the trees. But a counter-attack drove Captain Cockhill's column back from Bouilly while Second Lieutenant Storrey's men were captured en route to Bligny. Brigadier General Hampden had to send the 5th Devons forward to stabilise the line and they took 200 prisoners.

On 24 July the New Zealand cyclists and 9th Durhams cleared Marfaux and Cuitron while French tanks helped the 8th West Yorkshires take 200 prisoners and a dozen French guns in Bois du Petit Champ. After two quiet days, 187 Brigade advanced south of the Ardre while 186 Brigade held a flank north of the stream. Then the 2/4th KOYLIs, 2/4th York and Lancasters and 5th KOYLIs discovered that the Germans had withdrawn from Bois de Courton during the night. Only one prisoner was taken and he had been left behind to report the progress of the Yorkshiremen by telephone.

Early on 28 July the 5th Devons and 8th West Yorkshires moved quietly up the slopes of Mont de Bligny until the 'silent hillside suddenly became like a sheet of flame', but Captain Muller's men still cleared the summit. Lieutenant Colonel Brook's 2/4th Hampshire and Lieutenant Colonel Wilson's 2/4th Duke's advanced in section rushes through the cornfields north of the Ardre to take Bligny. The Yorkshiremen were 'suffering from extreme exhaustion' after nine days of fighting but an attack by the 2/5th West Yorkshires finally drove the Germans from the west side of Mont de Bligny.

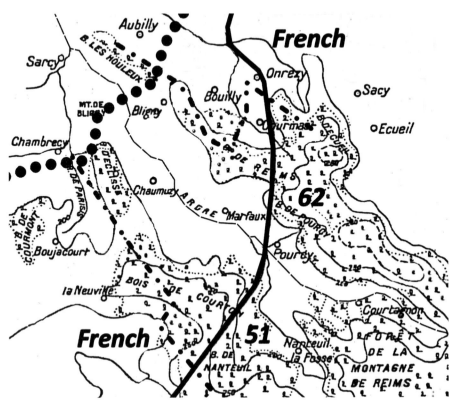

The counter-attack astride the River Ardre continued until 31 July.

The Western Counter-Offensive

The Crown Prince had asked to hold a shorter line between Reims and Soissons on 21 July, and while Ludendorff agreed he could withdraw his centre behind the Ourcq stream, he had to hold his flanks. Pétain believed 'an opportunity to obtain important results had arisen; it must not be allowed to escape. Let every man put his heart into it.' However, Tenth Army's left had been unable to advance south of Soissons while its right made a little progress towards Buzancy. General Mangin decided to force the issue by deploying the British 15th and 34th Divisions.

15th Division, 23 to 28 July, Buzancy

Major General Hamilton Reed, VC (awarded during the Boer war), took over the line opposite Buzancy from the French, but his officers were given small-scale maps making it difficult to find where they were supposed to deploy. The Scots had extra support from American guns but the poor maps meant their creeping barrage fell beyond the many machine-gun teams hiding in the long grass.

At 4.55 am on 23 July the advance was 'met by a withering machine-gun fire and at the same time the supports in the wood behind were hotly shelled.' The 10th Scottish Rifles formed a defensive flank but Lieutenant Colonel Hart was wounded as the 7th/8th KOSBs were cut down as they tried to reach the Crise stream. They reported 'no artillery support, being held up by machine-gun fire; casualties heavy.' Meanwhile, the 6th Camerons captured and then lost a sugar factory on the right.

The reliefs were delayed and movement around the front line attracted the attention of the enemy artillery; it was made worse by the fact that the Highlanders had no trenches to shelter in. For a second time, the American gunners overshot many of the German machine-gun teams.

The plan was for 44 Brigade to attack at 12.30 pm on 28 July, in the hope of catching the Germans resting after lunch. A two-minute barrage heralded the assault and the 1/5th Gordons advanced on the left flank while engineers accompanied the 8th Seaforths into Buzancy, armed with flamethrowers and explosive charges. A company of the 4/5th Black Watch captured one hundred prisoners around the chateau but the French had been unable to advance on the right. Lieutenant Colonel Bulloch sent Captain Murray's company forward to form a flank but a counter-attack drove the Scots back in 'a heart breaking failure'. Reed's men had been in many battles but the fight for Buzancy was considered to be 'the severest and most gruelling of them all'.

34th Division, 23 July, Hartennes

Major General Lothian Nicholson's command had been decimated during the German offensives on the Somme and along the Lys. The survivors spent May training American troops and then welcomed hundreds of young conscripts in June. They only had a month to train them before the rebuilt division faced its first battle. It took over the line facing Hartennes late on 22 July to find the trenches were shallow ditches while they had no idea where the enemy was. Despite the problems, the hope was that even a small attack would make the Germans retire again.

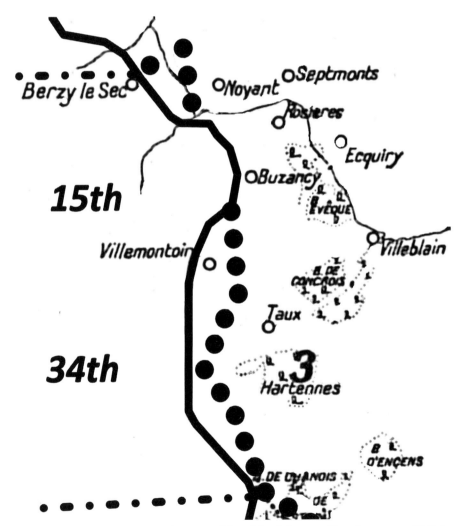

The counter-attack against the west side of the Marne salient began on 23 July.

Early rumours reported that the French were advancing on the flanks, so Nicholson warned his brigadiers to be ready to move and promised that fifty French tanks were heading their way. Unfortunately, no one saw the signal flares, the telephone lines had been cut and all the runners were hit. The first the assault troops knew the attack was underway was when the artillery opened fire.

Brigadier General Hilliam's men 'advanced through high standing corn' on time but the 1/1st Hertfords and 1/7th Cheshire could not enter Bois de Reugny. Brigadier General Woodcock's men advanced late and machine-gun fire ripped through the corn, pinning down the 2/4th Queen's while a counter-attack drove the 2nd Loyals back.

During the day Foch told Pétain to keep pushing because he wanted to threaten the west side of the Marne salient. But the Germans decided the issue when they withdrew during the night without being seen.

The division was called upon to attack a second time north of Grand Rozoy. It meant that Major General Nicholson's men had a long march of up to 10 miles during the night of 27/28 July. But the French failure to capture Butte de Chalmont on 28 July meant zero hour was put back to 4.10 am on 29 July. The advance began well behind 'a heavy rolling barrage in dense fog' and the French cleared Grand Rozoy on the left flank as the 2/4th Queen's reached the Courdoux road. The 4th Sussex advanced towards the crest of Hill 158 but Lieutenant Colonel Jourdain was killed as the 2nd Loyals consolidated the position. The 1/5th KOSBs were able to advance north-west of Beugneux while the 1/8th Scottish Rifles reached the foot of Hill 158.

The French gunners cheered as 18-pounders and 4.5-inch howitzers cantered forward during the planned halt, but poor communications with the heavy artillery meant there was insufficient support for the second part of the advance. The pause also gave the Germans time to counter 103 and 101 Brigades' advance beyond Beugneux. Brigadier General Chaplin asked for help after sending the 5th Argylls forward to reinforce the line against a counter-attack.

Major General Nicholson was anxious to take Hill 158 and Beugneux but neither two battalions of 102 Brigade nor the 2/4th Somersets (Pioneers) could stop a larger counter-attack which drove both the French and 34th Division back towards their start line.

The Marne Counter-Offensive Ends

Pétain had hoped for more progress on the flanks of the salient but he was pleased by the follow-up in the centre. He insisted on keeping up the pressure, to disrupt the German withdrawal to the River Vesle because he wanted to reopen the Marne railway soon as possible. But the French had been engaged for two weeks and Pétain complained he did not have 'a single fresh division in his precautionary reserve' and there were hardly any replacements left to make up the shortfall of 120,000 men. While he was concerned his armies were 'at the limit of our effort', so was Ludendorff. The next push on 1 August caught the Germans off their guard, as they prepared to withdraw again. This time their west sector would pull back behind the Aisne while the centre and east flank retired behind the Vesle.

34th Division, 1 August, Beugneux

Major General Nicholson's division was still opposite Beugneux and the plan was to repeat the same attack which had failed on 29 July. Smoke and mist left the officers relying on their compasses to guide the 4th Sussex and 2/4th Queen's past Grand Rozoy. The French were lagging behind on the left, so Brigadier General Woodcock sent forward a company of the 2nd Loyals to cover the flank. The 1/4th Cheshires continued the advance but Lieutenant Colonel Swindells was killed as they cleared le Mont Jour. Second Lieutenants Gillespie and French of the 5th KOSBs had to take command of the 5th Argylls after Lieutenant Colonel Barlow and all his officers were hit during the advance past Beugneux. Both battalions were stopped by enfilade fire from Servenay so Brigadier General Chaplin sent forward a company of the 8th Scottish Rifles to cover the flank until the French caught up. Major Whitehouse was killed as the 1/1st Hertfords tried to advance further.

Another attack by the 4th Sussex and the 2nd Loyals captured Hill 203 and Point 194 during the night. It meant Nicholson's observers would be able to overlook the German line of retreat the following morning. His division had suffered nearly 2,500 casualties by the time it withdrew from the Aisne.

15th Division, 1 August, Bois d'Hartennes

Major General Reed's men were to pass north of Bois d'Hartennes once the French had advanced past the south side. Contact planes and balloons fired rockets while 155mm batteries fired shells which exploded in black smoke at 8.25 am, signifying zero hour would be at 9 am. The 6th Camerons and 13th Royal Scots formed a defensive flank facing Villemontoire but the 'ragged and desultory' barrage failed to silence the machine-gun teams hiding in derelict tanks. Both the 10th Scottish Rifles and the 9th Royal Scots 'were almost massacred' and the survivors reported they could not advance until

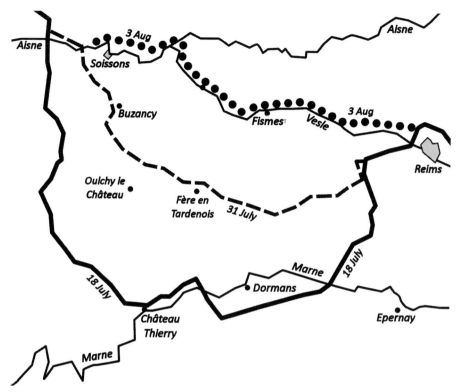

The German withdrawal towards the River Aisne, 31 July to 3 August.

the French silenced the machine guns enfilading their right flank. It never happened because a counter-attack forced the French out of Tigny.

Despite the failure and the high casualties, the attack on 1 August convinced the Germans to withdraw to the Vesle, so General Fayolle wanted to follow them up. That meant one more operation for Major General Reed's men. The orders reached 15th Division at midday and there was a scramble to prepare for an afternoon pursuit as the Germans abandoned Soissons and retired to the Blücher Position behind the Aisne and Vesle.

Both 45 and 44 Brigades entered Bois de Concrois and crossed the Crise stream. Only then could the exhausted Highlanders be relieved knowing 'their dash, their courage, and their devotion, had excited the admiration of the French troops in whose midst they fought'. The French would erect a monument on Buzancy plateau in honour of Reed's men; it said, 'Here the thistles of Scotland will bloom for ever among the roses of France.'

Chapter 3

Phantoms of the Imagination

Planning and Deploying for 8 August

The Preliminaries

Rawlinson's request to make a second, larger attack east of Amiens obviously played on Haig's mind. He asked for his ideas on 13 July and Rawlinson's plan for an attack, by three infantry corps supported by the cavalry corps, reached GHQ four days later. He proposed launching the attack around 10 August.

Foch discussed a larger, combined Anglo-French attack east of Amiens with Pétain, Haig and American, General John Pershing, on 24 July. The recent German attacks had dented the Allied line but they had not broken it. Casualties had been in the hundreds of thousands, leaving all nations looking for replacements, but Foch believed OHL had exhausted its reserve of divisions from the Eastern Front. He thought the German withdrawal from the Marne proved it was incapable of offensive action.

Foch wanted to attack at four points, to free up the railways which ran parallel to the Allied front line. First the French would continue to drive the Germans back from the Aisne, freeing the Châlons line. The British and French would then attack east of Amiens to remove the threat to the Boulogne line. The Americans would clear the St Mihiel salient, pushing the Germans away from the Nancy line. Finally, Foch proposed attacking in Flanders to force the Germans back from the Béthune coalfields and the Channel ports.

General Sir Henry Rawlinson and General Marie-Eugène Debeney joined a second meeting, two days later, where it was decided that the Fourth British Army and the First French Army would attack astride the Rivers Somme and Avre. Foch wanted to capitalise on the French success on the Marne and the plan was for the Australian Corps and Canadian Corps to advance next to the French XXXI Corps. The French First Army would be placed under Haig's control, so their attacks could be coordinated.

Haig and Debeney did not meet again, to maintain secrecy, while only a handful of senior officers were told, so they could start planning. More officers were included over the days that followed, so the details could be finalised. GHQ's formal operation order for a 20 mile wide attack was circulated on 29 July. There would be an initial advance of 6 miles followed by a second 6 mile advance towards Chaulnes and Roye.

Foch and Haig met their chiefs of staff on 3 August. The Généralissime wanted to attack east of Amiens immediately, while the Germans were being driven back from the Marne. They agreed Fourth Army and First Army would attack on 8 August, while Foch suggested that French Third Army could expand the frontage shortly afterwards.

Debeney and Rawlinson had issued brief orders to their corps commanders on 31 July. Fourth Army would attack with nine divisions and the Australian Corps and Canadian Corps would be fighting side-by-side for the first time. The Tank Corps would be providing nearly 450 tanks (their largest battle in the war). Rawlinson issued detailed instructions to Lieutenant Generals Richard Butler, John Monash and Arthur Currie on 6 August, giving them just thirty-six hours to prepare for battle.

The Final Planning

Haig met Rawlinson and Debeney at Fourth Army's Flixecourt headquarters on 5 August, telling them he wanted to reach the abandoned Amiens Defence Line, which dated from 1915, on the first day. It meant their infantry and heavy tanks had to advance 6 miles before the cavalry and light tanks could exploit the success.

The British III Corps would form a defensive flank across the Chipilly spur, between the Ancre and the Somme. The Australian left had to negotiate the meandering loops of the River Somme but the Australian right and the Canadian left would cross the Santerre plateau, ideal tank country. The Canadian right had to clear the wooded banks of the Luce stream.

General Debeney talked about an advance across a 20 mile front either side of Montdidier. The front would expand another 20 miles when General Georges Humbert's Third Army joined in the following day. Haig expected General Julian Byng's Third Army to join in a few days later, expanding the attack front by another 20 miles to the north.

Rawlinson and Debeney agreed Fourth Army would have no preliminary bombardment before it attacked at 4.20 am on the 8 August. The creeping barrage would guide the tanks and infantry through the enemy's front line while it was still dark but the sky would be getting light as they approached the first objective. The French had no tanks because they had all been deployed on the Marne, so General Marie-Eugène Debeney wanted a preliminary bombardment. It would start at 4.20 am, so as not to alert the Germans to Fourth Army's deployment.

Rawlinson would operate from Fourth Army headquarters at Flixecourt, 15 miles north-west of Amiens while Haig moved to GHQ's train, based at Wiry-au-Mont, 25 miles west of the city.

The German Situation

OHL had shifted reserves from the Amiens front to the Aisne, where Ludendorff planned to go on the defensive once the Marne salient had been evacuated. He believed the Allies would wait until the American divisions were ready to fight, which gave him time to train his own divisions.

General Hermann von Kuhl, Crown Prince Rupprecht's chief of staff, reported the defences astride the Somme were all in order at the beginning of August. He chose to abandon Second Army's bridgehead over the Ancre

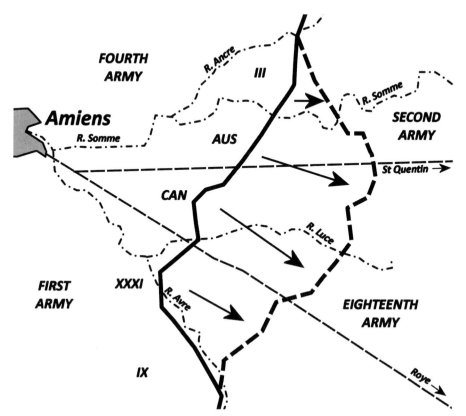

The Allied plan to attack east of Amiens on 8 August.

and Seventeenth Army's foothold across the Avre, to free up reserves. Ludendorff was also satisfied with the defences because OHL's maps were marked with 'reserve positions, switches and artillery positions shown in blue'. They all 'looked very nice' but most were 'but white tapes on the grass... Where to get the labour to do the work? The greater part of the blue was eye-wash.'

German Second Army would face Fourth Army's attack. Most of General Georg von der Marwitz's fourteen divisions were tired and understrength. The Forward Zone ran where the April battle had finished and the trenches were not always in the best defensive position. There was too little wire and too few dugouts, while the trenches dug back in 1915 and 1916 were dilapidated and many were 'facing the wrong way'.

As the Allies prepared for their attack on the Somme, Crown Prince Rupprecht was more interested in Flanders. He believed the British were planning to recapture the Lys salient and he was planning his own offensive in the area. He was meeting Ludendorff and his artillery commanders to discuss the preliminary bombardment when they heard the Allies had attacked on the Somme.

The Final Preparations

Surprise was a huge concern, and while it had been achieved at Cambrai, the previous November, this combined attack was four times the size, if the French contribution was included. The secrecy started right at the top with Downing Street in London. 'No previous mention of it had been made either to the War Office, the War Cabinet or to any other authorities in England, so that the gossips on the Home Front, for once, did not have an opportunity to give the soldier away.'

Rawlinson's instructions were issued between 31 July and 5 August and there was a huge emphasis on secrecy. Only a select few staff at each level of command were involved in the planning until the last moment. It was obvious to the infantry and gunners that they were being trained for a new offensive – but where? It was also apparent to the men moving shells and supplies into the area that an offensive was due – but when? Every man had a printed reminder pasted into his pay book; all it said was 'Keep Your Mouth Shut'.

All correspondence referred to a planned raid, while troop movements were connected to a relief of the French. Amiens had been cleared of citizens when the city was threatened by the German offensive back in March, but farmers and villagers east of the city were subjected to new curfews and cordons.

Fourth Army made sure it was business as usual behind the lines, so that enemy aerial observers saw nothing. Trains and buses carried troops to their camouflaged billets during the hours of darkness. For three nights, 'hour after hour, through a blinding torrent of rain, there moved an unending stream of ammunition wagons… wheel tyres were wrapped with rope, leather washers muffled the play of wheels and straw was laid along parts of the Bray–Corbie road.' The only troop movements made during the day were false ones behind other parts of the line. There was even an attempt to create a large amount of dust in the area of St Pol, to stage an imaginary tank training exercise.

The Artillery Arrives

Ten army field artillery brigades moved under camouflage during the nights before the attack. The Royal Air Force often flew over, to check nothing unusual could be seen. The artillery of two recently disbanded divisions increased the number of field guns and howitzers to 1,386. Thirteen heavy brigades and four siege batteries brought the number of medium, heavy and super-heavy guns to 684. The batteries had plenty to do before zero hour but they could not arouse suspicion. So they fired typical barrages, so Major General Charles Budworth could coordinate the registering of targets.

All the new arrivals stayed silent, waiting to fire at map references at zero hour, a technique first used en masse during the battle of Cambrai the previous November. Many guns would move to new emplacements hours before zero, to avoid the inevitable counter-battery barrages. Accurate surveying meant the battery commanders knew exactly where they were, while every gun had been tested to check the effects of wear on their efficiency. Regular weather reports allowed the gunners to adjust their ranges to allow for changes in air pressure.

The Infantry Moves into Position

The assault troops started arriving in Fourth Army's area late on 1 August, moving only at night. But no one knew what lay ahead until the day before the attack. Complicated reliefs had been planned to confuse the Germans and conceal what was really happening.

III Corps replaced the French between the Ancre and the Somme while the Australian Corps took over 4 miles of front around Hangard. Moving the Canadian Corps from the Arras area to the Somme posed problems because the four divisions always served together. Two Canadian battalions and two Canadian casualty clearing stations were sent to Flanders, helping to convince Crown Prince Rupprecht that Second Army was planning to recapture Kemmel Hill. Meanwhile, the rest of the Canadian Corps headed south on 7 August, only entering the line a few hours before zero.

Wireless communications were also manipulated all along the BEF's front to confuse the Germans. Radio traffic across Fourth Army remained the same, with arriving corps and divisions banned from making transmissions. Meanwhile, Second Army and First Army sent out false messages concerning attack plans.

The Tank Corps Deploys

The last time the Tank Corps had led a major attack had been Cambrai where it spearheaded the breaking of the Hindenburg Line. The tank crews would again be playing a leading role in the offensive. Brigadier General Courage's V Tank Brigade was reinforced by two battalions, numbering 342 Mark IV and Mark V tanks. There were also four supply companies, and while 66 Mark V* tanks would supply infantry units with ammunition and engineering stores, another 54 would support the tank companies. They would also carry machine-gun teams forward to occupy defensible points. Two Whippet battalions and a company of armoured cars would join the exploitation phase.

One road through Amiens was covered in sand to muffle the noise of tank tracks, while planes circled overhead to mask the sound of the engine noise. The crews then stayed hidden in woods or under camouflage during daylight hours. There was panic on 7 August when a shell blew up a supply tank loaded with petrol. An enemy observer spotted the smoke and the bombardment that followed wrecked twenty-five loaded supply tanks, turning the orchard where they had been hiding into a blazing inferno. The tanks made their final move to their deployment areas behind the infantry the following evening. Officers then checked the ½ mile route to the front line, while their crews made their final checks.

The Royal Air Force's Preparations

The RAF played a part in the BEF's deception plan. It increased aerial activity over Flanders at the end of July, to draw attention to Second Army's area. Squadrons switched to First Army and Third Army areas forty-eight hours before the attack, to unnerve the Germans by making them think there could be an attack between Arras and Albert.

Squadrons were also being moved to the Amiens area, and X, Y, I, III and IX Brigades would eventually deploy 800 planes to cover Fourth Army's attack. The French had assembled another 1,100 planes, giving the Allies a three-to-one advantage in the air. A total of 376 fighters would drive the

German Air Force (Deutsche Luftstreitkräfte) from the skies. The aerial observers could then hunt for batteries and other targets for the artillery. Others would report the progress made by the infantry and tanks, warning of approaching enemy troops.

Fast moving spotter planes armed with machine guns would go on long range reconnaissance missions, looking for targets for the heavy artillery and for the bombers. Eight observation balloons would do the same. Nearly 250 bombers would attack targets such as bridges, billets and supply dumps deep in enemy territory.

If possible, the German Air Force would be attacked while it was still on the ground. There would be attacks by 147 bombers and 376 fighters during the morning and afternoon. Towards evening, they would turn their attention to the railway sidings at Chaulnes and Péronne. Another 92 bombers would take over the task during the hours of darkness.

The German Reaction

There were concerns that Second and Eighteenth Armies would discover the attack on several occasions. Five Australian soldiers were taken prisoner during a raid near Domart. Suspicions were raised when the German Second Army withdrew west of the River Ancre on the British Fourth Army's left later the same day. At the same time, Eighteenth Army withdrew opposite French First Army. Both withdrawals made tactical sense but their timing was suspicious.

The German artillery fired short bursts all along the line every morning, demonstrating that they were 'apprehensive and nervy'. Then at dawn on 6 August they attacked south of Morlancourt in revenge for the Australian attack a week before. It came just as 58th Division was relieving part of 18th Division. The 7th Queen's and the 2nd Bedfords were holding 'numerous winding and puzzling trenches, captured from the Germans by the Australians… but they were only knee deep and the heavy rain had churned them into sticky messes…' The guides were late so 8th London Regiment was late and it meant the attack started while Lieutenant Colonel Percival's Bedfords were taking over from Major Baddeley's East Surreys.

The German artillery struck during the relief and then the infantry attacked in the dark and rain. Both 58th Division's left and 18th Division's right were driven back half a mile before the Bedfords and East Surreys helped shore up the line. A counter-attack by Lieutenant Colonel Turner's 6th Northants eventually recovered part of the lost ground.

The attack caused several problems, not least because it exhausted the troops earmarked to attack on 8 August. It also upset III Corps' barrage plan and the gunners had to recalculate their ranges to match the new front line. There were concerns one of the 230 prisoners taken would give something away; they did not. Some thought the German assault troops must have seen the piles of ammunition and stores stacked ready for the offensive; they had not. But the enemy remained on the alert, expecting 18th Division to retaliate. It did at dawn on 7 August as 54 Brigade cleared Cummins and Cloncurry Trenches, straightening out their jumping off line. The East Surreys, Northants and Bedfords captured their sectors but the 11th Royal Fusiliers could not, despite throwing the contents of over one hundred boxes of grenades at their enemy. Brigadier General Sadlier Jackson's tired men were then relieved by 36 Brigade of 12th Division.

The prisoners had said nothing, but General Marwitz thought Second Army could be attacked around Villers Bretonneux. Meanwhile, General Oskar von Hutier thought there were a lot of movements opposite German Eighteenth Army. But his aerial observers saw nothing and reports of wheeled traffic and tanks behind the Allied line were dismissed as 'phantoms of the imagination or nervousness'. All the precautions had paid off.

The infantry marched to their deployment positions, 'winding along their numerous approach tracks, constantly passing the black silent masses of waiting tanks and crowded guns'. There was a nervous energy in the air and one officer said the Germans were 'having their fun now but wait till our barrage starts' as their guns fired throughout the night. Then the codename 'Hell' was sent out because Méricourt was under shell fire, behind III Corps' line. Over 500 men would have to be evacuated with mustard gas burns.

The Australians were 'excited with their own realisation' that 'at last all five divisions of their National Army were attacking together and that the Canadian force was attacking beside them.' As zero hour approached, 'planes maintained their drone over all sectors of the German front to be attacked. Through this buzz the purr of the tank engines, throttled down, was inaudible, except to a few who were very close.' Then everyone settled down to wait for the signal to advance. 'Uncertainty was in the air and zero hour was awaited with the feeling that a stiff task was ahead. The thought running through all minds was: how much has the Boche learned of our plans? At 4.20 am the guns burst forth into a tornado of flame and sound upon an 11 mile front…'

Chapter 4

It All Looked a Certain, Confident Success

8 August

Lieutenant Generals Butler, Monash and Currie waited with baited breath as over 100,000 men marched into position beneath a moonless sky. The soldiers heard a few batteries firing their night barrages and they may have seen or heard some of the 435 tanks waiting to move off. There were concerns the Germans suspected something when they started shelling the Bois l'Abbé area at 3.30 am but it stopped just five minutes before zero hour. The jumping off tapes were usually 300 yards from the German front line but they were closer in III Corps' area, where the troops had been fighting to recover trenches for the past forty-eight hours.

The ground mist thickened as zero hour approached but planes flew overhead dropping phosphorus bombs, as their engines drowned out the noise of the tanks. A few minutes before zero hour the tanks crawled forward, the drivers coasting in second gear so as not to over-rev their engines. They crawled past the lines of waiting infantry just as the opening crash of the barrage echoed across the Somme countryside. 'The excited troops cheered the sound. Nearly every man lit a cigarette as all along the line the companies of the attacking brigades rose and moved forward.'

There were over 2,000 guns behind Fourth Army's front and another 1,600 supporting the French First Army. Around one in three fired a creeping barrage of shrapnel and smoke shells, 200 yards ahead of the tanks and infantry. A similar number hit the enemy batteries with a mixture of high explosive and gas shells, smashing the guns and incapacitating the crews. The rest hit the likely assembly points and approach routes behind the German lines.

Skirmishers formed 'a thin line intended to work as beaters, pointing out hostile posts to the tank crews…' Usually they could see little through the smoke and mist but they could hear the rattle of machine-gun fire. They guided the tanks towards the enemy positions, sometimes walking in front, sometimes riding on top, as the sound of their engines terrified the enemy.

'Some 150 yards behind were the main bodies of the leading battalions each on a two-company front, strung out in successive lines of tiny columns, in single file…' Another three waves advanced in columns, accompanied by the machine guns and trench mortar teams. The support battalions advanced in artillery formation, moving in a diamond pattern which could either deploy to the front or to the flank.

At least that was the plan. The smoke and mist made it difficult to keep formation and enemy fire split companies and platoons into small groups, while the terrain sometimes required a change of direction. Officers followed white tapes across no man's land before checking their compasses, remembering that their helmets and revolvers could affect the bearing. Others followed the nearest tank but many became disorientated in the smoke and dust. Most officers decided the best they could hope for was to try and follow the sound of the exploding shells forming the creeping barrage beyond the smoke.

'Again and again instances occurred of NCO's and even privates, taking charge of the situation when the officers had been killed, and carrying on successfully.' In the organised chaos the tank drivers often 'made for the sound of the nearest machine-guns'. The mist started to clear around ninety minutes after zero hour, the tank crews 'now steered by sight' towards the nearest machine-gun nest as the sun rose.

Every man carried his gas mask, water bottle and iron rations, he had 250 rounds of ammunition and two Mills bombs to attack with and an entrenching tool and two sandbags to defend himself with. Carrying parties brought up the rear but the elongated Mark V* tanks carried huge amounts of ammunition and entrenching tools. Tanks mounted with howitzers carried stores as well as their own shells while planes dropped boxes of ammunition for the machine-gun teams.

III Corps

Lieutenant Colonel Richard Butler's men had to advance across the plateau between the Ancre and the Somme. His left would go a short distance towards Morlancourt while his right secured the loop in the Somme between Cérisy and Méricourt. All three divisions had suffered many casualties during the March retreat across the Somme and there were too few experienced officers to train the replacements. Butler had also faced the problem of the trenches lost near Sailly-Lorette on 6 August. It meant 18th and 58th Division both had to dig new jumping off trenches while their artillery had to alter the bombardment programme. The 350 field guns and howitzers across III Corps' front opened fire at 4.20 am. Each brigade was led by twelve Mark V tanks while four supply tanks carried ammunition and supplies.

12th Division, Morlancourt, 8 August

The German artillery smothered 35 Brigade with gas during the night and Brigadier General Vincent had to be replaced by Brigadier General Beckwith. Zero hour was two hours later than the rest of Fourth Army and the infantry advanced through the mist and smoke at 6.20 am. Lieutenant Colonel Green's 9th Essex cleared the area next to the Ancre while Lieutenant Colonel Scarlett's 7th Norfolks fought their way through the trenches north-west of Morlancourt. The 1/1st Cambridge Regiment advanced towards the village with the help of a tank which had strayed from 18th Division's sector in the mist. Lieutenant Colonel Saint's men rounded up 300 prisoners following a counter-attack and then Captains Wallis and Hollis captured another 300 prisoners in Morlancourt.

18th (Eastern) Division, 8 August

The counter-attack on 6 August had caused so many casualties that Major General Richard Lee had to ask Lieutenant General Butler for help. He was given 36 Brigade from 12th Division and it took over Lee's right flank on the night of 7/8 August during a gas barrage. It left Brigadier General Owen's officers no time to check the ground north of Gressaire Wood.

Six tanks broke down while another lost direction and ended up in 12th Division's area but the rest helped 18th Division mop up the machine-gun teams. Only seventeen out of thirty-six returned, leaving too few for the following day. The 7th Queen's defeated German infantry about to advance across no man's land but they had lost their barrage. No tanks had appeared but Lieutenant Colonel Christopher Bushell VC (awarded during the March battle on the Somme) rallied his men and led them to Cloncurry Trench; he was killed by a sniper soon afterwards.

Both the 7th Sussex and 9th Royal Fusiliers were having a tough fight to recapture the lost trenches when Sergeant Barton and three men rushed the main strongpoint, taking thirty men prisoner. Despite all the brave attempts, the two battalions had suffered over 500 casualties and they had still not cleared the first objective.

The 10th Essex deployed late but Lieutenant Colonel Banks and Major Forbes encouraged their men to catch the barrage up with the maxim 'if in doubt, kill the Boche'. Many got lost in the mist but the rest took two batteries en route to the second objective as soon as it lifted. Banks eventually had so few men that his prisoners thought they would be shot. They handed over all their contraband and then removed their boots to prove they would not run away.

Lieutenant Colonel Richard's 7th Buffs secured the north flank and the Royal Fusiliers cleared the Corbie road so Captain Macdonald of the Queen's Own could advance behind two tanks. The 8th Berkshires were unable to clear Gressaire Wood, overlooking Chipilly spur and the River Somme, and had to fall back as soon as the mist cleared.

The 'young lads' of the 5th Berkshires followed the trampled corn through the fog to find the Essex but all but one of the tanks had turned back

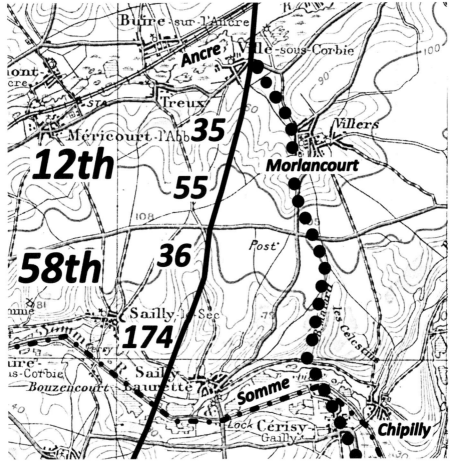

III Corps struggled to make progress between the Ancre and the Somme on 8 August.

because they were low on petrol. Lieutenant Colonel Hudson still advanced to the edge of Gressaire Wood only to find himself facing several machine guns when the mist lifted; over one hundred Berkshires were hit in just a few minutes. Lieutenant Colonel Banks and only eighty survivors of the Essex followed; a very depleted Queen's Own also retired.

58th (2/1st London) Division, Malard Wood, 8 August

'The barrage was beautiful, making a vivid red glow' in the early morning mist and the 7th London Regiment followed three tanks across the high ground north of Malard Wood. Five tanks helped Lieutenant Colonel Benson's 6th London Regiment make a pincer attack against the machine-gun posts around Malard Wood ravine and 'on our approach they were surrendered.' One German soldier disabled two tanks by putting bombs under the tank tracks before he was shot. The 2/10th London had taken prisoner most of the garrison of Sailly Lorette before two tanks caught up and they took many more along the river bank west of Cérisy.

Brigadier General Maxwell's men had taken their objective but they had become very mixed up in the mist. The 7th London Regiment had followed the slope down to the river to the north end of Malard Wood and it took time to redeploy them in the correct location. The mist was clearing by the time 173 Brigade caught up and 2/4th and 3rd London Regiment advanced beyond Malard Wood; few made it across the Chipilly spur.

Major General Frank Ramsey cancelled part of his barrage after a contact plane incorrectly reported British soldiers on the spur, leaving the 2/2nd London at the mercy of the German machine-gunners around Chipilly and Gressaire Wood. The 2/10th London fared little better along the river bank because their barrage landed too far ahead. An evening attempt to cross the spur by the 9th London Regiment failed despite accurate artillery support.

The Australian Corps

The corps had been formed following the battle of Third Ypres and Lieutenant General Monash had taken over in May 1918. This was the first time all five Australian divisions would fight together under their commander and the 'Diggers' were proud they were in the vanguard of the BEF's first major attack for nine months.

The 3rd and 2nd Australian Divisions would lead the advance to the first objective, while over 1,000 field guns fired the creeping barrage and nearly 100 heavy calibre guns shelled distant targets. Then the 4th and 5th

Australian Divisions would head for the final objective, the Amiens Outer Defence Line. Twenty-four batteries would canter forward to bombard the second objective. There would be no creeping barrage during this stage but aeroplanes would drop smoke bombs in front of villages and strongpoints to mask the machine guns.

The First Wave

The 3rd Australian Division deployed south of the River Somme while the 2nd Australian Division took its place alongside, north of the Amiens–Chaulnes railway. National pride increased when they realised they were going to be fighting next to the other colonial corps: the Canadian Corps. The two divisions advanced at 4.20 am, heading for the first objective between Cérisy and Lamotte-en-Santerre, a distance of 2 miles.

3rd Australian Division, South Bank of the Somme

The 11 Brigade lost the barrage as they struggled in the mist covering the Somme valley. Two platoons of 39th Battalion cleared the narrow strip of land between the river and the canal, seizing bridges en route. Captain Jack led 42nd Battalion along the Cérisy road but the meandering of the river meant his men had to negotiate several reed beds. The 44th Battalion crossed the high ground where Captain Longmore claimed 'it was impossible to see one's own outstretched hand and any form of control except self-control was out of the question.' Tanks silenced machine-gun posts as Lieutenant Colonel Heron's 41st Australian headed into the Cérisy valley capturing 200 men and a dozen field guns.

There was a disaster early on in 9 Brigade's sector when a shell hit 35th Battalion's headquarters, hitting most of Major Carr's staff. Captain Yates was a casualty but Captain Coghill made sure his men tackled the machine-gun posts which were 'scattered, as if from a pepper-pot, along the main German line'. The 33rd Battalion cleared both Hazel Wood and Accroche Wood and Lieutenant Colonel Lord was pleased to hear the first objective had been taken 'with hardly any stubborn resistance; the fog had rendered it most difficult and where the tanks appeared most of the Germans were terrified.' The Australians had found many hiding 'in dugouts and shelters and the fog helped even more than elsewhere. Parties were on them before they attempted resistance and most surrendered without a shot.'

Major Grant's men advanced onto Gailly Ridge as many guns fell silent and 34th Battalion found 'gunners, doubtless overawed by the tanks, now sitting on the gun trails, apparently waiting to be captured'. Altogether 3rd Division had captured five batteries of field guns, one battery of 4.2-inch guns and two 5.9-inch howitzers. The tanks had provided excellent support in the mist and eighteen out of twenty-four rallied in Cérisy valley.

2nd Australian Division, Lamotte and Marcelcave

Both 20th and 19th Battalions were supposed to advance at an angle to the main St Quentin road but it was diverting them east. The 'cheering Australians pulled the garrison out of' the Inner Amiens Defence Line and 18th Battalion captured two battalion headquarters and a dozen field guns around Warfusée-Lamotte. Lieutenant Colonel Sadler's 17th Battalion took another 200 prisoners and a dozen howitzers around Lamotte-en-Santerre.

Twenty-three tanks of the 2nd Battalion led 27th and 28th Battalion parallel to the Nesle road and also took a dozen field guns. Part of 28th Battalion was pinned down near Card Copse until Lieutenant Alfred Gaby negotiated the wire and captured fifty prisoners with just his pistol. Gaby was killed only three days later; he was posthumously awarded the Victoria

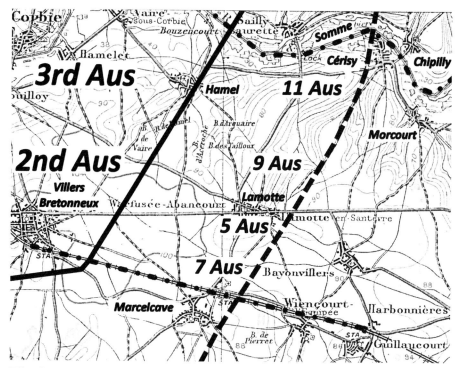

The Australian Corps' advance to the first objective.

Cross. The first the Germans knew 26th Battalion was approaching was when they saw tanks crawling past their positions and infantry charging out of the mist; hardly any escaped. Only four out of twenty-three tanks were lost but Brigadier General Wisdom's men had to withdraw because the Australian batteries were firing short. It took time for the runners to get the message back in the mist.

After several hours groping around in the mist, it 'lifted like a curtain, gradually disclosing a scene that would never be forgotten by those who saw it. The Somme valley came into view, the gentle sunlight, still tempered by the haze, bathing the steep wooded slopes and folds of the northern riverside and the more gradual, long grass or wheat covered spurs of the southern bank.'

The Australians could see scouts directing tanks towards machine-gun nests while small columns of men followed across the fields. The roads were filled with 'battery after battery of field and horse artillery, chains jingling, horses' heads and manes tossing'. Sometimes the gunners cantered to a new position, unhooked their guns and opened fire.

Around one hundred Mark IV and Mark V tanks had assembled behind the line, 'many having the colours of their infantry painted on their sides or on plaques hung by chains from their fronts'. Another one hundred Whippets were waiting to accompany the cavalry. At the allotted time they crawled forward like 'elephants accompanying an Oriental army'. The hundreds of prisoners being escorted to the rear looked on in awe as the tanks and gun teams moved forward and one officer said, 'it all looked a certain, confident success.'

The Second Wave

The mist was clearing as the second wave of divisions advanced in artillery formation. The 4th Australian Division would move another 2 miles along the south bank of the Somme, to Morcourt, while 5th Australian Division advanced through Bayonvillers. Their final objective was the Outer Amiens Defence Line between Proyart and Harbonnières. Monash had 1st Australian Division in reserve if he needed to reinforce any sector.

The second wave of divisions also had an impressive number of tanks: forty-eight fighting tanks and thirty-six Mark V* tanks carrying supplies and machine-gun teams to defensive positions. The tanks had towed twelve cars from the 17th Armoured Car Company forward and the 1 Cavalry Brigade and the Whippet tanks were on standby for the exploitation stage.

4th Australian Division, Cérisy and Morcourt

At the appointed time, Major General Ewen Sinclair-Maclagan's men 'got up and cheered in lines of sections in file with rifles slung and with the tanks between them'. They advanced at a steady pace along the south bank to the Somme, moving down into gullies and up over ridges.

The 15th Battalion attacked Cérisy but it was under machine-gun fire from Chipilly across the river until the mist lifted and the heavy batteries could target them. Tanks could not negotiate the canal side road, so they turned back, climbed out of the valley and tackled Morcourt head on. The 'German infantry were instructed to attack tanks by firing at the loop-bolts and also by getting behind the tanks and throwing bundles of bombs on to their backs.' It was 'rather like catching birds by putting salt on their tails' and all but one of the tanks were knocked out. A 'senior officer sped past in a motor-car but two officers trying to follow him on their horses were shot' as 14th Battalion closed in on Morcourt. Company Sergeant Major Day then covered the bridge with his Lewis gun so no one could escape across the river, and Lieutenant Colonel Crowther's men rounded up 300 prisoners.

A single tank joined 13th Battalion's advance along Morcourt valley and Sergeant Sexton (real name Buckley) continued shooting 'his Lewis gun from the hip until the Germans ceased fire'. His comrades then 'found among canteens, stores, transport lines, and shelters, teeming with unresisting Germans, more souvenirs than it had time to collect'. They also captured wagons loaded with all sorts of contraband, including the entire contents of a pay office.

Lieutenant Colonel Johnson's leading companies skirted the woods, while the support companies mopped up, and one man painted 'captured by 45th Battalion AIF' on twenty-nine field guns. The tanks sometimes struggled to negotiate the undulating terrain and one even rolled over while climbing a slope. Eventually, the 'only way they could help their infantry was by lying along the valley's edge firing their 6-pounders and machine-guns.' Lieutenant Vincent soon caught up and saw the 'Germans running, throwing away arms and equipment or plundering a canteen which, with engineer shops, clothing stores, and various offices, lay along the western slope'. His men shot a few and the rest (around 200) put their hands up.

Captain Kemp and Lieutenant Kemp of 46th Battalion charged into the south end of the valley, finding more men milling around the canteens and stores, waiting to surrender. Two soldiers were detailed to escort no less than

180 back and when one asked if they could help themselves to new uniforms and boots, the guard replied, 'you can do what you bloody well like as long as you don't run away.'

On 4 Brigade's front, four Mark V* tanks broke down before the advance began, while the remaining four were knocked out climbing a steep slope. Lieutenant Colonel Drake Brockman led 16th Battalion towards Méricourt only to withdraw his flank after his men came under fire from Chipilly spur across the river. Three tanks were knocked out as 48th Battalion fought past Morcourt and the Australian artillery could not see to help Lieutenant Colonel Perry's men through the haze before the Germans withdrew towards Proyart.

5th Australian Division, Bayonvillers and Harbonnières

The German artillery were firing wildly as Major General Talbot Hobbs' men advanced behind twenty-four Mark V tanks. The 'Germans leapt out, raised their hands above their heads, and waited to be collected when a monster came within 100 yards.' They were then 'ransacked for souvenirs by

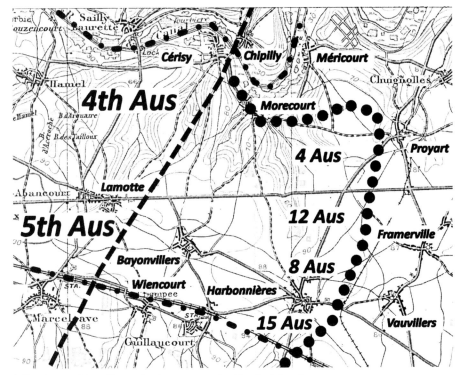

The Australian Corps' advance to the final objective.

the infantry… some posts actually had their watches or other articles ready before the troops came up.' The advance continued at 'a sharp walking pace' towards the bend in the Somme, under machine-gun fire from the Chipilly spur on the other side of the river. The Lewis guns silenced the single anti-tank gun in front of 30th Battalion, and the tanks put down suppressive fire as Lieutenant Colonel Street's men headed for Cérisy.

One German artillery officer had posted observers in the trees and they could see the tanks crawling across towards Morcourt above the smoke. His two field guns disabled seven tanks before Lieutenant Colonel Freeman's 31st Battalion outflanked them and then 'their crews, who had been lying in a turnip field, stood up and surrendered.' A 4.2-inch gun battery targeted the rest of the tanks until Lieutenant Arnold's Whippet machine-gunned the crews.

A single tank crawled towards the Morcourt valley and 'nosed around the bushes and huts' while the 'Germans were running about like ants from a disturbed nest'. Gun batteries limbered and galloped away, passing the enemy infantry running down the Roman road. Brigadier General Tivey sent 32nd Battalion forward to fill the gap between 30th and 31st Battalions and it took hundreds of prisoners in the Brioche valley, beyond Morcourt.

Only one tank was knocked out as Lieutenant Colonel Scanlan's 59th Battalion captured a field battery. At the same time, 58th Battalion suppressed the machine guns in Bayonvillers until six tanks helped Captains Loughnan and Tait round up 120 prisoners. The 57th Battalion captured its own battery of 5.9-inch howitzers north-east of Marcelcave but Lieutenant Colonel Denehy had to call a halt south Bayonvillers because the supporting barrage was falling short.

Denehy's men cheered when the troopers of 1 Cavalry Brigade trotted past, accompanied by Whippets, looking to head deep into German territory. Lieutenant Colonel Ing's Queen's Bays charged the Germans in the valley south of Harbonnières while a tank helped 59th and 57th Battalions capture many in the village. An Australian national flag provided by General Monash was soon fluttering from Harbonnières church tower.

The 15 Brigade was soon consolidating the Outer Defence Line, a 500 yard deep defensive zone which had not been touched for over two years. A foray towards Vauvillers was stopped by heavy fire, proving that there was still hard fighting ahead, but Major General Hobbs knew most of his final objective was secure by mid-morning.

As the Australians dug in, someone spotted an abandoned huge railway gun in no man's land. Lieutenant Burrow's engineers of 8th Field Company unhooked the line of carriages, raised steam in the locomotive and shunted the gun and its ammunition trucks behind the Australian line. It would end up on display in Sydney.

An aeroplane dropped a flare to warn about troops gathering around Framerville, so Brigadier General Elliott sent the Queen's Bays and Mark V* tanks carrying machine-gun detachments forward to reinforce the line. The counter-attack failed to materialise but 15 Brigade was still unable to capture its section of the Amiens Outer Defence Line. There was a strong enemy presence in Harbonnières, the Canadians' Brigade were nowhere to be seen on the right and General Hobbs' had run out of tanks.

The Exploitation Wave

17th Armoured Car Battalion

Twelve armoured cars drove down the Roman road as soon as the barrage lifted. Time and again the crews used axes and chains to drag felled trees aside. At the south end of the Morcourt valley they found 'a camping ground for German reserves. The valley sides were terraced with shelter bivouacs, huts for headquarters, and horse standings.' The armoured cars fired into the mass of sheltering men as field guns of 16 Brigade, Royal Horse Artillery, fired shrapnel shells into the valley. The armoured cars then continued past the ammunition dumps and stores lining the Roman road; they found a train in the Le Grand Ravin valley. The armoured cars were eventually turned back by a road block, and while some engaged German transport around Proyart and Chuignolles, the rest explored Rainecourt and Framerville to the south. They all returned to the Roman road and spent the rest of the day patrolling the roads in front of the 5th Australian Division's position.

1 Cavalry Brigade, Framerville and Harbonnières

The Australians shouted 'give it to them' as Brigadier General Sewell's troopers trotted through the line around Bayonvillers. The 11th Hussars and 5th Dragoon Guards then cantered towards the unoccupied Outer Defence Line north of Harbonnières and captured a damaged railway gun before taking their objective opposite Framerville. Some turned south and captured three field batteries near Vauvillers before dismounting to engage the retiring enemy. Three Whippets were knocked out and the Queen's Bays made three unsuccessful charges south of Harbonnières. Lieutenant Colonel Terrot's 5th Dragoon Guards joined them near the Chaulnes railway, while Mark V* tanks delivered machine-gun teams to the front line.

By the early afternoon Lieutenant General Monash could report that the Australian Corps had captured nearly 8,000 men and 173 guns. His men had advanced around 7 miles to the Amiens Outer Defence while armoured cars and cavalry were searching the countryside ahead.

The Canadian Corps

Lieutenant General Currie's troops had only just arrived on the Somme and they deployed across a 4 mile wide front between the Chaulnes railway and the Roye road a few hours before zero hour. The 2nd, 1st and 3rd Canadian Divisions would advance up to 3 miles to the first objective. The 4th Canadian Division and 32nd Division would then head for the Amiens Outer Defence Line, some 4 miles away. Currie's men were supported by the four tank battalions of Brigadier General Hankey's IV Brigade.

The First Wave

The 2nd Canadian Division started from a narrow sector south of Villers Bretonneux, where the line faced south. The 1st Canadian Division would advance east though Hangard Wood while the 3rd Canadian Division would move astride the Luce steam. The assault battalions marched towards the front line during the early hours of 8 August and the final one was in position only twenty minutes before zero hour. Divisions reported their assembly was complete with the code word 'Llandovery Castle', a Canadian hospital ship torpedoed a month earlier with the loss of nearly 250 lives. The Germans were unaware the entire Canadian Corps had deployed for battle. There was no preliminary bombardment and then 'exactly at 4:20 the barrage opened with the thunder of more than nine hundred guns and immediately the assaulting infantry pressed forward.'

2nd Canadian Division, through Marcelcave and Guillaucourt

Major General Henry Burstall held an awkward sector south of Villers Bretonneux, facing at forty-five degrees to the line of attack. The frontage would halve during the advance so he had deployed his three brigades one behind the other. The tanks struggled to find Brigadier General Rennie's 4 Brigade in the mist but the barrage had demoralised the Germans around Marcelcave. On the left, the 19th Battalion had 'almost better than could be hoped for' assistance from the Australians, as their Lewis guns cut down the retiring Germans. It allowed the Canadians to go forward, 'advancing on parade to their objective to the admiration of all.' Lieutenant Percy-Eade led the seven tanks of 14th Battalion into the village while the rest of 21st Battalion shot up a howitzer battery and silenced a strongpoint to the south. Nine tanks were engaged in a fierce battle for Morgemont Wood and Cancelette Wood. But only two were left by the time 18th Battalion reached the first objective in 'one of the finest features of the day'.

Brigadier General Ross had welcomed ten tanks as 5 Brigade headed for the second objective but several were hit and the rest had to take evasive action, using up precious fuel. Five of the captured artillery pieces helped support 24th Battalion's attack on Guillaucourt, but four out of nine Whippets were knocked out or disabled. The surviving tanks helped 26th Battalion clear Snipe and Pierret Woods before many prisoners and heavy guns were taken in the valley beyond.

The tanks then joined 6 Brigade en route to the final objective, followed by the guns of the 5th Canadian Artillery Brigade, which were making their fifth move of the day. Cavalry regiments and Whippet tanks had already passed through the area and Brigadier General Bell's men found few Germans around Caix. The 29th and 31st Battalions joined them along the Amiens Defence Line. The only resistance came on the left, where a small group of Germans held along the railway line until after dusk.

Brigadier General Legard was detailed to help 2nd Canadian Division but half of his Whippets had been knocked out capturing Guillaucourt by the time 9 Cavalry Brigade caught up with the infantry. The squadrons dispersed a large a group of Germans preparing to counter-attack, ending resistance south of the Roye road. A contact plane told the Whippets and they drove back to tell Legard. He at once ordered the 15th and 19th Hussars to take up the pursuit and they cantered to the Amiens Outer Defence Line. After making contact with the cavalry moving ahead of the Australians, to their left, they were joined by the 2nd Cavalry Brigade on their right. They all then waited for the infantry to catch up.

1st Canadian Division, 8 August, Hangard Wood and Aubercourt

Major General Archibald MacDonnell had deployed the 3 Brigade opposite Hangard Wood. The creeping barrage hit 13th Battalion but Brigadier General Tuxford's three battalions still advanced on time. Twenty-one tanks led the infantry, driving straight towards any firing in the mist. As 14th Battalion cleared the ground north of Hangard Wood, Corporal Herman Good ran forward when some of his 13th Battalion were pinned down in Hangard Wood. He went on to capture a battery of 5-inch guns with just three men to help him and would be awarded the Victoria Cross. Private John Croak was injured capturing another machine gun firing at 13th Battalion but he refused to have his wounds dressed and instead led a charge, capturing another three. He died of his wounds the following day and would be posthumously awarded the Victoria Cross.

The tanks silenced eight machine guns as 14th Battalion moved into Morgemont Wood and they were about to charge a strongpoint on the east side when the Germans ran for Marcelcave. Meanwhile, 16th Battalion had been clearing the wood along the north bank of the Luce stream where the undergrowth was too thick for tanks. Stokes mortars hit Aubercourt before a tank helped the infantry capture a regimental headquarters in a nearby quarry. A fresh company of tanks joined the final advance but the mist had cleared by now and only twelve reached the first objective.

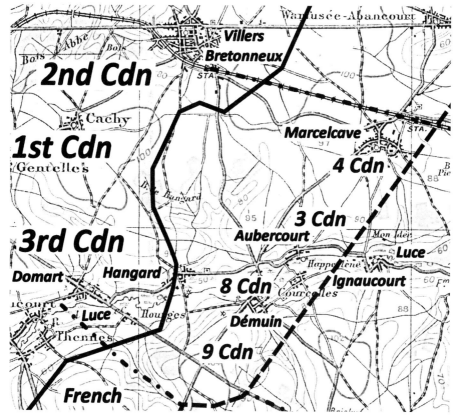

The Canadian Corps' advance to the first objective.

Brigadier General Griesbach had only been allocated six tanks, so 1 Brigade's three battalions often had to rely on their Lewis guns to suppress the enemy as they advanced. Half of 3rd Battalion had lost its way in the mist and the rest struggled when two tanks were knocked out clearing Lemaire Wood and Ruisseau Wood, north of the Luce. Meanwhile, 4th Battalion cleared the thick woodland along the banks on their own. Tanks silenced the machine guns in Cancelette Wood and then crossed the stream to help 2nd Battalion clear Ignaucourt. The contact planes could see the Germans abandoning their positions around Cayeux-en-Santerre as the mist cleared. Another five tanks were hit but the eleven 'runners' were still doing sterling work, silencing machine-gun nests ahead of the infantry. By 11 am 1 Brigade was along the second objective, around Cayeux.

It was now the turn of 2 Brigade but 7th Battalion was delayed crossing the Luce. Brigadier General Loomis instructed 10th Battalion to advance along the north bank through Caix to the Outer Amiens Defence Line. The 7th Battalion soon caught up but it had to form a flank facing south, where 4th Canadian Division was delayed.

3rd Canadian Division, 8 August, Domart to Mezières

Three tank companies of 5th Battalion assembled around Domart on the Roye road and the crews had to follow the Luce, negotiating the gullies and spurs adjacent to the stream. The artillery deployed around the tank assembly point fired a bombardment at 4.08 am and the drivers pulled away in second gear to keep their engines as quiet as possible.

Eight of the tanks were delayed in the mist but they caught up with 1st Canadian Mounted Rifles around Hangard, helping them to Cemetery Copse. The Démuin bridge was down so one tank dropped a crib into the Luce and fourteen could cross the stream. So far five tanks had been knocked out but they had helped the infantry to clear Démuin. The 2nd Canadian Mounted Rifles passed through and advanced to Courcelles on the south bank, seeing many Germans running before them. Another tank was lost but the surviving eight held the Démuin bridgehead while the engineers built a bridge for the artillery.

Brigadier General Ormond's men were deployed astride the Amiens–Roye road, facing the enemy-held high ground south of the Luce. So 9 Brigade's battalions deployed in the dead ground close to the German trench. One company of tanks had also crossed the stream but the German counter-barrage at zero hour forced the crews to scatter and three bogged down in the mud. The rest found the enemy was allowing 'themselves to be overrun, many surrendering without firing a shot.' Half a company of tanks crossed the Luce stream at Thennes, in the French sector, before turning north to help 9 Brigade. Another four headed south to help the French but only one reached Villers-aux-Érables.

Corporal Harry Miner silenced three machine guns as 58th Battalion followed the south bank of the Luce stream past Rifle Wood. He was mortally wounded as he turned one on its former owners; he would be posthumously awarded the Victoria Cross. Six tanks were hit as 116th Battalion's leading company lost all its officers in front of Hamon Wood. The survivors pushed onto the high ground beyond, as 58th Battalion cleared Courcelles on the left. At the same time, six tanks helped 43rd Battalion round up 250 prisoners around Rifle Wood, Holland Wood and Vignette Wood, south of the Roye road.

Artillery limbers crossed the Luce bridge as the three battalions of 7 Brigade filed across the footbridges. They cheered the cavalry and guns going forward and glared at the columns of dejected prisoners headed to the rear. Six fresh tanks found only thirteen survivors of the first wave waiting for them; the rest had been knocked out, had broken down or were ditched along the banks of the Luce.

Brigadier General Dyer's men advanced from Hamon Wood at 8.20 am and 49th Battalion then faced little opposition in the fields south of Ignaucourt after a brisk fight for Cerfs Wood. A tank helped 42nd Battalion capture three batteries and half a dozen guns were turned back on the enemy. Four tanks led the advance across Hill 102 towards Beaucourt, in 'a route march enlivened by the sight of the panic-stricken enemy running in every direction'.

A few tanks helped the Royal Canadian Regiment clear Jean Wood and Wheelbarrow Wood, next to the Roye road. Meanwhile Brutinel's Independent Force were cooperating with the French on the right flank and they saw the Germans abandoning Mezières, so some of the Canadian infantry moved towards the village to stop them escaping.

4th Canadian Division, Beaucourt

Major General David Watson's men had to cross the Luce before they could deploy along the Démuin–Moreuil road. The 12 and 11 Brigades crossed at Démuin and Domart to find only eight tanks waiting for them, because thirty-four machines had been knocked out or broken down. The order to advance through 3rd Canadian Division was issued at 12.10 pm but they then had to halt along the Ignaucourt–Mézières road for another hour until thirty tanks of 1st Battalion caught up. They cheered the Whippets and cavalry moving through their position during the wait.

The Mark V* tanks were to carry machine-gun teams to the third objective and then half would return. But the rough ride meant many 'suffered severely from the unaccustomed heat and fumes from the engines; many became sick, and a number fainted'. Half of the teams decided it was safer to dismount and advance on foot.

Both the 38th and 78th Battalions discovered that the cavalry had driven most of the Germans before them, and Lieutenant James Tait's group tackled a dozen machine guns firing on 78th Battalion. They rounded up prisoners along the north edge of Beaucourt Wood. Brigadier General MacBrien's men eventually joined the 7 Cavalry Brigade along the Amiens Outer Defence Line south of Caix.

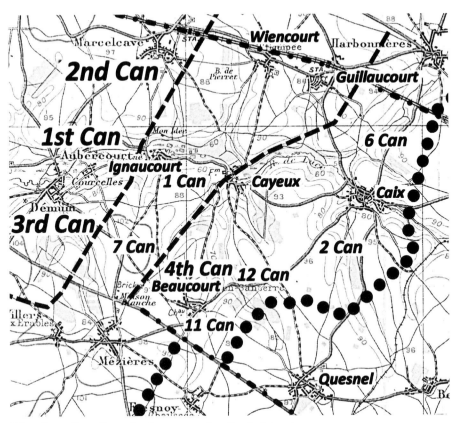

The Canadian Corps' advance to the final objective.

The 102nd and 54th Battalions found the Canadian Cavalry Brigade around Beaucourt village but they came under heavy fire from the wood beyond. The three tanks were knocked out as 54th Battalion advanced to the edge of wood and then 102nd Battalion rounded up 160 prisoners inside.

A battery south of the wood then knocked out ten tanks in quick succession, so 54th Battalion could not reach Le Quesnel. Brigadier General Odlum sent 75th Battalion forward but there was so much fire that a frontal attack was ruled out. Eventually 11 Brigade established a line supported by armoured cars, in contact with the French on the Roye road.

Cooperation with the French on the Right Flank

Brigadier General Brutinel had assembled a mobile force from his Canadian Machine Gun Corps. The 1st and 2nd Canadian Motor Machine-Gun Brigades had machine guns mounted on motorcycle sidecars. The Canadian Cyclist Battalion would act as scouts while lorry-mounted mortars provided support. Brutinel's Force deployed on Fourth Army's right flank and passed through 3rd Canadian Division, deploying along the Roye road facing Mezières.

The French only had a small number of light Renault tanks available because they had lost most of their heavy Schneider and Saint-Chamond tanks on the Marne in July. So General Debeney chose to use a preliminary bombardment before his First French Army advanced forty-five minutes after the Canadian Corps. A small liaison force of Canadian and French infantry cleared a ravine on the Corps boundary before deploying along the Roye road.

XXXI Corps' attack around Moreuil Wood, Morisel and Moreuil extended Fourth Army's attack. An afternoon advance cleared the Santerre plateau as far as Fresnoy and Plessier but the wait for the guns meant they could not reach Arvillers, as Debeney had wanted. The Germans were waiting for IX Corps' attack at 8 am. The French troops struggled to cross the Avre and they could not get to La Neuville and Braches until XXXI Corps had cleared Genouville Wood. To the south, both X and XXXV Corps continued to fire, to convince the Germans the attack front could be widened.

3rd Cavalry Division, Amiens Outer Defence Line

Major General Anthony Harman's cavalry needed extra firepower beyond the final objective, so sixteen Whippets had been attached to his three brigades. But there had been no time to practice tactics and it was soon clear that the tanks were too slow to help the cavalry.

The Canadian Cavalry Brigade passed Morgemont Wood and crossed the Luce around Ignaucourt. There was little artillery fire as Brigadier General Paterson's troopers trotted forward because the Canadian batteries were deploying forward while the German ones were falling back. But the clearing mist revealed dozens of limbers and wagons jockeying for position with columns of tanks en route to their deployment and rally areas. Columns of walking wounded were escorting prisoners to the rear as they carried the seriously injured Canadians on stretchers. Whippets accompanied Lieutenant Colonel Paterson's 7 Cavalry Brigade and Lieutenant Colonel Whitmore's 6 Cavalry Brigade as they passed through the Canadian infantry around Cayeux during the afternoon.

Machine guns opened up beyond the village and one squadron of the 7th Dragoon Guards cantered into a wood while a second cut off the escaping Germans and a battery of field guns. The 17th Lancers and some of the Whippets then stopped a counter-attack before heading for the Amiens Defence Line. But there was no one on their right flank and they were forced to withdraw under heavy fire from Le Quesnel. The problem was, the 6th Dragoons had been pinned down in front of Beaucourt because seven Whippets had been hit or had broken down.

The Canadian Cavalry Brigade and two companies of Whippet tanks had gone in search of Brutinel's Force on the right flank. The Royal Canadian Dragoons and Lord Strathcona's Horse followed the Roye road to Fresnoy before turning north. The appearance of the cavalry and Whippet tanks made 300 Germans surrender in Beaucourt but those in the adjacent wood held on until the Canadian infantry arrived.

The Canadian Corps had advanced 8 miles across the Santerre plateau and it had taken nearly all of its final objective. It had captured over 5,000 men and 161 guns of all calibres. Infantry casualties had been as low as 3,500 but only five of the tanks would be ready to fight the following morning.

Fourth Army Summary

The ground mist began to clear around 8 am and the RAF's observers could see the roads behind the German line were getting busy with traffic. By midday, Major General John Salmond decided it was time to cancel his bombing plan and order as many planes as possible to attack the bridges over the River Somme, to hit the traffic moving east. The decision turned out to be a disastrous one.

The German Air Force was sending as many planes as it could to the skies over Fourth Army and the low cloud was squeezing the planes into a limited amount of air space. The German pilots chased the Allied pilots with ease as they focused on hitting the bridges rather than defending themselves. Over 200 planes flew over the Somme but none of the bridges were damaged, never mind destroyed. But forty-four aeroplanes were shot down while another fifty-two returned to their aerodromes in a damaged condition.

So far, Fourth Army's divisions had suffered less than 9,000 casualties. The number of prisoners was far higher, with Fourth Army taking 12,400 while the French had captured 3,350. Haig was pleased with the early reports but later ones were not as optimistic. Feedback from the Australian Corps and Canadian Corps was good but Rawlinson was concerned that III Corps was in difficulty, north of the River Somme. Haig wanted the French to deploy their cavalry on the British right flank, but the roads were too congested. He visited Debeney's headquarters to hear that the French First Army had not reached its objectives.

Haig then returned to his headquarters where Foch gave him a summary of the day's events. There had been great successes in the centre of Fourth Army but there had been failures on the flanks. Rawlinson gave instructions to renew the advance the following day but there were problems. The Tank Corps had lost one in four tanks while many more were in the workshops. The Royal Air Force had also suffered many losses.

The German Reaction

The attack had taken Ludendorff and Army Group commander Böhn by surprise. The Allies had driven part of Second Army and Eighteenth Army back up to 8 miles and 'the front line divisions which had been struck between the Somme and the Avre were nearly completely annihilated.' Battalions had 'quite shrunk to nothing, barely any infantry left' while many were 'surrounded and had to lay down their arms'. Many batteries had also been knocked out or captured.

Generals Marwitz and Hutier had thrown their reserves into the breach but they had come under air attack and long range artillery bombardments as they struggled to get forward along the crowded roads. Stragglers were full of tales of defeat while the reserves had few maps and little knowledge of the ground.

Ludendorff later referred to 8 August as a 'black day' for the German Army (one of several). 'As the sun set on 8 August the greatest defeat which the German Army had suffered since the beginning of the War was an accomplished fact.' The number of men killed, wounded or captured would top over 27,000.

Chapter 5

We have Nearly Reached the Limit of our Powers of Resistance

9 to 20 August

Fourth Army

A quiet night followed the noise and excitement of 8 August. Rawlinson's general instructions for 9 August were simple: 'Having secured the old Amiens defence line, Fourth Army will push forward tomorrow and establish itself on the general line Roye–Chaulnes–Bray-sur-Somme–Dernancourt.' Only this time there would be no surprise, there were fewer tanks available and the Germans had rushed up seven divisions to reinforce their line.

General Butler was to decide when III Corps was ready to advance north of the River Somme. General Currie would do the same on Fourth Army's right flank, knowing he was supported by the Cavalry Corps. General Monash had to conform the Australian Corps' advance with the attacks to his flanks. The freedom to decide zero hour and the vast number of redeployments meant there were delays on 9 and 10 August. The Germans were busy moving divisions to the threatened area but Fourth Army only had one. Rawlinson also knew that he faced a wide area of old trenches and wire and the Germans could make a stand anywhere.

III Corps

The attack on 8 August had proved that the Germans were holding the area between the Ancre and the Somme in strength. Lieutenant General Butler planned to capture the outposts holding the north end of the Chipilly spur at first light, following an advance against the old Amiens defences at 10 am. But he wanted 131st American Regiment (as strong as a British brigade) and it took until mid-afternoon to reorganise the front line.

12th Division, 9 to 13 August, Morlancourt to Méaulte

Major General Harold Higginson was originally told that 37 Brigade's pincer attack on Morlancourt was to be made at 4.30 am but the time was postponed to 5.30 pm to give time for an American regiment to enter the line. Brigadier General Incledon-Webber managed to halt the 6th Queen's Own and 6th Queen's in time but the 6th Buffs did not get the message and Lieutenant Colonel Smeltzer's men had to be recalled. They had encountered little resistance south of the village, but the long delay had allowed the Germans time to reinforce Morlancourt and they were waiting for 37 Brigade.

One tank was knocked out as it crawled forward too early and the firing alerted the enemy. Lieutenant Colonel Dawson led the 6th Queen's Own towards the Amiens Outer Defence Line on horseback while Sergeant Thomas Harris silenced two machine-gun posts. He was killed charging a third and would be posthumously awarded the Victoria Cross. The Queen's advanced late and Captain Paish braved heavy machine-gun fire to run across to a tank to convince the crew to help his men silence a strongpoint. The Buffs were also late but Privates Caldwell and Wallace silenced the crew of a field gun and a tank helped capture 350 prisoners. Lieutenant Colonel Saint's Cambridge Regiment was able to clear Morlancourt after Company Sergeant Major Betts captured thirty men and four machine guns; he would be awarded the Military Cross.

Higginson expected the Germans to hold Hill 105, opposite his right flank, on 10 August. Brigadier General Maxwell-Scott and 58th Division's GSO1, Lieutenant Colonel Davies, were planning a coordinated attack when they heard the Germans were abandoning their trenches south of the hill. Maxwell-Scott ordered Lieutenant Colonel Goodland to move the 5th Berkshires forward while Davies told the Londoners the same.

The 6th Queen's, the 9th Essex and the 6th Buffs advanced across the ridge north of Hill 105 at 6 pm but a counter-attack forced the six tanks to withdraw, taking Lieutenant Colonel Sweltzer's Buffs with them. At dawn the following morning, Lieutenant Colonel Van Someren's 9th Royal Fusiliers captured their objective around Méaulte but Lieutenant Colonel Thompson's 7th Sussex could not hold theirs.

58th Division, Chipilly Spur to Morlancourt, 9 and 10 August

Major General Frank Ramsey's men were 'absolutely fagged out and sick of it' but they 'somehow moved off into the wood and got into position' when they received last minute orders to capture Chipilly spur. The attack was then postponed, and while the barrage was cancelled, 174 Brigade's battalions advanced at different times behind just three tanks.

Lieutenant Colonel Benson's 6th London Regiment was the first to be pinned down by enfilade fire from Les Célestins Wood, while Lieutenant Johnstone's 7th London Regiment were stopped en route to Gressaire Wood. Part of the 2/10th London reinforced the left flank and the guns finally opened fired in support; only they were firing short.

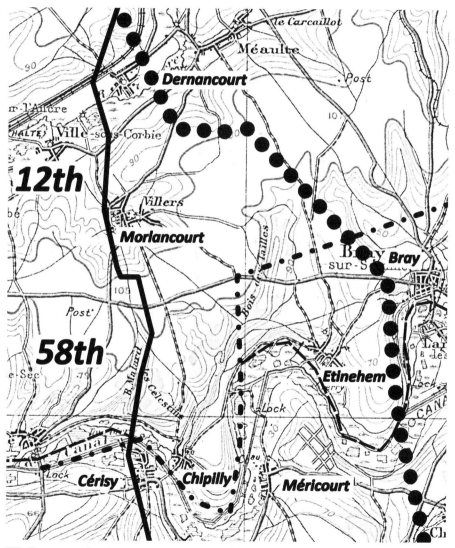

III Corps made slow progress across the Morlancourt ridge between 9 and 20 August.

The rest of the division advanced at 5.30 pm towards the Amiens Defence Line. Lieutenant Colonel Derviche-Jones's 8th and Lieutenant Colonel Chart's 12th London Regiment advanced behind five tanks across Hill 105. The orders reached Lieutenant Colonel Sanborn's 131st Regiment late, so the Americans had to run alongside the tanks through Malard Wood to catch up with the barrage. A smoke screen failed to cover Captain Richmond's 1st Battalion and Major Gale's 2nd Battalion, so they were both pinned down. Major Allen's 3rd Battalion and Lieutenant Colonel Johnstone's 7th London Regiment helped them capture the sector headquarters in Gressaire Wood after dusk.

The 2/2nd, 3rd, and 2/4th London Regiments were hit by crossfire from Chipilly and Gressaire Wood as soon as they left Malard Wood. Brigadier General Corkran had to wait until they had both been cleared before sending 173 Brigade forward again after dusk. The barrage had missed the machine guns around Chipilly, so the gunners fired smoke while Australian soldiers led the Londoners along the river bank behind the enemy position. A company of 3rd Battalion of the American 131st Regiment and three companies of the 4th Australian Division joined in, using captured machine guns to fire at the enemy as they ran from Chipilly spur, and around 200 were rounded up.

Patrols later discovered Germans were retiring towards the Amiens Defence Line, but their rearguards fired on 175 Brigade and 131st American Regiment as they moved cautiously forward. They found around seventy guns and howitzers in Gressaire Wood, all abandoned because their limbers had been unable to rescue them. Major General Frank Ramsey was pleased to hear that the 9th London Regiment had helped 131st American Regiment clear Bois de Tailles. He also heard the Londoners had been unable to reach the Amiens Defence Line south of Hill 105, but the Americans had cleared it along the river bank.

Haig visited III Corps headquarters on 11 August, to find that Lieutenant General Butler had been unable to sleep due to the stress of battle. He had served as deputy chief of staff at GHQ for over two years, so Haig knew him well and made him rest. Lieutenant General Alexander Godley (from XXII Corps) took his place at III Corps for the time being.

The Australian Corps

After all the activity on 8 August, the 'next morning almost the whole battle-front remained surprisingly tranquil until nearly noon' on 9 August. Lieutenant General Monash had to wait until III Corps had reached Bray-sur-Somme north of the Somme before he could send his left through Chuignolles.

Rawlinson realised the meandering Somme needed to be tackled by one corps, so the Australian Corps took over the north side of the river. Lieutenant General Monash's plan was for the 3rd Australian Division to relieve part of III Corps and 4th Australian Division astride the river. The 2nd and 1st Australian Divisions would advance through 5th Australian Division, as the front widened out beyond the Amiens Defence Line. At each stage Monash promised that 'a strong body of tanks would assist, in order to minimise casualties. The artillery support [would] be considerable.' Monash issued the orders to advance at 10 am on 9 August but his subordinate headquarters were no longer connected by telephone lines now they were moving in the open. Lieutenant General Currie postponed the attack for an hour but he was still concerned that the Australians would not be ready in time. He was assured that they would be, even though 5th Australian Division would be continuing the attack, because 1st Australian Division was not ready to take over the line.

4th Australian Division, 10 August, North of the Somme

Major General Sinclair-Maclagan took over the Chipilly spur from 58th Division before dawn on 10 August. Monash's plan was to make a pincer attack either side of the Somme river later that night. Four tanks accompanied 13 Brigade's advance north of the river but they soon returned because they had only been sent forward to scare the Germans with the noise of their engines.

Lieutenant Colonel Arell's 49th Battalion made a north facing flank while Lieutenant Colonel Salisbury's 50th Battalion dug in along the Étinehem spur. A flare illuminated the area so the Germans withdrew from the north end while 51st Battalion was able to occupy an empty Étinehem the following morning. The 13 Brigade cleared the rest of Étinehem spur early on 13 August and 62-year-old Colonel Sanborn of the 2nd Battalion, 131st US Regiment, took control of the area the following night.

3rd Australian Division, 10 August, Astride the Somme

Lieutenant General Monash's plan was for Major General John Gellibrand's division to make a night attack with tanks, believing 'the German [was] in a condition of great confusion; we have only to hit him without warning and roll him up.' At the same time, 'several armoured cars dashing eastward along the Roman road with headlights full on' would provide a diversion. Lieutenant Colonels Heseltine and Knox-Knight received the orders 'with some amazement' while the tank officers 'thought the job was mad'.

Officers thought 'someone's confidence had overreached itself after the overwhelming success of 8th August,' while the other ranks just thought 'the enterprise was ridiculous and stupid'.

The tanks were only going to be deployed to make noise, not to become engaged in the fighting, but Brigadier General McNicoll misunderstood the plan and Major Grounds told his crews to lead the attack, as they normally did. It left Captain Hickey struggling to find a route across the battlefield and onto the road in the dark. Lieutenant Colonel Knox-Knight was nervous as 38th and 37th Battalion approached the enemy line between Proyart and Rainecourt, believing there would 'be a train load of VCs waiting for us when we get back if it is a success, but we won't want them if we get through with our lives.'

The German response began with a plane flying low over the Roman road, dropping bombs, sending the infantry diving for cover in the ditches. Then flares lit up the sky for the machine guns and anti-tank rifles, as the tanks fired blindly back into the darkness. Lieutenant Ashmead reported, 'the battalion's cut to pieces, it is no use going further,' as it struggled to deploy into the fields. Some of the tanks turned back, finding the drivers and animals of the transport 'strewn over the roadway'. The German artillery finished off the attack with high explosive and gas shells. It took until dawn to extract everyone and any sign of movement attracted a stream of bullets.

Little happened north of the Somme on 11 August and the artillery dealt with the German attempts to reinforce their line by 'dribbling' small parties forward. Men from the American 131st Regiment helped 51st Battalion secure the north end of the Étinehem spur ready to attack at 1 am the following morning.

As 50th Battalion reached La Neuville on the east side, 51st Battalion moved down the spur. A bayonet charge took around 350 prisoners while 43rd Battalion cleared Méricourt south of the river. Later that evening, 37th Battalion moved silently into the Proyart, seizing part of the village. To the south, Sergeant Percy Statton pinned down two machine-gun posts with Lewis gun fire, so 40th Battalion could advance. Later he silenced two crews pinning down an adjacent battalion with his revolver after the men sent to deal with them were hit. Statton would be awarded the Victoria Cross.

2nd Australian Division, 9 to 11 August, Framerville

Major General Charles Rosenthal received his orders to pass through 5th Australian Division's left late and the field artillery deployed too late to fire a creeping barrage. The officers received 'hurried verbal instructions as to the objective and boundaries but some of the tank officers had no time to ascertain either'. All the while German planes strafed and bombed the assault troops as they assembled.

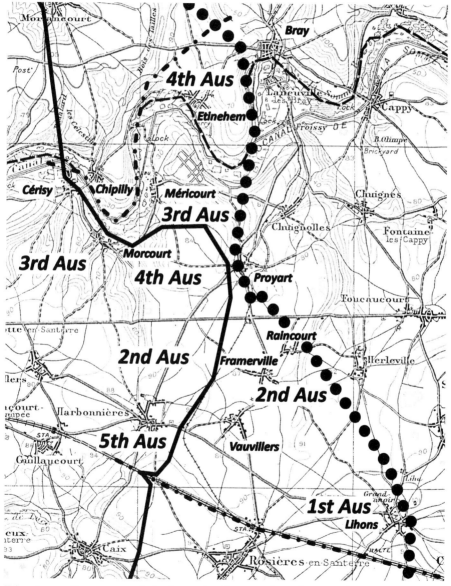

The Australians struggled along the Somme but they made good progress towards Lihons.

Most of the Germans fled as the attack developed, but 15th and 17th Battalions still took 300 prisoners around Framerville. Fifteen tanks led the advance but the German machine-gunners did not realise most were supply tanks because hardly any fighting tanks were still running. The anti-tank gunners did not discriminate and eleven were knocked out. The 27th Battalion became spread out between Framerville and Vauvillers but the Germans fled at the sight of the supply tanks. Two tanks were put out of action as Lieutenant Colonel Davis's 25th Battalion came under heavy fire as they helped 1st Australian Division form a flank south of Vauvillers.

There were plenty of guns to support Major General Rosenthal's next attack but there were no tanks left. The 20th Battalion came under enfilade fire from the left as they advanced south of the St Quentin road and the 28th Battalion helped Lieutenant Colonel Forbes' men form a defensive flank in time to stop a counter-attack from Proyart. The men of 19th Battalion 'found the Germans withdrawing, apparently by order, and stopping at intervals to fire' through Rainecourt until the mist lifted and then their machine-gun teams opened fire. As 28th Battalion cleared a 'screen of light machine guns' south-east of Framerville, 26th Battalion met no one in the mist. But snipers were able to target the Australians as soon as it lifted. A short advance east of Framerville the following day was followed by a lull in the fighting. A final attack was made by 6 Brigade on 18 August, and while it took Herleville, it was later forced to retire.

5th Australian Division, 9 August, Framerville and Vauvillers

Major General Talbot Hobbs' frontage would widen as it advanced beyond the Amiens Defence Line, so the plan was for the 1st Australian Division to pass through his right. But late orders and a German bombardment delayed the deployment. The supporting barrage had finished and the smoke screen had dispersed by the time 29th Battalion advanced toward Vauvillers. A hidden anti-tank gun knocked out six of Major Bennewith's tanks and many of Lieutenant Colonel McArthur's men were hit as they cleared the Amiens Defence Line south of the St Quentin road.

There was no sign of the 1st Australian Division on 5th Australian Division's right, so Brigadier General Elliott asked for permission to advance next to the Canadians. Only 15 Brigade 'was given no objective', the tanks did not turn up and there had been no time to arrange a barrage. Elliott was also unaware that the cavalry patrols in front of the Canadians had withdrawn, allowing the Germans to reoccupy their trenches on his right flank.

The hasty plan resulted in both the 58th and the 60th Battalions being pinned down as they crossed the Amiens Defence Line. Lieutenant Deane then had to cover the south flank until the Canadians turned up and they then handed over a tank so Lieutenant Cookson could advance along the railway line. The battalions of 1st and 2nd Australian Divisions reached the Harbonnières area a couple of hours later but the Germans were planning to withdraw because 8 Brigade was already behind their flank. Elliott's men charged as soon as they saw signs of a retirement, taking around 440 prisoners around Vauvillers.

1st Australian Division, 9 to 11 August, Lihons

Major General William Glasgow's orders to pass through 5th Australian Division's right were issued late. Motorcars and motorcyclists toured the battalion headquarters but runners then had to find the companies as they marched forward. It made the attack late and, again, there was no time to prepare the field artillery, so the infantry relied on the tanks for support.

Brigadier General Heane's 2 Brigade eventually passed through 15 Brigade en route to Lihons hill. Lieutenant Colonel Herrod's 7th Battalion faced considerable opposition and every one of Major Laskey's fourteen tanks were knocked out. Eventually Captain Phillips had to follow old trenches to get behind the German position.

Two batteries opened fire as 8th Battalion approached Crépey Wood and 'it was butchery for the tanks' as another five were knocked out. Lieutenant Colonel Mitchell's men persevered and Private Robert Beatham and Lance Corporal Nottingham silenced four machine-gun teams before turning the weapons on their enemy. An injured Beatham was killed taking another post and was posthumously awarded the Victoria Cross while Nottingham was awarded the Distinguished Conduct Medal.

Brigadier General Bennett received his orders late, so 3 Brigade could only take over part of 2 Brigade's front on 10 August. All the tank crews were exhausted, while the artillery fired too far ahead because of the short notice. Then 'an aeroplane with black German crosses came over very low, and circled, a man leaning out from its side. It fired two white flares and its machine gun chattered, some of the troops firing back with their Lewis guns at the shoulder.'

The enemy barrage fell on the Australians as they advanced at 8 am towards Lihons, and Lieutenant Colonel Colvin was killed as 25th Battalion helped 11th Battalion form a flank near Vauvillers. The 11th lost seven officers in minutes, 'men whom neither the AIF nor Australia could afford to lose.' Lieutenant Colonel Mullen's 9th Battalion failed to get around Crépey Wood until 10th Battalion joined in and they then had to stop a counter-attack. Lieutenant Colonel Luxton's 5th Battalion and Lieutenant Colonel Ulrich's 6th Battalion lost heavily as they advanced towards Lihons.

Part of the problem was the heavy enfilade fire across the railway, where the Canadians had not received the revised orders to advance. They had been addressed to the 'Australian Division on our flank' and had ended up with 5th Australian Division in reserve by mistake. Major General Hobbs understandably thought a copy had been sent to all divisions.

Major General William Glasgow prepared his infantry for a 4 am advance on 11 August but only six of the nine tanks could find them in the mist. Four soon broke down because they had been used time and again over the previous four days. Eleven officers were hit as 11th Battalion covered the north flank. An enemy plane then directed a mustard gas bombardment onto Crépey Wood and Augur Wood as Lieutenant Penrose's 9th Battalion passed through. Counter-attacks threatened to cut off Lihons until Lieutenant Colonel Neligan's 10th Battalion helped 11th Battalion restore the line. Meanwhile, Lieutenant Colonel Luxton's 9th Battalion entered Lihons, rescuing around 900 civilians hiding from the battle. Lieutenant Colonel Mitchell discovered the Canadians were not moving on his right as 8th Battalion advanced parallel with the Nesle railway but Lieutenant Colonel Ulrich had led 6th Battalion onto the hill south of Lihons hill by dusk.

After a week of almost continuous fighting Lieutenant Colonel Monash was able to call a halt. The Australian Corps had captured 8,767 prisoners and over one hundred guns.

The Canadian Corps

A change of heart by Fourth Army headquarters disrupted Lieutenant Colonel Arthur Currie's plans for 9 August. Originally, 32nd Division was going to join his Canadian Corps but Rawlinson decided not to commit his reserve divisions just yet during the evening. It meant that 3rd Canadian Division had to return to the front line, to attack for a second day running. It took many hours to inform by motor car and despatch rider because everyone was on the move. It meant the advance did not start until 4.30 pm, leaving insufficient daylight to capture the next objective. It had also given the Germans time to move up reserves to their new line of defence, about 1 mile ahead of the Amiens Defence Line.

The Left Flank, Rosières and Méharicourt

2nd Canadian Division, 9 August, Rosières

Both 29th and 31st Battalions came under fire as they advanced next to the Nesle railway, towards Rosières. It increased as they moved up the open slope because the troops on the flanks were late. Brigadier General Bell's men ended up pinned down for an hour as they waited for their tanks to catch up. They were late because they had nowhere safe to assemble, until smoke grenades were used to hide them.

Five tanks broke down or were knocked out but the remaining two 'took out one machine-gun nest after another' as planes strafed and bombed the German positions. One tank was hit helping 29th Battalion clear Rosières while the final tank was knocked out as 31st Battalion advanced to the south. Then 28th Battalion captured a sugar factory before 27th Battalion joined the advance towards Méharicourt.

Brigadier General Ross had been waiting for his fifteen tanks to arrive before allowing 5 Canadian Brigade to advance but Major General Burstall urged him to send his men forward to help 6 Canadian Brigade. A contact plane had reported Vrély was abandoned but machine-gun fire told a different story. Scouts led 22nd and 25th Battalions along sunken roads and ditches, pointing out enemy positions to the Lewis gunners. Lieutenant Jean Brillant was seriously wounded as he rushed and silenced the crew of a field gun firing at the 22nd Battalion. He continued to lead his men until he collapsed and died the following day; he was posthumously awarded the Victoria Cross.

By mid-afternoon both battalions were beyond Vrély but a squadron of the 9th Lancers were driven back by machine-gun fire as they cantered towards Fouquescourt. Two Whippets were knocked out before the other four withdrew. The advance was also compromised when a shell hit 5 Brigade's headquarters, injuring Brigadier General Ross; Lieutenant Colonel Tremblay, 22nd Battalion's commanding officer, took over.

Major General Henry Burstall was instructed to consolidate his position in the old trenches around Méharicourt, while 4th Canadian Division pushed through his right flank towards the village.

The Centre Sector, Vrély to Fouquescourt

1st Canadian Division, Vrély, 9 August

The plan was for 2 Canadian Brigade to side-slip south of the Luce stream, a difficult move which took far longer than expected. Brigadier General

Loomis twice arranged for the attack to be postponed but the gunners did not hear of the second change, leaving 8th and 5th Battalions to advance without artillery support. The twelve tanks were also late and it was some time before they caught the infantry up.

The 8th Battalion came under a lot of machine-gun fire from Hatchet Wood which hit many, including their commanding officer, Major Raddall. Corporal Frederick Coppins led four men forward when his platoon was pinned down, but they were killed and he was wounded as he silenced the machine gun. Corporal Alexander Brereton also silenced a couple of machine-gun posts, so the rest of his platoon could take out the rest. Both Coppins and Brereton would be awarded the Victoria Cross. The 8th Battalion continued on its way but the 16th Lancers could not silence German machine-gunners firing from a copse; there had been 400 casualties around Vrély.

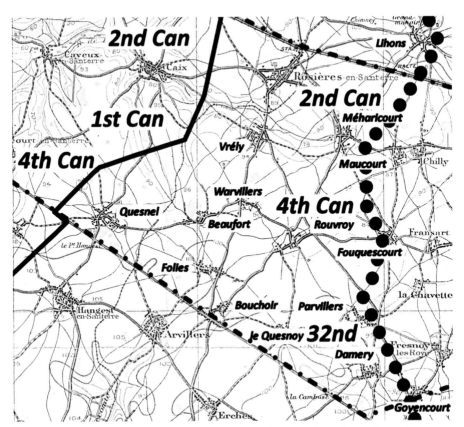

The Canadians cleared the Amiens Defence Line but then German reinforcements arrived.

The 5th Battalion advanced faster because it encountered less resistance, so Major Pyman had to wait until the 8th Battalion had caught up on his flank. His men then came under machine-gun fire as they approached Warvillers and the adjacent wood. A squadron of the 5th Lancers cantered around the north side coming under fire as they negotiated several barbed wire fences. Sergeant Raphael Zengel silenced one machine-gun team and continued to direct fire when he recovered from a shell burst; he would be awarded the Victoria Cross. Both 8th and 6th Battalions had advanced another mile between Méharicourt and Rouvroy-en-Santerre by dusk.

Major General Glasgow postponed 1 Canadian Brigade's advance until 1.15 pm to allow the artillery to prepare its barrage. The 2nd Battalion advanced beside in small rushes through Beaufort Chateau woods, only to come under fire from the old British trenches. Seven Whippets helped clear the village and Marmites Farm, so the infantry could continue towards Rouvroy. Meanwhile, 1st Battalion had worked their way through Folies before waiting for 4th Battalion to advance up to Rouvroy with the tanks. Brigadier General Griesbach sent the 3rd Battalion forward later and it cleared the village after dusk.

4th Canadian Division, 10 and 11 August, Chilly, Hallu and Fouquescourt

The twelve tanks were late so zero hour was delayed by two hours, giving the artillery more time to bombard the old British trenches between Chilly and Fouquescourt. There were no detailed maps of the old French trenches so the Canadians were going to have to move slowly and carefully.

On the left, 85th Battalion came under enfilade fire because the Australians were held up in front of Lihons. The 72nd Battalion drove the Germans out of Maucourt and then the late tanks helped them advance through old French trenches around Chilly, en route to Hallu and Fransart.

Artillery fire knocked out three tanks while machine-gun fire from Maucourt and Fouquescourt scythed through 44th and 46th Battalions. Both 47th and 44th Battalions were clearing Fouquescourt when a bombardment drove them out. Two tanks then turned up, and while one was knocked out, the other led Brigadier General Hayter's men back into Fouquescourt. More tanks turned up during the evening, securing the line.

Artillery fire interfered with 12 Canadian Brigade's deployment around Hallu the following day and then the Canadian artillery did not see the SOS signals when the Germans attacked. Lieutenant James Tait rallied his company as 78th Battalion retired to the railway, but he led them back west of the village, silencing a machine gun which allowed his men to capture another twelve. Tait was wounded during another counter-attack but he stayed with his men until he died. It was his second brave deed in four days and he would be posthumously awarded the Victoria Cross.

Despite Tait's efforts, ground had been lost and Brigadier General MacBrien did not try to advance again until the troops on his flanks had moved up. Eight tanks came forward to help the support battalions attack the old trench system for a second time, and while 78th Battalion re-entered Hallu, a counter-attack drove 38th Battalion back towards Chilly.

Both 12 and 10 Canadian Brigades were late starting on 11 August, and the German guns were hammering their jumping-off line around Fransart and Rouvroy before they were ready. The Canadian artillery did not see the signal for an SOS barrage when the enemy infantry advanced from Hallu Wood.

Hallu village was lost but otherwise 78th and 50th Battalions held on. No counter-attack was made 'in view of General Rawlinson's policy of not pushing the attack in the face of strong opposition'.

3rd Canadian Division, Parvillers and Damery, 12 to 14 August

Major General Lipsett's men were once more back in the line, clearing the old trenches between Fouquescourt and Parvillers. Lieutenant Thomas Dinesen silenced five machine guns around Quarry Wood and Middle Wood single-handedly on 12 August. His courage and leadership resulted in 42nd Battalion capturing 1 mile of trenches; he would be awarded the Victoria Cross. Middle Wood was lost the following day but the PPCLI captured Parvillers. Sergeant Robert Span was killed holding off a counter-attack with his Lewis gun while his comrades escaped. He was posthumously awarded the Victoria Cross.

Both 7 and 9 Canadian Brigades kept up the pressure, clearing Middle Wood, Blücher and Hermann Woods on 14 August. They then made a Chinese attack against the front of Damery while the real attack cleared the village; over 150 prisoners were seized during a failed counter-attack. The Royal Canadian Corps and 116th Battalion eventually took Parvillers the following day. The 52nd Battalion stopped the counter-attack that followed, 'mowing down large numbers of Germans as they marched forward in massed formation;' over 200 prisoners were taken. Damery fell soon after and the French then took Z Wood.

1st Canadian Division, Fransart, 16 to 19 August

Major General Macdonell's men took over from 3rd Canadian Division on 16 August, and while 19th Battalion secured Fransart, 13th Battalion could not take La Chavatte until the following morning. Lieutenant General

Currie was considering how to take Fresnoy when he was instructed to hand over his 7 mile sector between Chilly and Goyencourt to the French.

The Canadian Corps had taken 9,200 prisoners and captured nearly 200 guns in just twelve days. It had advanced over 15 miles, most of them covered during the first two days of the offensive, and had suffered just over 11,000 casualties. Currie told his men, 'This magnificent victory has been won because your training was good, your discipline was good and your leadership was good'. But there was no time to rest because the Canadian Corps would spend the next two weeks moving north to First Army, where it would attack east of Arras.

The Right Flank, Le Quesnel to Damery

4th Canadian Division, Le Quesnel, 9 August

Major General David Watson's men made the first attack on 9 August. The 11 Canadian Brigade and Brutinel's Independent Force had to capture Le Quesnoy, the only part of the original Canadian Corps objective remaining in German hands. Zero hour had been set for 4.30 am but the telephone lines were not secure so all messages had to be distributed by runners, cyclists or mounted messengers.

Brigadier General Odlum struggled to give his orders out in time in the dark. The 87th Battalion was nowhere to be seen on the left when 75th Battalion advanced towards Le Quesnel five minutes after zero hour. The despatch rider carrying the order for the artillery could not find the batteries, so they did not start firing until five minutes after the infantry advanced. But the problems over timing confused the Germans as well and the Canadians captured a divisional headquarters in the village.

Two of 87th Battalion's companies appeared over an hour later and they cleared the north and east sides of Le Quesnel while 75th Battalion moved through the wood to the south. Five tanks were sent to deal with a group of stubborn Germans in the Amiens Outer Defence Line but two had been knocked out by the time they withdrew. Only then could 3rd Canadian Division start passing through, en route to the next objective. Meanwhile Major General David Watson had to prepare to attack through the Canadian Corps' centre.

3rd Canadian Division, 9 to 16 August, Folies, Bouchoir and Parvillers

Major General Louis Lipsett was to advance beyond Le Quesnel but he only had one brigade left capable of offensive action. It meant the rest of the

Canadian Corps had to shuffle sideways to compensate for its short front, delaying all the divisions. Meanwhile, Brigadier General Draper assembled 8 Canadian Brigade with seven tanks around Beaucourt-en-Santerre, 3 miles behind 4th Canadian Division's line.

Draper was to advance as soon as 4th Canadian Division cleared Le Quesnel but that took until the afternoon. The only benefit of the delay was that the French had caught up south of the road. Two tanks were knocked out as the 4th Mounted Rifles moved past the north side of Folies but a third joined them during the advance to Bouchoir. Two tanks and a number of motorcycle-mounted machine guns helped the 5th Mounted Rifles bypass the south side of the village before seven Whippets and the Royal Scots Greys cleared it.

Major General Lipsett's Canadians attacked again at 4.20 am on 10 August. The 1st Mounted Rifles advanced to the old French trenches in front of Parvillers while eight tanks accompanied the 2nd Mounted Rifles en route to Le Quesnoy. Four were knocked out but the hamlet was taken, opening the way for 32nd Division to attack the old trenches systems beyond.

32nd Division, 10 and 11 August, Fouquescourt, Le Quesnoy, Parvillers and Damery

Major General Thomas Lambert's artillery had been hit by a bombing raid during the night, so they were not ready to fire until 10.30 am. His infantry took over the line between Rouvroy and Le Quesnoy on the right of the corps line, and they faced an old French front line where the Germans were expected to hold on.

Sixteen heavy tanks were late while the seven Whippets struggled to cross the old trenches around Rouvroy. An officer from 6th Tank Battalion went forward to see what the problem was, only to discover that they had all ditched and anti-tank guns had already knocked out four.

Eight tanks led 97 Brigade towards Parvillers and there was plenty of machine-gun fire until the 5th Border Regiment and the 10th Argylls got through the wire, and then the Germans ran. But all but one of the tanks had been knocked out and machine-gun fire from the old German trenches stopped Brigadier General Girdwood's men cutting through the old entanglements around Fouquescourt and Parvillers.

The 15th Lancashire Fusiliers helped the Canadians clear Le Quesnoy but they missed a machine-gun post in Wood 99 and it had wounded Major Uniacke before Lieutenant Colonel Utterson's 16th Lancashire Fusiliers silenced it. Captain Gill and Major Mandelburg gathered all the stragglers they could find and then advanced towards Parvillers. All eight tanks were knocked out before Major Knott captured a battery of field guns but a lot of the Lancashire Fusiliers had been hit. The right flank was in danger because the French were struggling, so Brigadier General Minshull-Ford sent the 2nd Manchesters forward to help consolidate the position.

Both Knott and Lieutenant Colonel Kutterson were hit and Captains Gill and Smith were unable to hold Square Wood, even though an extra four tanks were sent forward to help the Lancashire Fusiliers. When Major General Lambert heard that his battalions were exhausted, most of his tanks had been knocked out and his artillery was short of ammunition, he still had to tell his two brigadiers to prepare to attack the following morning.

Brigadier General Evans (14 Canadian Brigade's commander) had been given 32nd Division's battalions so he could capture Parvillers and Damery on 11 August. The plan was for the machine-gunners and artillery to hammer the villages while sixteen tanks led the infantry past. The guns would then extend their range while they turned back to attack the ruins from the rear. At least that was the plan.

Zero hour had to be postponed by an hour to 9.30 am because neither the infantry nor the tanks were ready. Some of the tanks were late while the barrage landed too far ahead, missing many machine-gun and mortar teams hiding in ditches and shell holes. Machine-gun fire from La Chavatte hit the 2nd KOYLIs as they followed tanks towards Parvillers. But three ditched and another three were knocked out by an anti-tank gun, so the two survivors fell back. All eight tanks leading the 5/6th Royal Scots 'were wrecked while crossing our front line'. Many of Lieutenant Colonel Fraser's men, including Captains Darling and MacCrae, were hit as they cut though the wire in front of Damery. The 1st Dorsets were also unable to capture Z Wood because the French were struggling south of the Roye road.

As news of the problems came in, Currie became worried that 32nd Division would use up its scant reserves. Major General Lambert rode out to order Brigadier Evans and Minshull-Ford to cancel further attacks and then again to tell them to dig in. During the afternoon it looked as if the Germans were abandoning Damery, so Brigadier General Evans ordered the 15th HLI forward. The movement drew fire from the enemy lines, so the attack was cancelled. The 3rd Canadian Division relieved 32nd Division during the night.

2nd Cavalry Division, 10 August, Fouquescourt

Brigadier General Rankin had orders to head for Nesle but the 4 Cavalry Brigade could not get past Fouquescourt.

3rd Cavalry Division, 10 August, Damery

Lieutenant General Currie told Major General Lipsett to capture the high ground north of Roye, hoping the sight of his cavalry would make the Germans abandon the town. So Brigadier General Paterson sent his Canadian Cavalry Brigade along the main road into Roye, the only road passable for horses. The leading squadron of the Fort Garry Horse came under fire from Damery and Z Wood, north of the road, so they galloped forward, jumping over wire fences and trenches to reach Goyencourt. The rest of the regiment were cut down as they charged Z Wood. Brigadier General Evans VC (awarded in the Ypres Salient in October 1917) advised Paterson to send no more of his troopers forward.

Summary

Foch visited Haig on 9 August and believed the Germans were sufficiently demoralised for the British Fourth Army and French First Army to renew the attack the following day. But Haig was convinced the Germans were still capable of putting up a fight and suggested attacking between Arras and Albert instead. So they agreed Third Army would attack Seventeenth Army's line, to see if it would withdraw towards Bapaume.

Haig went on to discuss Fourth Army's next move with Rawlinson, only to hear he was against further attacks. His divisions were tired and he was running out of tanks while the Germans had plenty of old trench systems to defend. He even said, 'are you commanding the British Army or is Marshal Foch' when he heard the Généralissime's assessment of the enemy. Haig met Rawlinson again on 11 August, to hear that more reinforcements had reached the old trench system on the western edge of the 1916 battlefield; so many in fact that German Second Army had more divisions than British Fourth Army. The Germans were holding. So now was the time to regroup the infantry, move up the artillery and repair the tanks.

Haig visited Rawlinson to hear that Fourth Army's engineers and labour units had to extend the roads and railways so the heavy artillery and their ammunition could be moved forward. The Tank Corps also needed time to repair and service the huge number of tanks disabled, and the crews needed to rest as well. Haig then heard from Lieutenant General Monash how the Australian Corps were faring after four days hard fighting. He also visited the five Australian divisions to hear how they had taken thousands of prisoners while their own casualties had been comparatively light. But he could also see the Diggers were tired and they needed time to rest and reorganise.

Haig issued an order for Fourth Army to resume the attack on 15 August but the plans were changed when the Généralissime visited GHQ's train late on 11 August. Foch was accompanied by his chief staff officer General Maxine Weygand, and his artillery advisor General Pierre Desticker. They suggested attacking different points of the German line to make Ludendorff spread his reserves. The agreed plan was for the British Third Army to advance north of the Somme while the French Tenth Army made an assault east of the Oise. Haig then warned Byng to be ready to extend the BEF's offensive front as far north as Bucquoy.

The French

Haig wanted the French to do more and he asked them to take over part of the Canadian Corps' line late on 9 August. But Debeney would only take over a small sector, so it did not upset his plans for the advance on Noyon. IX Corps had advanced alongside the Canadians as far as Arvillers and Davenscourt and then First Army extended its attack by pushing X Corps south of Montdidier, forcing the Germans to abandon the ruined town during the night. There was a general retirement opposite First Army on 10 August and Third Army was able to join in, crossing the River Matz. By now it was 'no longer a case of methodical, slow and carefully mounted attacks with a debauch of artillery fire, but of strong reconnaissances working by encirclement and pushing forward rapidly.' The advance finally stopped when Eighteenth Army occupied the old French trenches between Roye and the Laigue Forest. By the end of 11 August, First Army had advanced around 9 miles while Third Army had pushed its line forward over 6 miles.

The Germans

Reinforcements were arriving in great numbers to shore up the German line but they found the front line units all mixed up, not sure when or where the next attack would come from. Few artillery batteries had orders and the crews were just waiting for targets to appear. Meanwhile, the logistics staff were abandoning their depots, so anyone could help themselves.

'There was general excitement and fear of renewed air attacks… In the early hours of 10 August no one could give a clear idea of the actual position at the front; no one knew anything about troops on right and left, or about the divisions in position… individuals and all ranks in large parties were wandering wildly about, but soon for the most part finding their way to the rear... only here and there were a few isolated batteries in soldierly array, ready to support the reinforcing troops.'

On 11 August, Ludendorff told Kaiser Wilhelm II that the German Army had suffered a heavy defeat. Officers were struggling to control their men and there were reports of large groups surrendering to only a few men. News of the offensive was spreading and there were rumours that soldiers were planning strikes. Ludendorff even offered to resign but the Kaiser refused to accept and instead said, 'I see that we must strike a balance. We have nearly reached the limit of our powers of resistance; the war must be ended.'

Ludendorff grouped Ninth Army, Second Army and the Eighteenth Army into a new Army Group under General Max von Böhn the following day, so they could coordinate a defensive plan to hold the Hindenburg Line if they needed to fall back to it. But nothing had been done to the defensive line since Operation Michael nearly six months earlier and nothing had been done to preserve it. There were too few labour units and too little time to repair the entanglements and trenches if the Allies kept pushing.

Böhn's chief of staff, Major General Fritz von Lossberg, visited OHL headquarters only to find the quartermaster general in a despondent mood. Lossberg had suggested sending divisions back to the Hindenburg Line so they could prepare the position, but Ludendorff refused because he did not want to make such a large withdrawal which would be bad for morale. Instead he talked of building a new defensive position east of the old Somme battlefield, between Combles and Péronne, and along the River Somme and Somme–Oise Canal down to Noyon. But the chosen line was only 10 miles behind the front in places and Lossberg argued that it would take too many men too long to build. The stand-off meant that the Hindenburg Line was never repaired and no new defensive line was started.

The fighting died down across the Somme after 11 August but Fourth Army kept probing and pushing to keep the Germans under pressure. Ludendorff went as far as to report that '20 August was another black day. In some places the men could no longer stand the tremendous artillery barrages and tank attacks.'

The Meetings

General John Pershing was anxious to assemble the American Expeditionary Force as soon as possible so it could prepare to attack the St Mihiel salient south-east of Verdun. He met Haig on 12 August and asked for the American divisions currently training with the BEF. Haig wanted some to fight alongside British divisions first but he agreed they would be returned as soon as they finished their current spell in the line.

Haig then met Rawlinson, Byng and Debeney telling them he was anxious to renew the attack as soon as possible and he suggested 15 August. Both Rawlinson and Debeney said they faced a new defensive line and fresh reserves, so they wanted more time. Haig asked them for more information on the situation before agreeing to a postponement. Byng was told to expect reinforcements, so Third Army could attack between Arras and Albert, around the 21 August. He was expecting the Germans to fall back to the Somme at some point and Third Army had to be ready to advance north of Péronne to outflank the river, where it ran north to south across Fourth Army's line of advance.

Haig met Rawlinson again two days later and he was shown aerial photographs of the problems ahead of Fourth Army. The ground was littered with trenches and entanglements dating from the 1916 battles. He was also told that prisoners reported fresh German divisions had reached the area astride the Somme.

Byng reported the Germans had abandoned a 1 mile deep strip across an 8 mile front between Bucquoy and Hamel on 15 August. They had evacuated Serre and Beaumont Hamel and occupied the high ground between Puisieux and Beaucourt. The news prompted Haig to meet both Horne and Byng to discuss an extension of the BEF's operations. He wanted First Army to capture the high ground east of Arras while Third Army advanced across the north half of the 1916 battlefield towards Bapaume.

Haig and his chief of staff, Lieutenant General Herbert Lawrence, then visited Foch to explain the developing situation. The Généralissime suggested attacks by First and Fourth Armies, looking to prompt a withdrawal from the River Ancre, opposite Third Army. He would have liked to have attacked immediately but accepted that the Germans' defences had to be shelled if there was to be any chance of success. Foch also admitted that the First French Army was short of ammunition but they agreed that Debeney's command would return to General Pétain's control.

On 17 August Foch asked Haig to renew the offensive on 20 August but Pershing was again asking for his American divisions back. Foch agreed three would start transferring as soon as possible, leaving the BEF short of reserves. As a compromise he agreed the French would start relieving part of the BEF's line. It meant Haig could send the Canadian Corps to First Army, ready to attack east of Arras.

Two days later, Haig reminded Byng he was about to receive extra divisions and tanks and they agreed Third Army would start crossing the Ancre on 21 August. First Army would make fake preparations around Arras while its artillery shelled the enemy line to the north as a diversion. Third Army's flanks would attack the next day and Fourth Army would help capture the Thiepval heights. The Australian Corps would extend the attack south of the river the following day.

The renewal of the BEF's offensive was preceded by a successful attack by the French Tenth Army on 20 August. It advanced up to 2 miles across a 12-mile front between the River Oise and Soissons. Ludendorff referred to it as another black day for the German Army.

The King's Visit

His Majesty King George V had arrived in France on 5 August. Over the week that followed he visited Second, First, Third and Fifth Armies, missing out Fourth Army because it was busy fighting on the Somme. His Majesty was introduced to groups of 100 men at a time from each corps at their respective army headquarters. He also visited King Albert, commander-in-chief of the Belgian Army.

Chapter 6

The Finest Attack in Open Warfare

21 to 23 August

The time was ripe to widen the attack. The French Tenth Army would attack south on 20 August while the British Third Army would join in to the north the following day. General Sir Julian Byng assembled eight divisions in three corps across Third Army's 10 mile wide front between Arras and Albert. Haig told him to push fast but there were concerns because '50 per cent of the infantry were said to be boys, who would do well if the first action in which they took part was a success.' Several hundred artillery pieces had assembled in secret and they would open fire at zero hour: 4.55 am.

Dozens of tanks and armoured cars found it difficult to find their start points in the pre-dawn fog. The older Mark IV tanks would lead the infantry to the first objective, the newer Mark V tanks would continue to the second, while the Whippets and armoured cars would go to the exploitation line. Both VI and IV Corps had 'gun-carrying tanks' which had a 6-inch howitzer mounted on a tank chassis; the world's first self-propelled gun.

The Germans were sure something was afoot and their artillery hit the assembly areas with gas shells; the 23rd Royal Fusiliers alone suffered nearly 400 casualties near Ayette. General Otto von Below had withdrawn most of his troops out of the danger zone, deepening Seventeenth Army's outpost zone to 2 miles. It meant that Third Army would encounter camouflaged machine-gun posts and hidden anti-tank guns during the first day. They then faced the main line of defence along the Arras–Albert railway line, where cuttings and embankments restricted the tanks.

Third Army

At 4.55 am on 21 August, the second stage of the BEF's offensive began and there was little the Germans could do to stop the onslaught.

'The hostile brigades rolled forward behind a mighty curtain of fire and thoroughly smothered the very mixed up German combatants, who had to defend themselves simultaneously against infantry, squadrons of tanks, cavalry and aircraft. What did it matter if here and there our guns blew up a tank, if our machine guns shot an attacking cavalry detachment to pieces, if our fighter aeroplanes shot down several hostile machines? The enemy filled the gaps in the twinkling of an eye…'

VI Corps

Lieutenant General Sir Aylmer Haldane's men found it difficult to move in the correct direction in the mist but casualties were low because the Germans could not see their enemy until it was too late. Around 1,200 prisoners had been taken by the time the mist lifted but the enemy showed no sign of withdrawing, so a halt was called on the second objective.

59th Division, St Martin and Hénin, 21 August

Major General Sir Robert Whigham's patrols found only outposts around Hénin and St Martin because the mainline ran across Hénin Hill.

52nd Division, Hénin Hill, 22 and 23 August

Major General John Hill's artillery had been given insufficient time to register targets around Hénin Hill while Brigadier General Leggett's men had no time to reconnoitre because their guides got lost. Nine tanks struggled to catch the 1/7th Scottish Rifles and the 1/7th and 1/4th Royal Scots up in the mist but they did not have to attack the main defence line on Hénin Hill. Instead they formed a flank from Mercatel back to Boiry Becquerelle while Major Slater made sure the 1/4th Royal Scots cleared the trench next to the Cojeul stream.

Guards Division, 21 to 23 August, Moyenneville and Hamelincourt

The Germans were alert because prisoners had reported the time 2 Guards Brigade was to cross the Cojeul stream. The five tanks could not find Lieutenant Colonel Brand's 1st Coldstream Guards as they attacked Moyenneville but one tank helped Lieutenant Colonel MacKenzie's 1st Scots Guards take one hundred prisoners south of the village.

The 3rd Grenadier Guards crossed the railway and pushed on south of Hamelincourt. The tank crews had been gassed and the cavalry could not find a way through the maze of trenches. Lieutenant Colonel Thorne's men stopped a counter-attack with a 'prompt and effective reply by the British guns, combined with the steady rifle, Lewis-gun and machine-gun fire of the infantry.'

56th Division, 23 August, Boiry Becquerelle and Boyelles

Major General Sir Amyatt Hull took over the Guards' left sector during the night but his men had a long march wearing gas masks. They then 'assembled in the dark and attacked in the morning, never having seen the ground before. The artillery was no better off than the infantry.' Zero hour was set for 5.7 am, and while the twenty-one tanks were late, 168 Brigade, 'by working forward and then to a flank, evidently much demoralised the enemy.' The 1/14th London Regiment captured over one hundred prisoners in Boiry Becquerelle, while the 1/4th and 1/13th London Regiment took over one hundred prisoners around Boyelles.

The afternoon advance had mixed results. The 1/14th London struggled to capture Boiry Redoubt, but 4th London Regiment seized Boyelles Reserve Trench. Lieutenant Colonel Shaw was killed consolidating 1/13th London Regiment's new position around Bank Copse. Despite the rushed deployment, Brigadier General Loch reported his men had taken around 660 prisoners.

The Guards Division, 23 August, Hamelincourt

The 3rd Grenadier Guards had to advance early on 23 August to assist 3rd Division's assault on Gomiécourt. The German artillery retaliated and the 1st Scots Guards had to endure an hour long counter-barrage before they could move. Only three out of eight tanks accompanied the Scots Guards through Hamelincourt where 'the Germans appeared to be taken completely by surprise and surrendered freely; the earth seemed to open and give up Germans.'

The 1st Coldstream Guards reached Hally Copse and Boyelles Reserve Trench along the Sensée stream first, but it was some time before the 1st Scots Guards and the 1st Grenadiers secured the left flank. Lieutenant Colonel Bailey's 1st Grenadier Guards took 200 prisoners along Mory Switch in what was 'the finest attack in open warfare that has ever been made'. It brought the Guards' total to over 1,250 prisoners in just three days.

2nd Division, 21 August, Courcelles, Ervillers and Gomiécourt

All twelve tanks reached 99 Brigade south of Ayette but the artillery had to concentrate on hitting Moyenneville and Courcelles rather than trying to form a creeping barrage in the mist. The 1st Berkshires advanced towards Courcelles but the fog made it impossible to smell mustard gas and nearly 400 men of the 23rd Royal Fusiliers were hospitalised after advancing through an infected area. Even so, Brigadier General Ironside was able to report the attack had gone 'like clockwork' and his men had taken 200 prisoners. They dug in while eight Vickers teams (called 'guns of opportunity') kept watch as 3rd Division headed for the second objective.

3rd Division, 21 August, Courcelles, Ervillers and Gomiécourt

Major General Cyril Deverell's men passed through 2nd Division heading for the Arras–Albert railway east of Courcelles. Thick mist and smoke made

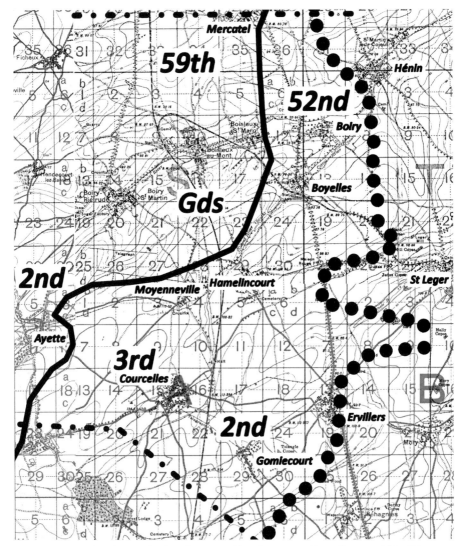

VI Corps broke through the German line between Boyelles and Ervillers.

'advancing only practicable by compass bearing', but it also blinded the German machine-gun teams.

The tanks were late but the 7th Shropshires and the 1st Royal Scots Fusiliers still reached the railway and 'the final assault was made with the bayonet, the enemy being driven out with great slaughter.' Captains Barrett and Van Gruisen were killed as the 13th King's reached the railway. Captain Steel and Captain Scanlan of the 1st Northumberland Fusiliers took 150 prisoners but they still struggled to reach the railway south of Courcelles, even with help from Major Tower's company of the 4th Royal Fusiliers.

Eventually the tank commander, Lieutenant Colonel Richard West, collected all the stragglers he could find and led them to the objective; he would be awarded the Victoria Cross. A counter-attack threatened to surround the 1st Northumberland Fusiliers but they retook the objective along with sixty prisoners.

General Haldane wanted to push his right flank forward, so Brigadier General Lawson's 2nd Cavalry Brigade was sent to explore the area. Both the 4th Dragoon Guards and 8th Hussars came under fire, losing one hundred troopers and many more horses before they withdrew.

Major General Deverell was told to capture Gomiécourt at 4 am on 22 August but the twelve tanks struggled to cross the railway because it ran along cuttings and embankments.

Four tanks were hit when the 1st Gordons and 7th Shropshires came under fire from Ervillers. Lieutenant Colonel Henderson had watched as the 2nd Royal Scots 'faded away in a manner similar to that of the Cheshire cat in Alice in Wonderland'. He later sent two companies forward to help the Shropshires reach the railway south of Courcelles.

Private Hugh McIver chased an enemy scout 'like a man possessed' before killing a machine-gun team, encouraging another twenty to put up their hands. He later bravely stopped a British tank firing at his comrades. McIver would be killed in action with the Royal Scots on 2 September 1918; he was posthumously awarded the Victoria Cross. Brigadier General Fisher's men eventually rounded up over a hundred prisoners around Ervillers.

Two Whippet tanks were knocked out as the 8th King's Own and 2nd Suffolks captured 300 prisoners, resulting in Haig mentioning 76 Brigade in his special order of the day. The remaining six Whippets could not subdue the machine guns beyond the village when the mist cleared, so a further advance was postponed.

2nd Division, 22 August, Mory, Béhagnies, Sapignies and Gomiécourt

Major General Cecil Pereira's men had to pass through 3rd Division at 11 am on 22 August. The heavy guns successfully targeted the villages but the creeping barrage proved to be too slow for the Whippets. It was also too fast for the infantry, so the field gunners had to pause it in front of Mory, Béhagnies and Sapignies until they caught up.

The 1st King's and 2nd South Staffords crossed the railway east of Courcelles with six Whippets only to come under fire from Mory Copse. Two tanks were knocked out and the two battalions suffered around 600 casualties before the attack was called off. One anti-tank gun knocked out three Whippets, forcing another four to drive south to avoid it. It left only two to accompany 2nd HLI's advance around the north side of Gomiécourt. They were unable to silence the machine-gun fire coming from Béhagnies and Lieutenant Colonel William Brodie VC (awarded for bravery in November 1914) was one of the many hit. But the 24th Royal Fusiliers 'pushed on in a determined manner, with drill like precision, steady bearing and unfaltering pace' until they too were pinned down in front of Sapignies. A brave Lewis gun team eventually stalked and killed the two gun teams, allowing the HLI and Royal Fusiliers to secure their objective.

Brigadier General Ironside had orders to protect the flank with 99 Brigade. The 1st KRRC deployed facing Gomiécourt while a single Whippet engaged several machine-gun posts. 'The guns were often placed in depth and as soon as the foremost gun was either captured or put out of action, a retirement was made to the next gun.' Even so, the KRRC seized over 400 prisoners in the sunken road along 2nd Division's south flank.

IV Corps

Lieutenant General Montague Harper's men faced the Ancre valley around Achiet-le-Petit and Miraumont, where the Germans had 'orders to hold to the last'. The creeping barrage could only cover the advance to the first objective while the plan to move two brigades of artillery forward had to be cancelled because of enemy bombardments and air attacks.

Most of the twenty-two tanks lost their way in the fog but the poor conditions allowed 37th Division's infantry to get close to the machine-gun posts. Then 63rd Division and 5th Division advanced to the final objective with twenty-four Mark V tanks and twenty-four Whippets. Another twelve Whippets, six armoured cars and 9 Cavalry Brigade would exploit beyond the Arras–Albert railway.

37th Division, 21 August, Ablainzevelle and Bucquoy

All but four of the tanks accompanied the infantry in the morning fog, help-ing the 1st Hertfords to clear Ablainzevelle while the 13th Royal Fusiliers advanced from Bucquoy. The German machine-gun teams 'fought with great determination and continued to fire until their guns were run over by the tanks'. Major General Hugh Bruce-Williams' men eventually took over 350 prisoners.

63rd Division, Logeast Wood, 21 August

Major General Charles Lawrie's late change in the order of the battalions meant the advance on 21 August started later than 5th Division's. Commander Daniel Beak would silence four enemy positions in front of the Drake Battalion, allowing the Hawke Battalion to advance through Logeast Wood as well. The German plan to withdraw then ended in confusion as 188 Brigade bypassed units in the mist. Several tanks were knocked out when it cleared and the cut-off enemy groups counter-attacked the Marines and the Anson Battalion. It forced Major General Lawrie to withdraw his flanks after dusk.

Major General Lawrie's men stopped three attacks the following day and Lieutenant Colonel Fletcher made sure the Marines held on while the 2nd Irish Regiment stopped the only break-in north of Achiet-le-Petit. They were relieved by 37th Division during the night.

5th Division, 21 August, Irles

Six tanks advanced along the road from Bucquoy and Lieutenant Colonel Roddy's 1st Cheshires had soon cleared Achiet-le-Petit. Most of the tanks were knocked out on the far side of the ruins but Major Busfield and Captain Groves still reached the railway. The 16th Warwicks found they were in danger of being shot at by the six tanks moving amongst them. The fog cleared as they climbed the ridge beyond the railway line and Lieutenant Colonel Deakin helped shoot down a battery of 5.9-inch howitzers before the Warwicks turned the guns on their former owners. A counter-attack threatened to cut off the Cheshires where the 63rd Division was lagging behind on the left, so Major Walker eventually had to withdraw after his battalion suffered over 300 casualties.

The 1st DCLI and the 1st Devons had a tough fight along the railway line south of Achiet-le-Petit, so the 1st East Surreys moved up to help. The delay meant the mist had cleared by the time Brigadier General Norton's men crossed, and all his tanks were knocked out by anti-tank guns guarding the level crossings. The 12th Gloucesters then had to extend 95 Brigade's flank back to the New Zealand Division, which was half a mile behind.

Major General John Ponsonby's division was ahead of his flanks but some patrols struck lucky as they explored the Irles area on 22 August. Lance Corporal George Onions and Private Henry Eades saw a large group of enemy soldiers approaching the 1st Devons, so the pair hid before driving them into a trench where they forced them to surrender. The two soldiers returned with 240 prisoners and 'the sight of this column advancing in fours caused a great stir.' The battalion headquarters manned a trench to face the threat before Lieutenant Colonel Halford 'detected that the column was unarmed through his glasses and headed by Onions strolling along with rifle slung and Eades doing whipper in' at the rear. The East Surreys even queried 'why the Devons had taken to practising ceremonial drill on the

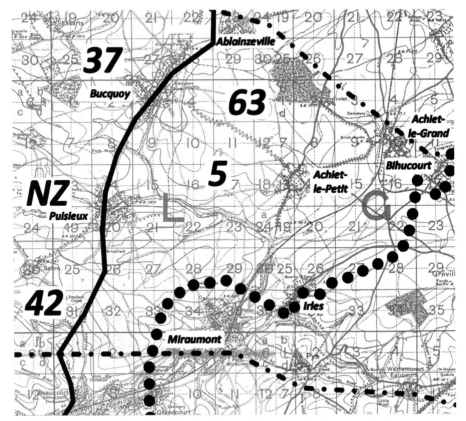

IV Corps' left reached Achiet-le-Grand but the right struggled to capture Miraumont.

battlefield.' Onions would be later awarded the Victoria Cross. Eades was recommended for the Distinguished Conduct Medal but he died of wounds before he received it. Around the same time, the 12th Gloucesters sent two platoons ahead of their line to enfilade an enemy position. They too rounded up some 180 prisoners.

37th Division, 23 August, Achiet-le-Grand and Bihucourt

The plan was to renew the advance towards Achiet-le-Grand and Bihucourt at 11 am on 23 August. Six tanks crawled to crossing places over the railway as the 13th KRRC and 13th Rifle Brigade found 'the enemy had planted machine guns on average one to every 20 yards.' They took several hundred prisoners in the dugouts along a cutting but there was a tough fight for a brickworks. The 8th Somersets then pushed into Achiet-le-Grand while the 10th Royal Fusiliers continued into Bihucourt.

The 13th Royal Fusiliers used their Lewis guns and trench mortars to put down suppressive fire against the brickworks west of Achiet-le-Grand while a group deployed on the flank, forcing the 400 strong garrison to surrender. But the new 1/1st Hertfords' commander had headed in the wrong direction and they ended up pinned down alongside the 1st Essex west of the railway until Captain Mathieson found a tank to help them. The south edge of Bihucourt was reached during the afternoon as the Royal Fusiliers and Essex made an advance 'most gallant' but the Hertfords could not reach Grévillers.

Byng told Harper to make a third attack during the evening but the artillery had no idea where the infantry were, so the barrage landed far ahead of the 11th Royal Fusiliers. It missed the machine guns close to the front line and they shot down 63 and 112 Brigades as they advanced towards Biefvillers. Everyone was back at their start line by the time it was dark.

5th Division, 21 to 23 August, Achiet-le-Petit and Loupart Wood

All the tanks were being repaired and the late zero hour at 11 am meant the mist had cleared. The German machine guns along the railway cutting shot down Captains Millais' and West's companies as the 1st Bedfords cut through the wire. Two tanks, which had wandered out of 37th Division's area, helped the Bedfords get through the three entanglements but Lieutenant Colonel Courtenay was killed leading the final charge. The 16th Warwicks lost heavily as they cleared the trenches en route to the objective, so Brigadier General Oldman sent Lieutenant Colonel Humphries' 1st Norfolks to reinforce them.

Lieutenant Colonel Minogue's 1st East Surreys reached their objective but Lieutenant Colonel Colt's 12th Gloucesters lost the barrage while crossing the railway cutting. At one location 'twenty-three machine guns were captured on a 50 yard front, each with a great heap of empty cartridges by its side.' Brigadier General Norton sent the 1st DCLI forward to help but Major Dent could not reach Irles. Captain Honywill's company of the 1st Devons cleared it during the evening.

Major General Ponsonby instructed 13 Brigade to advance towards Loupart Wood at 7.30 pm but he had no idea if Irles had been taken, so the artillery was instructed not to shell it. Lieutenant Colonel Miller's 15th Warwicks and Lieutenant Colonel Wilberforce's 14th Warwicks made good progress towards Loupart Wood, 'which had stared them in the face since the beginning', but most of Lieutenant Colonel Johnstone 1st Queen's Own lost direction and only a single platoon reached Irles. Lieutenant Colonel Colt was severely wounded as he led the 12th Gloucesters through the village. Brigadier General Jones could report his men had taken their objective but his right flank was exposed because Miraumont was still in German hands.

New Zealand Division, 21 to 23 August, Puisieux and Irles

The 3 Rifle Brigade advanced beyond Puisieux because 'the surprise so studiously aimed at was completely realised' in the thick fog. Corporal Neilson silenced two machine guns at the north end of the village, allowing 4th Rifle Brigade to capture over one hundred prisoners, while the 3rd Rifle Brigade silenced five machine guns on the south side. The two battalions then advanced east, taking another one hundred prisoners, only they went too far in the fog and had to withdraw to a safer line when it lifted.

The Germans counter-attacked from Miraumont early the following morning, driving the 3rd Rifles back until Lance Corporal Milne secured the flank by shooting twenty and taking five prisoners. Dozens more were killed at dawn and around 300 were driven north into the hands of 5th Division. The Rifles could then establish a line overlooking the railway.

At 2.30 am on 23 August, a preliminary operation by the 1st Rifles seized the high ground north of Miraumont. The battalion then advanced towards the village at 11 am, coming under fire from Irles across the Ancre valley.

42nd Division, 21 August, Beauregard Dovecot

Major General Arthur Solly-Flood's men had to clear the north bank of the Ancre and Miraumont. A company of the 1/5th Lancashire Fusiliers were pinned down around the Lozenge on Hill 140 in the mist until Lance Sergeant Ned Smith silenced a machine-gun post. He later helped another of Lieutenant Colonel Castle's platoons capture its objective and would be awarded the Victoria Cross.

Captain Hartley led the 1/7th Lancashire Fusiliers onto a ridge called Beauregard Dovecote in the mist but many were hit when the mist lifted and Lieutenant Colonel Brewis had to order a withdrawal. The seizure of Hill 140 had allowed the 1/6th and 1/7th Manchesters to clear the ridge above the River Ancre, overlooking Miraumont.

Captain Sington finally secured Beauregard Dovecote, another observation point over the Ancre valley, early the following morning. The Lancashire men stopped several counter-attacks on 22 August but machine-gun fire across the valley forced the 1/5th and 1/7th Lancashire Fusiliers to withdraw out of sight. The final counter-attack was broken up because the German barrage fell short.

Captains Bird and Harrison of the 1/8th Lancashire Fusiliers helped the 1/10th Manchester retake Beauregard Dovecote ridge during the early hours of 23 August. It secured the observation post over Miraumont that Brigadier General Fargus wanted.

V Corps

Lieutenant General Cameron Shute's men faced across the quagmire that once was the River Ancre between Grandcourt and Aveluy. 'The river was high and had overflowed wide stretches of the long marshy island between its branches and the causeways and bridges over it had been damaged or destroyed.' The Germans were holding the old trenches on the far bank. Shute's plan was to cross around Beaucourt and Hamel on his left while his right flank waited for III Corps to advance onto the Thiepval heights from the south.

21st Division, 21 to 23 August, Beaucourt

All three brigades explored the Ancre between Beaucourt and Hamel on 21 August. The 12/13th Northumberland Fusiliers crossed near Beaucourt and took Logging Trench but the 1st East Yorkshires could not secure a foothold on the far bank. The 6th and 7th Leicesters crossed around St Pierre Divion only to be driven back when the fog lifted. A counter-attack drove the 12th/13th Northumberland Fusiliers back a little way the following day, but the 6th Leicesters crossed again and contacted the

Northumberland Fusiliers. It meant 17th Division had a foothold to take over during the night.

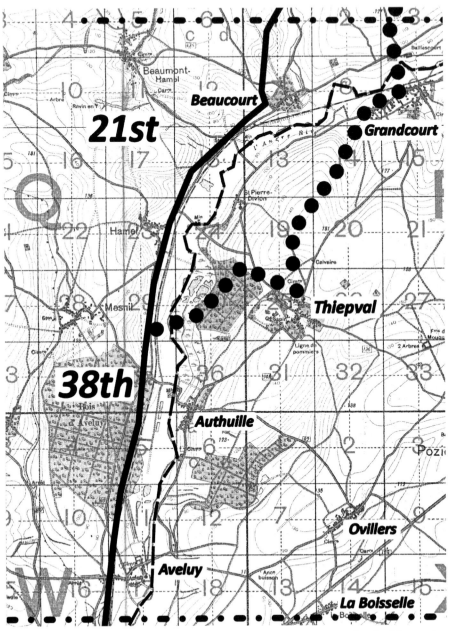

V Corps pushed its left across the River Ancre to get a foothold on the Thiepval heights.

17th Division, 23 August, Crossing the Ancre

The 6th Dorsets crossed first and 'dribbled over in small parties in single file and under continual fire. All were soaked to the waist and some to the arm pits.' They cleared Logging Support and Common Trench while the artillery and machine guns hit the Germans higher up the slope. The engineers could then build bridges, so the 10th West Yorkshires and 7th East Yorkshires could cross.

38th (Welsh) Division, 23 August, Crossing the Ancre

Early on 22 August, Second Lieutenant Williams led a party of the 14th Welsh across the Ancre, into Thiepval wood and then held on while Captain Glyn and Lieutenant Williams led the 15th Welsh 'through water up to their chest under fire'. In the centre 2nd Welsh Fusiliers, 17th Welsh Fusiliers and 10th SWB crossed and entered Authuille Wood at Crucifix Corner. Two of 1st Battalion's tanks crossed the Aveluy causeway but Captains Vaughan and Williams were wounded as the 13th Welsh Fusiliers captured 200 Germans on Usna Hill. Lieutenant Colonel Collier sent reinforcements from the 14th Welsh Fusiliers to help hold the line around La Boisselle.

Fourth Army

Haig issued orders for Fourth Army's next attack on 15 August and Rawlinson forwarded the instructions to his corps commanders four days later. III Corps would advance between the Ancre and Somme rivers on 22 August, joined by the Australian Corps' left as they pushed east. But they faced the old Somme battlefield: 'for 8 miles in breadth and over 25 in width that wilderness, most like a long abandoned, stoneless graveyard, was grid-ironed by old trenches while bands of rusty entanglements here and there marked the main trench-lines of 1916.'

III Corps

Lieutenant General Alexander Godley's men had to clear Albert, to help Third Army's right along the Ancre. There were suspicions the Germans were expecting an attack so 'a fire of Lewis guns was kept up all night to prevent his hearing the arrival of the tanks.' The Germans were indeed sure they were about to be attacked 'and their troops were distributed in depth in order to meet it'. Their artillery fired an observed barrage of gas and high explosive shells at the assembly areas until the mist formed, so they had to resort to firing from their maps, missing their targets.

18th (Eastern) Division, 22 and 23 August, Albert and the Chapes Spur

Major General Richard Lee had to form a defensive flank east of Albert. The 8th East Surreys worked their way through Albert in the mist in three stages. First, they cleared the town up to the Ancre and regrouped. They then cleared the rest of the town, reorganising a second time before attacking a line of strongpoints beyond the east edge. There were many tunnels and cellars to clear but Albert was declared safe by mid-morning. Lieutenant Colonel Symons' engineers then removed 136 mines and charges from the roads and bridges and there were no accidents.

The 8th East Surreys then followed a narrow-gauge railway east of Albert, heading for Bécourt Wood. Brigadier General Wood mistakenly thought Tara Hill had been captured so he cancelled a barrage, and Captain Whitmarsh's company was hit by enfilade fire as the 7th Buffs attacked Black Wood.

South of Albert, Brigadier General Sadleir-Jackson had sent scouts to find bridging points across the Ancre during the night. Sergeant Robinson swam across to fix one footbridge for the 6th Northants while Private Hughes did the same for the 11th Royal Fusiliers. It meant the two battalions could cross the river before dawn.

A barrage covered the advance from the river while tanks of 4th Battalion followed the Northants across the Dernancourt causeway towards Vivier Mill. Enfilade fire from Albert pinned the Royal Fusiliers down but Captain Doake of the 2nd Bedfords captured Shamrock Hill beyond during the afternoon. The Northants continued their advance north of Méaulte, capturing 670 prisoners including an entire battalion headquarters. The brigade had also found eighty machine guns 'disposed in pairs and in depth along the whole front'. The final casualty of the day was Brigadier General Sadleir-Jackson who was wounded when he went 'forward to secure a better control of the situation.'

A barrage by all the available artillery, trench mortars and machine guns helped the 7th Buffs straighten the line during the early hours of 23 August. The 2nd Bedfords and 6th Northants could then advance onto Chapes spur before dawn. Captain Bland silenced three machine guns as the 10th Essex approached Bécourt Wood and six tanks crawled forward, 'rolling over many machine-gun nests.'

12th (Eastern) Division, 22 and 23 August, Méaulte and Bécourt

Major General Harold Higginson's men advanced along the south bank of the River Ancre behind a line of smoke and shrapnel shells. Most of the tanks broke down or were late but one followed Lieutenant Colonel Goodland's 5th Berkshires up Becordel's main street and two crawled around the sides of the village.

Elsewhere, the barrage moved too fast and the infantry congregated in the mist. Three tanks caught up as the 7th Sussex and the 9th Royal Fusiliers captured two field batteries. Another helped Lieutenant Colonel Smeltzer's 6th Buffs clear Bécourt but it had to withdraw as soon as the mist cleared. Two tanks broke down and a gas bombardment made another three late but the 7th Norfolks and 1/1st Cambridge overcame strong resistance as they advanced south-east of Méaulte. The 9th Essex were pinned down as they came over the crest at the north end of Happy Valley while a counter-attack

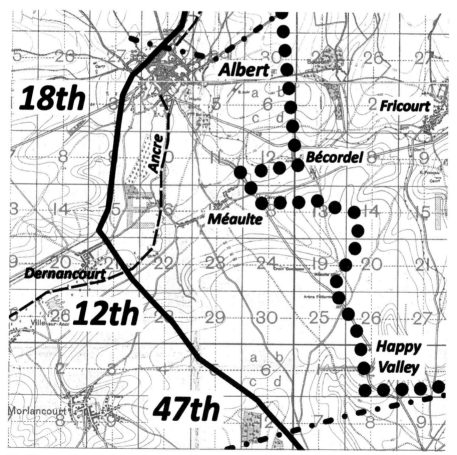

III Corps advanced along the Morlancourt ridge between the Ancre and the Somme.

drove Lieutenant Colonel Russell Johnson's men back until Lieutenant Colonel Dawson reinforced them with the 6th Queen's Own.

47th (2nd London) Division, 22 and 23 August, Happy Valley

Ten Mark V tanks joined Major General Sir George Gorringe's men as they left the old Amiens defences north of the River Somme at 4.45 am. The 1/19th and 1/20th London advanced through the mist and smoke, finding the Germans willing to surrender in Happy Valley, but poor map reading meant they dug in half a mile west of their objective. It was sometime before Brigadier General Mildren realised, and an accurate barrage hit his men as soon as the mist lifted. It was fortunate that four supply tanks had carried entrenching tools forward so the Londoners could dig in.

The map reading error meant that 142 Brigade deployed too far back, so the Londoners had no hope of catching the barrage up. Only one out of six tanks joined the advance and neither the 1/24th London Regiment nor the 1/23rd London Regiment could reach the north end of Happy Valley. The 1/22nd London Regiment contacted the Australians on the right but Lieutenant Colonel Pargiter's men were under heavy fire from Hill 105 and Ceylon Wood. The situation became desperate when the mist had lifted and observation balloons made it dangerous to carry ammunition forward. A supply tank eventually reached Lieutenant Colonel Tolerton's 23rd London Regiment but it drew fire and 'for a time became a death trap for the unloading parties.'

The Whippets had broken down so the 1/1st Northumberland Hussars entered Happy Valley from the south alone and cantered behind the German line. They came under fire from all directions as they tried to find a way around the wire entanglements and only twenty-three troopers 'and many riderless horses galloped back along the ridge, cut to pieces by the machine-gunners there'. The futile charge 'exhibited to thousands of onlookers the stupidity of those who had ordered this impossible attempt'.

A counter-attack during the afternoon hit the gap between 12th and 47th Divisions at the head of Happy Valley. Brigadier General McDouall had only 600 tired men spread out across 2 miles and they were all short of ammunition. Both the 1/24th and 1/23rd London Regiments were driven back but Captain Oakley made sure the 1/22nd London Regiment held on long enough for reinforcements to reach him. Men from the 140 Brigade and the 11 Brigade also held the chalk pit which anchored 47th Division's right flank. A few Londoners were taken prisoner but captured documents revealed that they gave nothing away. They 'were apparently excellently schooled in the way they should behave if captured, and they gave very clever, evasive answers. The captured sergeant refused to give absolutely any information.'

As the fighting raged on the ground, another battle was going on in the skies. Andrew Beauchamp-Proctor shot down one observation balloon and forced another five crews to jump to safety. They were just a handful of the forty-three planes and balloons he had shot down so far, contributing to his award of the Victoria Cross.

The Australian Corps

On 18 August, Rawlinson told Monash to prepare for an attack three days later. He wanted to improve the position around Bray-sur-Somme, north of the Somme, while pushing to the far side of the Chuignes valley, south of the river.

3rd Australian Division, 22 August, Bray-sur-Somme

Major General Gellibrand wanted to encircle Bray-sur-Somme and the engineers made 'an excellent job' of repairing the Cérisy bridge so that tanks could cross the river and support 9 Brigade. Zero hour was set for 4.45 am but the Germans spotted the troops assembling in the bright moonlight and their artillery hit the deployment area. Mist and smoke hid Brigadier General Goddard's troops and the Germans 'could speak of nothing but the rapidity with which our men were on them and round their machine guns'. Twenty-four tanks from 13th and 2nd Battalions accompanied 33rd and 35th Battalions but a pause on the first objective allowed the enemy to regroup. Lieutenant Colonel Morshead's 33rd Battalion captured a battalion headquarters while Lieutenant Colonel White's 35th Battalion encountered tougher resistance beyond Bray.

The 3rd Pioneer Battalion had been deployed because the infantry battalions were so understrength. They saw the Germans evacuating Froissy Beacon, so they sent men across in boats and cleared the reed beds between the river and the canal. Footbridges were launched across the river, so the Neuville spur could be cleared by nightfall.

1st Australian Division, 23 August, Chuignolles

Two tanks led Captain Withy's company of 1st Battalion across the spur north-west of Chuignolles. Captain Steen followed two tanks around the village but Captain McDermid's men lagged behind the tanks and came under fire from Arcy Wood. The Germans in Robert and Matto Woods surrendered to 4th Battalion when they saw more tanks crawling towards them.

Major General Glasgow organised a new barrage for 1 Brigade's advance towards Cappy and Chuignes. One tank helped 1st Battalion clear Garenne Wood and Marly Woods and Major Street's men shot many Germans as they tried to escape. But Captain Cormack was killed while 3rd Battalion was pinned down until the Germans abandoned Chuignes.

Some of the twelve Mark V tanks allocated to 2 Brigade were late while others were knocked out en route to St Martin's Wood. Both Captains Burke and O'Sullivan were killed leading 5th Battalion but Lieutenant Robchester's tank followed a tramway through the woods and silenced twenty machine guns. Plateau Wood was taken with the help of 7th Battalion but 6th Battalion lost the barrage south of the Rye road. Lieutenant William Joynt took charge of his company of 8th Battalion when his commanding officer was killed and he then regrouped 6th Battalion. He led a bayonet attack through St Denis Wood while a tank circled around it; the eighty prisoners would have seen that its 'sides were pitted with bright new bullet marks'. Joynt finally led the advance through Plateau Wood; he would be awarded the Victoria Cross.

Disaster struck while 3 Brigade waited near St Germain Wood for 59th Battalion (from 15 Brigade) to clear Luc Wood and Long Wood. An enemy shell hit an ammunition dump and 150 men were hit in the explosions that followed. Five tanks were then knocked out as the smoke cleared but artillery fire allowed 59th Battalion to clear Marly Woods and reach the river.

Meanwhile, the tanks could not cross Herleville valley, so 9th Battalion chased the Germans from Froissy Beacon and along the canal bank as the Germans 'ran through those woods like water through grass'. The men of 12th Battalion had to crawl through the crops under fire from the Froissy heights, but they were still able to clear Garenne Wood and the woods around Chuignolles. All along the line the Germans were falling back to defensive positions consisting of nothing more than 'isolated shell-holes and little wooden notice boards on short poles with the pretentious inscription Second Main Line of Resistance'.

32nd Division, 23 August, Herleville

Major General Thomas Lambert was to advance beyond the woods around La Vallée and Le Gran Ravin, south of the main Roye road. His men deployed under a sky lit by moonlight and flares before advancing behind a creeping barrage, strafing planes and a line of Mark V tanks at 4.45 am.

Twelve tanks led the 10th Argylls and 2nd KOYLIs towards Herleville but firing from the nearby woods created a gap and the company of Argylls sent to cover it lost all their officers. The situation was secured when five tanks helped 8th Australian Battalion clear the Herleville wood area and the KOYLIs clear Herleville village after the 1/5th Border Regiment reinforced the area.

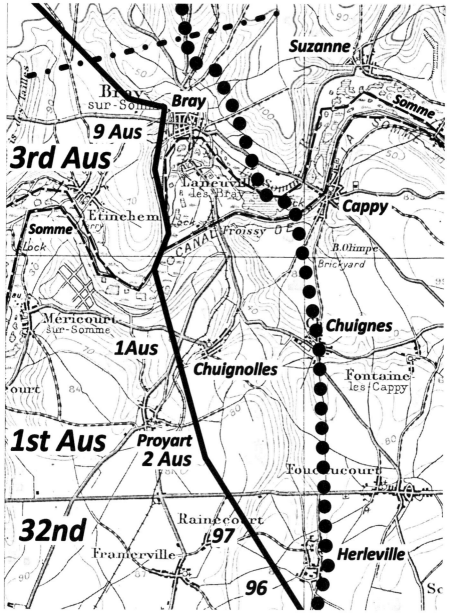

The Australian Corps made slow progress either side of the River Somme.

Lieutenant Colonel MacDonald's 16th Lancashire Fusiliers were pinned down in front of Star Wood until a bombing party from 16th Australian Battalion turned up. Lieutenant Lawrence McCarthy ran forward to silence a machine-gun post and then cleared 500 yards of trench in 'the most effective piece of individual fighting in the history of the AIF'. After throwing all his own bombs and all the German ones, 'a bloodstained handkerchief waved from the sap'. Around forty men surrendered and 'closed in on him from all sides and patted him on the back'. The British press referred to McCarthy's award of the Victoria Cross as the 'super-VC'.

The Germans retaliated the following morning by firing thousands of mustard gas shells at 32nd Division's area. Nearly 450 men had to be sent to the rear for treatment.

Summary

While there was plenty of good news from the front line, there was bad news from the home front. Secretary of State for War Lord Alfred Milner had visited GHQ on 21 August with news of a shortage of conscripts, leaving the BEF facing a manpower crisis as it was extending its attack front. Haig had switched fronts because the Germans were rushing their reinforcements south of the Somme and he asked General Debeney to attack on his right flank. However, French First Army had just taken over part of Fourth Army's line and would not be ready until 23 August.

German OHL was also facing a manpower crisis. Time and again, front line units were being overrun and the replacements were young and inexperienced. At times 'it was really impossible to talk about companies; they were merely weak platoons.' One officer lamented how his regiment had 'lost its old, good stock: all three battalion staffs, all the company commanders, all the medical officers, the greater part of the excellent telephone detachment and more than 600 men. It had previously lost 300 in the Lihons-Proyart fighting.'

Third Army's success meant that Fourth Army could increase its pressure south of the river and Haig wanted Byng and Rawlinson to be bolder when considering objectives. Despite Milner's warnings, he told them: 'risks, which a month before would have been criminal to incur, ought now to be taken as a duty.'

Chapter 7

A Sense we had Reached Success at Last

24 to 26 August

First Army

Haig had warned General Sir Henry Horne to be ready to follow up a German withdrawal east of Arras as early as 15 August. Two days later GHQ received Horne's plan for First Army's advance astride the River Scarpe if it happened. GHQ instructed Horne to extend the BEF's offensive north following Third Army's advance towards Bapaume. First Army would attack on 26 August, aiming to break the Drocourt–Quéant Line, or Wotan Stellung, some 8 miles to the east. The Canadian Corps could then wheel south-east and take the Hindenburg Line opposite General Byng's Third Army in the rear.

VIII Corps

Lieutenant General Sir Aylmer Hunter-Weston had to push along the north bank of the Scarpe, to support the Canadian Corps' advance across the river. The main objective was to capture Greenland Hill between Gavrelle and Roeux.

51st Division, 24 to 26 August, Greenland Hill

Brigadier General Oldfield was commanding while Major General George Carter-Campbell was on leave. The 7th Black Watch could not capture Hyderabad Redoubt early on 24 August but it did clear Pippen Trench. Then came instructions to capture Greenland Hill, north of the Scarpe, on 26 August. The 6th Black Watch was ready to advance at 5 am but enemy troops were spotted moving in no man's land in the darkness. Simultaneous barrages from the British and German guns scattered them, and the 6th Black Watch were able to capture Newton Trench.

The Canadian Corps

Lieutenant General Arthur Currie's men had just been engaged on the Somme but they had little time to rest because they started moving north on 19 August and took over General Horne's line east of Arras over the next few days. Currie told his divisional commanders of First Army's plans on 22 August and their men immediately set about probing the German lines in what they referred to as 'hole-boring'. The 31st Battalion had captured a sugar factory, south of Neuville Vitasse, as early as 23 August and the German commander abandoned the village later that night because he believed 'the commitment of the Canadians had been recognised'.

The field artillery opened fire at 3 am on 26 August and the infantry followed the shell explosions as close as they dared. Nine tanks were allocated to each of the two Canadian divisions but they were 'not to be used ahead of the infantry unless definite resistance demanded their employment'. The infantry rarely needed their help. Two squadrons of aerial observers took to the air at dawn to find targets for the heavy artillery while another four squadrons looked for targets to strafe and bomb.

3rd Canadian Division, 26 August, Monchy-le-Preux

The 4th Mounted Rifles followed the river bank and then the 2nd Mounted Rifles turned south behind Orange Hill. Finally, the 1st and 5th Mounted Rifles

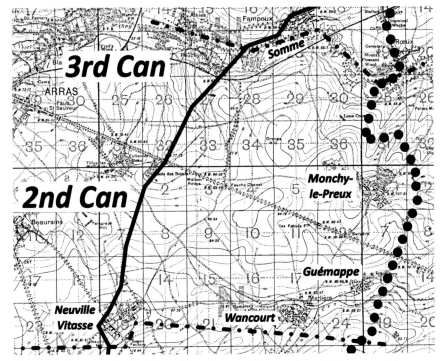

After moving north, the Canadian Corps advanced quickly east of Arras.

made a pincer attack on high ground around Monchy-le-Preux. Lieutenant Charles Rutherford found himself ahead of the 5th Mounted Rifles when he spotted a large group of Germans outside a pillbox. He persuaded all forty-five of them to surrender with just his revolver. He later attacked another pillbox, taking thirty-five prisoners. Rutherford would be awarded the Victoria Cross. Next came eight tanks, accompanying the Royal Canadian Regiment and the PPCLI as they headed for the woods east of Monchy. But four were knocked out and the infantry were pinned down after advancing half a mile. At the same time the 42nd Battalion tried to clear the trenches south of the village.

2nd Canadian Division, 26 and 27 August, Chapel Hill, Guémappe, Vis-en-Artois and Chérisy

Several tanks were knocked out by artillery fire as 20th Battalion crossed Chapel Hill under a machine-gun barrage at dawn on 26 August. The 21st Battalion then crossed the Cojeul stream at Guémappe under enfilade fire from Monchy hill to the north. Meanwhile Brigadier General Bell formed a defensive flank with Neuville Vitasse east of 6 Brigade.

Late in the morning, Major General Henry Burstall was instructed to get over the Cojeul stream, beyond Wancourt, and both the 28th and 27th Battalions crossed in the afternoon. They came under fire on the ridge beyond but still managed to clear Egret Trench.

Third Army

VI Corps faced an advance towards the Hindenburg Line around Bullecourt, IV Corps had to capture Bapaume, while V Corps had to escape the Ancre valley and advance across the 1916 battlefield. General Byng had the 1st and 2nd Cavalry Divisions waiting in reserve, ready to take advantage of any withdrawal.

VI and XVII Corps

General Byng's plan was to take Hénin Hill on his left flank, so he could see over the Cojeul valley. Lieutenant General Haldane would hand over two divisions to Lieutenant General Sir Charles Fergusson on 25 August, so XVII Corps' staff could prepare to attack the Hindenburg Line.

The area had been fought over the previous March and there were 'thick belts of old wire, rusty and torn in places, still protecting (inversely) the battered and tumbled trenches, many of which were capable of being turned to good account'. However, 'the Boche resistance was devoid of sting and there seemed to be almost more sport than danger in hunting the enemy.'

52nd Division, 24 to 26 August, St Martin and Hénin

Major General John Hill had to reach the Hindenburg Line, where it crossed the Cojeul stream. The left, the 1/7th Scottish Rifles and 1/7th Royal Scots advanced 1 mile through St Martin but the 1/6th and 1/5th HLI was stopped by wire covering Hénin on the south bank of the stream. Lieutenant David MacIntyre, adjutant of the 1/6th HLI, led the cutting attempt and then charged a machine-gun team, so the Highlanders could continue their advance. He would be awarded the Victoria Cross. The Highland Light Infantry then climbed Hénin Hill only to find their heavy guns were shelling it. They asked the artillery to stop firing only to find Germans waiting for them when the advance resumed and they were pinned down in front of the Hindenburg Line wire.

Major General John Hill gave Brigadier General Forbes-Robertson the difficult task of clearing the Hindenburg Line where it crossed the Cojeul valley on 26 August.

'The Hindenburg system was such a labyrinth of deep trenches and a birdcage of wire entanglements, new and old, in use and deserted, that the mind finds itself in wandering mazes lost when it attempts analysis or a timetable or a comparison of orders with results.'

The 1/4th and 1/5th Scots Fusiliers entered the formidable position at St Martin at 3 am, contacting the 2nd Canadian Division near Wancourt. Many Germans 'threw down their weapons with a readiness that was almost indecent and gladly surrendered'.

The 1/7th Royal Scots and 1/5th Scots Fusiliers covered the gap between the Canadians and 52nd Division, as the Scots Fusiliers bombed their way south-east. Then nine tanks joined Lieutenant Colonel Dashwood-Tandy's 1/4th KOSBs as they crossed the Cojeul stream and climbed Hénin Hill on the right.

56th Division, 24 to 26 August, Croisilles

Ten tanks helped the 1/1st London, 1/7th Middlesex and 1/8th Middlesex clear Ledger Reserve and Summit Trench but prisoners reported three fresh divisions were moving to the area. Brigadier General Freeth was warned to approach Croisilles with care while 169 Brigade moved up behind 167 Brigade, ready to meet the counter-attack.

Patrols followed trenches to learn the village had been evacuated, while an airman reported a tank crawling around Croisilles. Lieutenant Colonel Pank later discovered that the Germans were still in the ruins, while the tank had been disabled. The 1/8th Middlesex's patrols had also seen fresh entanglements covering the ruins but Hull ordered Freeth to attack anyway.

The six tanks sent to assist 167 Brigade were late, and while Croisilles Trench had 'been shown as an organised and deep defensive work', the Londoners discovered it was 'only 2 feet deep and quite useless as a reorganising point'. Freeth had no option but to recall his men to Summit Trench. Major General Amyatt Hull asked for the tanks back but they were being serviced, so the attack was scaled down to an assault on Croisilles. The village was hit by gas shells throughout the night but patrols reported it was 'full of machine guns', so the artillery hammered it with high-explosive through the day.

Lieutenant General Sir Charles Fergusson had taken over 56th Division on 25 August and he wanted to attack the following day. At 3 am 167 Brigade advanced but 'the wire was uncut (in some spots there were five belts) and the machine guns in Croisilles poured a devastating hail of bullets on the assault troops.' After 52nd Division cleared Hénin Hill to the north, Hull was told to keep probing Croisilles. The 2nd London Regiment made 'a stealth raid with two platoons but the experiment was bad, as the platoons were almost wiped out.'

The Guards Division, 24 to 26 August, St Léger

Major General Geoffrey Feilding's plan was to pinch out St Léger and the 3 Guards Brigade advanced across the Sensée valley at 7 am. Most of the German infantry fled but the machine-gun teams 'clung to their positions with a tenacity of purpose worthy of the highest praise'. Lieutenant Colonel Dene was wounded before zero hour but Captain Bonn made sure the 1st Welsh Guards advanced north of the village, pausing only when they were hit by their support barrage. They eventually reached Léger Reserve Trench but an attempt to go further was thwarted.

Lieutenant Colonel Stirling's 2nd Scots Guards had taken around one hundred prisoners before they were pinned down by machine-gun fire south of St Léger. But the 1st Grenadier Guards faced the biggest challenge because 2nd Division was delayed on the right flank. Machine-gun fire pinned them down and then others returned to Mory Copse to snipe at Major Bailey's men.

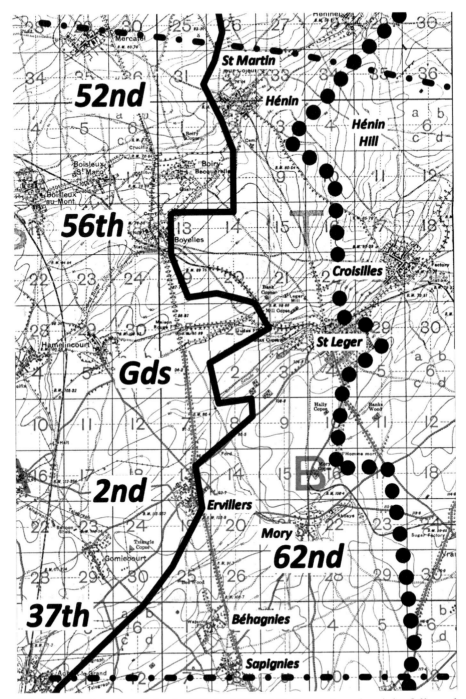

VI Corps' left had to fight for Hénin hill and St Leger but the right followed up a withdrawal.

The three battalions of the 3 Guards Brigade had become separated astride the Sensée stream. Brigadier General Follett had been promised a company of tanks but while Third Army had set zero hour for 9 am, Major General Feilding ordered the guardsmen to advance at 4.30 am by mistake. Few of the tanks found the infantry in the morning mist but the Germans were surprised by the early attack.

The Germans fled from their trenches north of St Léger when they saw the 1st Welsh Guards but they returned when they saw the guardsmen were delayed cutting through the wire. Only one tank reached the 2nd Scots Guards and they were unable to take Banks Trench, south-east of St Léger. The 1st Grenadier Guards were pinned down by fire from Banks Trench when the mist cleared and two out of three tanks had been knocked out by the time they were ordered to retire to Mory Switch.

Plans to advance through St Léger Wood were cancelled because the guardsmen 'had done all that was humanly possible', until patrols discovered the Germans had abandoned it. Brigadier General Champion de Crespigny then made the 2nd Coldstream Guards and 2nd Grenadier Guards occupy the wood before they returned.

2nd Division, 24 and 25 August, Mory, Béhagnies and Sapignies

The Germans spotted the 1st King's in the bright moonlight and they failed to reach the copse north of Mory before dawn on 24 August. 'A long skirmishing line of men of the Guards Division was seen advancing without opposition' mid-morning but Lieutenant Colonel King's men were again stopped by heavy fire. Major General Pereira arranged for 99 Brigade to try again and six tanks helped the surviving King's take one hundred prisoners as they 'chanced a flank move'. The 1st Berkshires had also advanced but the 23rd Royal Fusiliers were pinned down in front of Mory.

Brigadier General Osborn planned a two stage attack against Sapignies on 25 August. A heavy bombardment hit Béhagnies while a Whippet helped the 2nd HLI clear a sunken lane in 'a grim bayonet fight' before dawn. The 24th Royal Fusiliers then cleared the village so the 2nd Ox and Bucks could outflank Sapignies from the north. Many Germans 'were discovered asleep in their dug-outs and surrendered without a struggle; those attempting to escape were shot down.'

62nd Division, 25 and 26 August, Mory and Favreuil

Major General Walter Braithwaite was to cross the Sensée valley but there were difficulties relieving 2nd Division around Mory. Brigadier General

Reddie was allowed to set 187 Brigade's zero hour and he told his battalion commanders to assemble at 5th KOYLIs headquarters. Unfortunately, Lieutenant Colonel Hart received the message too late and the 2/4th York and Lancasters advanced at 9 am while he was away. 'The absence of the creeping barrage seemed a curious omission but the Hallamshires had been in many an awkward predicament before and no one thought of holding them up.' It was impossible to recall them, so Reddie told Lieutenant Colonel Peter to follow with the 5th KOYLIs. The York and Lancasters passed through Mory Copse while the 5th KOYLIs cleared Mory. On 186 Brigade's front the 5th Duke's were stopped by crossfire from Mory and Favreuil.

A counter-attack was driving the York and Lancasters' right flank back during the afternoon until Captain Ellis's company of the Dukes shored up the line. A bayonet charge by Lieutenant Spencer's company of the 2/4th KOYLIs stopped the attack while Lieutenant Holland's company drove the enemy back. A later counter-attack against Mory copse was stopped after Captain Skirrow 'knocked out the crew of a machine gun with his revolver.' The 5th Duke's were also hit by a counter-attack and Brigadier General Burnett had to allow Lieutenant Colonel Walker to withdraw his right flank. Captain Geldhard's company of the 2/4th Duke's were met by 'about thirty of the enemy coming down the road with their hands in the air shouting "kamerad" when they counter-attacked'. The SOS barrage effectively dispersed the German forces and prisoners stated that they had lost half their number. After a miserable night, Brigadier General Reddie realised the Guards Division were advancing earlier than expected, so the 5th KOYLIs were sent forward and they joined Lieutenant Colonel Brook's 2/4th Hampshires on the objective.

IV Corps

Lieutenant General Sir Montague Harper's left and centre were across the Ancre between Achiet-le-Grand and Irles but his right had been unable to clear Miraumont. His left was to advance through Biefvillers, looking to outflank Bapaume from the north, while his right was to cut off Miraumont.

37th Division, 24 and 25 August, Biefvillers, Avesnes and Favreuil

Major General Hugh Bruce Williams wanted to capture Biefvillers but his artillery orders were delayed and the infantry had to advance unsupported through the mist at 4.30 am. Machine-gun fire stopped the 8th Lincolns reaching Sapignies but two tanks helped the 8th Somersets enter Biefvillers. The village then came under a heavy bombardment and it had to be evacuated following the death of Lieutenant Colonel Hardyman. Patrols from the New Zealand Division later found that the Germans had not reoccupied the village.

Major General Bruce Williams organised another attack at 5 am the following morning. The 4th Middlesex and 8th Lincolns advanced south of Sapignies but the Germans' SOS barrage stopped the 13th KRRC and 13th Rifle Brigade entering Avesnes for some time. A second frontal attack at dusk was cancelled because 'it was suspected that the divisional telegraph message ordering the attack must have been tapped'. Instead Brigadier General Challenor had the 10th Royal Fusiliers bomb down a trench towards Favreuil before the 13th Rifle Brigade and New Zealanders made a pincer attack; they rounded up 150 prisoners between them.

5th Division, 26 August, Beugnâtre

Brigadier General Jones's 13 Brigade relieved 37th Division during a rainy night but the companies 'were very much mixed, guides were not available and the positions were difficult to ascertain.' Lieutenant Howatt was killed locating an enemy trench but his patrol returned with nearly fifty prisoners. The 2nd KOSBs were pinned down and Major Dudgeon was wounded when they attacked Beugnâtre at dawn. Major Lake took command 'undaunted by difficulties' and cleared the village with the help of Lieutenant Colonel Wilberforce's 14th Welsh Fusiliers. They were then 'rewarded by splendid targets of Germans, who were running away in their hundreds.' 'Major Lake was badly wounded twice but refused to be carried off the field until he knew all was secure on his flanks.' Major General John Ponsonby now had to wait until Bapaume was taken.

New Zealand Division, 24 August, Grévillers

Eight Mark IVs and three Whippets advanced with the 2nd Auckland and 1st Wellington at 4.30 am. There had been no artillery barrage and it was some time before the Germans realised the New Zealanders were advancing towards them through the mist. Two tanks led the 2nd Auckland Battalion past Grévillers where the 'garrison was taken completely by surprise, and some even were interrupted at breakfast.' They were just a few of the 350 prisoners taken by the New Zealanders.

The engineer Sergeant Samuel Forsyth silenced three machine guns near at Grévillers. He was then wounded and the tank he was leading was knocked out, but he continued advancing until the enemy retired. Forsyth was later killed by a sniper and he would be posthumously awarded the Victoria Cross. Machine-gun fire from Loupart Wood stopped the Auckland Battalion getting beyond the village and it was midday before four tanks helped the 1st Wellington Battalion enter it.

Five Mark IVs and ten Whippets led the advance towards Bapaume. Major Wilson's 2nd Canterbury Battalion discovered Biefvillers had been abandoned and pushed on alongside the 2nd Otago Battalion until a barrage knocked out four tanks around Avesnes. Lieutenant Colonel Pennycook was killed trying to locate enemy posts but Lance Corporal Grant and Private Sims stayed behind with their machine gun when the Otagos withdrew on the exposed ridge.

Major General Andrew Russell planned an attack for 5 am on 25 August but German planes spotted 2 Brigade assembling, so their route to the front was drenched with gas which delayed the tanks. The 1st Otago Battalion and the 1st Canterbury Battalion were busy silencing machine-gun nests when eight Mark V tanks turned up; four of them would be knocked out around Monument Wood. Then the 'mist lifted with unforgettable suddenness and there was bright sunshine' not long after the New Zealanders reached Avesnes. The Germans around Bapaume could now pin down the infantry while the fifteen Whippets had to withdraw to a safe distance. The 2nd Canterbury Battalion eventually cleared Monument Wood and part of Favreuil during the evening.

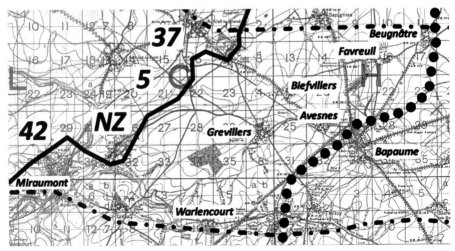

IV Corps followed the Germans up to Beugnâtre, Bapaume and Thilloy.

Brigadier General Melvill had instructions to approach Bapaume and then wait for the situation to develop on the flanks. There was no barrage and the 2nd Wellington Battalion soon reached the south side of the town, only to hear that 63rd Division was struggling to clear Thilloy on their right flank.

Russell's plan was to advance around the flanks of Bapaume without a barrage early on 26 August. Captain McClurg captured many machine guns along a sunken road as Lieutenant Colonel Beere's 4th Rifle Brigade approached Beugnâtre. Both the 2nd Rifle and 3rd Rifle Brigade used 'fighting patrols dribbling forward and scuppering the German machine-gun nests' to get closer to the Beugnâtre Road. Brigadier General Hart reported his patrols could not get into Bapaume, and planning for a dusk attack was rushed, so the 2nd Rifle Brigade found the Germans waiting for them.

The 2nd Wellington Battalion could not make much progress south of Bapaume because 63rd Division could not clear Thilloy. So the 1st Auckland Battalion moved up and Sergeant Reginald Judson silenced four machine-gun crews before jumping out of a trench and running over the top to get at the rest. He killed two men and the rest ran, so he returned with their two machine guns. Judson would be awarded the Victoria Cross.

63rd Division, 24 to 26 August, Loupart Wood

At midday Major General Lawrie was instructed to advance south-east through Grévillers and Loupart Wood to outflank the Germans facing the New Zealand Division. The plan was to advance at 7.30 pm, but 189 Brigade's battalions and the eight tanks were delayed on the busy tracks, and there were no maps available. No one knew who held Loupart Wood so Brigadier General De Pree rode ahead with his battalion commanders to discover there was heavy machine-gun fire coming from Warlencourt. A 'severe bombing attack, directed on the Hawke and Hood Battalions by a swarm of low-flying planes' was the final straw and the attack was called off. Brigadier General De Pree was sacked by Major General Lawrie for letting a possible opportunity slip by, and while it was 'impossible to say what the results of the attack might have been, it [was] sufficient to say that high authorities a few days later came to the conclusion that the decision was justified'.

Another attack in thick mist at 5 am on 25 August was made without tanks past the south-west side of Bapaume. The 1st Royal Marines reached Ligny-Thilloy but a counter-attack drove them back onto the 2nd Irish Regiment.

Lieutenant Commander Sprange was killed at the head of the Anson Battalion but Captain Scott and Lieutenant Paterson eventually led their men beyond Thilloy. Lieutenant Commander Fish and Commander Jones were hit while clearing the trenches south-west of Loupart Wood and both the Hood and Hawke Battalions were pinned down by the machine guns on the Butte du Warlencourt until the Drake Battalion arrived. Commander Daniel Beak then made sure Lieutenant Commander Blackmore and Lieutenant Colonel Maudsley renewed the advance across the Albert–Bapaume road. Beak and one of his runners would later silence a nest of machine guns and take ten prisoners; he would be awarded the Victoria Cross. Lieutenants Dodds and Stevenson made sure the Hawk Battalion cleared Le Barque on the right flank.

Harper still wanted 63rd Division to get past the south side of Bapaume and zero hour was set for 6.30 am on 26 August. Major General Lawrie's men discovered that the Germans were determined to hold on around Thilloy area, while Bapaume was cleared of stores. Neither 188 nor 189 Brigades could make any progress.

42nd Division, 24 to 26 August, Miraumont

Patrols had failed to get into Miraumont during the night but the Germans withdrew as soon as 21st Division cleared the high ground south of the Ancre. The Manchester battalions of 127 Brigade crossed the stream first, to clear the south half of the village, and then 126 Brigade mopped up the north part. Between them they took nearly 550 prisoners but, more importantly, they had freed up Third Army's centre. The advance reached Pys by dusk, and while 126 Brigade came under machine-gun fire from Warlencourt, 127 Brigade threw back a flank to meet 21st Division.

V Corps

Lieutenant General Cameron Shute planned a pincer attack to clear the Thiepval ridge, starting at 1 am on 24 August.

21st Division, 24 to 26 August, Grandcourt to Eaucourt l'Abbaye

General Byng wanted to secure the high ground east of Grandcourt, to threaten Miraumont. Major General David Campbell gave Brigadier General McCulloch instructions to extend 64 Brigade's bridgehead east of the Ancre before dawn on 24 August. The plan soon went wrong as one company lost its way, another did not receive its orders and the machine guns failed to turn up. The 1st East Yorkshires and 9th KOYLIs were hit by their supporting barrage as they crossed Battery Valley and then by enemy fire from Thiepval ridge but they still overran the outposts covering Grandcourt. McCulloch then waited three hours for the 15th Durhams to catch up and 'the Germans fled in all directions, discarding rifles and equipment' when the advance resumed.

McCulloch had been badly wounded in the final charge and Lieutenant Colonel Holroyd-Smyth of the Durhams discovered his position was 'practically surrounded by the enemy' at first light. Captain Longden was killed shouting 'Come on the Durhams' during one attack while Holroyd-Smyth ignored calls to surrender. The Germans abandoned Grandcourt and Miraumont when the rest of 21st Division started moving up the Ancre valley, allowing 42nd Division to move forward on IV Corps' right.

At 6 am the following morning, Brigadier General Gater led the 12th/13th Northumberland Fusiliers and 1st Lincolns by compass through the morning mist. They were passing Eaucourt l'Abbaye when a German balloon saw them above the mist and directed machine-gun fire onto them. Some of the 2nd Lincolns outflanked the German position north of Le Sars and then 110 Brigade continued the advance 'at a fast pace' along the Bapaume road to the Butte de Warlencourt. Heavy rain delayed 64 Brigade and the barrage had moved on towards Factory Corner before Lieutenant Colonel Holroyd-Smyth's men were ready to advance on 26 August.

17th Division, 24 to 26 August, Thiepval Heights

The attack continued at 1 am on 24 August but the 6th Dorsets faced a struggle for Cast Trench en route to the summit of Thiepval Ridge. The 10th West Yorkshires faced a similar situation until Second Lieutenant Braithwaite ran through the British barrage to take 120 prisoners in Cannon Trench. The 7th East Yorkshires helped the Dorsets reach Stuff Redoubt and all three battalions then cleared Schwaben Redoubts and Thiepval, taking another one hundred prisoners.

Major General Robertson's men had taken their objective but 21st Division was pinned down in Battery Valley to the north while there was also no sign of 38th Division to the south. Even so, Lieutenant General Shute urged Robertson to keep advancing towards Courcelette, hoping it would trigger a German withdrawal.

The problem was 50 Brigade headed south-east rather than east, across the 1916 battlefield, due to 'the complete novelty of open warfare' and a lack of landmarks. Brigadier General Gwyn-Thomas's staff could see they were heading the wrong way from across the Ancre but no one saw their warning flag signals. A mounted staff officer cantered across the valley and onto the Thiepval heights but he could not catch the advancing troops up. So Gwyn-Thomas moved his headquarters across the river only to lose contact with divisional headquarters and his three battalions.

Brigadier General Allason had also taken 52 Brigade forward but it moved in the correct direction towards Courcelette, locating 50 Brigade on its flank at Pozières. The two brigades soon found themselves under attack but it was stopped with the help of one of the 18-pounders which had risked crossing the 'narrow creaking causeways and bridges' across the Ancre. The mistake in direction resulted in 21st Division facing a counter-attack across Battery Valley which nearly cut off 110 Brigade near Le Sars. But 50 Brigade had managed to contact 38th Division on the right, taking many prisoners around Ovillers.

One officer later wrote: 'I had a feeling of elation such as I had never known before in war… now there was a sense we had reached success at last.' There may have been a feeling of success at the front but it was a nightmare for the troops along the logistics chain. They had to carry everything across the Ancre before finding their way across the 1916 battlefield in 'a game of hide-and-seek in the dark'.

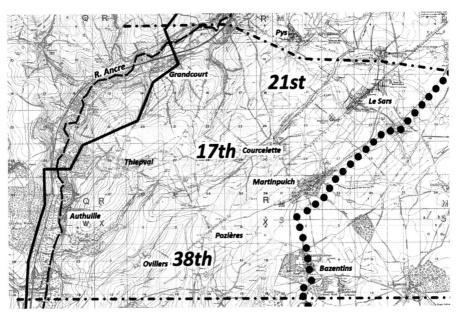

The Germans abandoned most of the 1916 battlefield in a couple of days ahead of V Corps.

It took all night to complete the reliefs but 38th Division replaced 50 Brigade while 51 Brigade filled the gap north of Pozières. The advance resumed at 4 am on 25 August, and while Brigadier General Dudgeon's men forced the rearguard out of Courcelette, Brigadier General Allason soon reported that Martinpuich was clear. The two brigades found the Germans waiting for them around Eaucourt l'Abbaye and High Wood. The artillery was short of ammunition, so the crews wheeled their guns forward so that the infantry could point out the enemy machine guns. A counter-attack aimed at Martinpuich then hit Lieutenant Colonel Cotton's 10th Lancashire Fusiliers, but Sergeant Harold Colley helped defend the flank. Only three men out of two platoons were left standing and Colley would die of his wounds the following day; he was posthumously awarded the Victoria Cross. Allason eventually had to deploy the 10th West Yorkshires on his right flank because 38th Division was held up around Bazentin-le-Petit.

Rain delayed the early start on 26 August and 51 Brigade faced a tough fight to clear Eaucourt l'Abbaye. Brigadier General Allason's men were unable to get any further because the Germans were making a stand around Ligny-Thilloy. Meanwhile 52 Brigade was unable to advance due to machine-gun fire from High Wood. Brigadier General Dudgeon sent the 12th Manchesters south to outflank the tangle of tree stumps; they took over one hundred prisoners.

38th Division, Thiepval, Ovillers and La Boisselle, 24 to 26 August

Major General Thomas Cubitt planned converging attacks against Thiepval heights. The 15th Welsh crossed a bridge in the dark and entered Thiepval Wood but the 14th Welsh were still wading across at zero hour. The advance started at 1 am in bright moonlight. The German machine-gunners aimed at the river crossings, unaware most of the Welsh were already across. The 15th and 14th Welsh climbed the slopes to the site of Thiepval but Lieutenants Charlton and Turner were wounded as the 2nd Welsh Fusiliers rounded up 200 prisoners in Authuille Wood. The 17th Welsh Fusiliers advanced across Usna Hill at the same time but they could not clear the trenches in front of Ovillers and found themselves isolated. They ignored the calls to surrender before the 10th SWBs arrived to rescue them. The 14th and 16th Welsh Fusiliers advanced from Tara Hill and rounded up one hundred prisoners around Y Sap crater and La Boisselle.

Lieutenant General Shute wanted 38th Division to clear Ovillers but Major General Cubitt did not know how far 114 Brigade had gone beyond Thiepval. Brigadier General Hulke had been told that Pozières had been cleared but his 2nd Welsh Fusiliers were still pinned down in front of it, so he decided against making a frontal attack against Ovillers. Instead the 17th Welsh Fusiliers and the 10th SWBs bypassed the ruins to the north and Germans withdrew at dusk. The 14th Welsh Fusiliers struggled to clear the old trenches west of Contalmaison while machine-gun fire pinned down the 16th Welsh Fusiliers for a time. By nightfall, Cubitt was able to report that the 38th Division had taken all its objectives and nearly 650 prisoners.

All three brigades moved forward at 2.30 am the following morning. The 114 Brigade cleared Pozières but machine-gun fire stopped it reaching High Wood, while Lieutenant Colonel Cockburn's 2nd Welsh Fusiliers silenced resistance around Bazentin-le-Petit 115 Brigade and the 14th Welsh Fusiliers cleared Bazentin-le-Grand.

Although Contalmaison was cleared, many Germans had been missed in the dark and some tried to capture 113 Brigade headquarters until a company of the 13th Welsh Fusiliers rescued Brigadier General Rhys Price's staff. During the evening, the 16th Welsh Fusiliers sent patrols through Mametz Wood, 'which was only lightly held'. It was just over two years since the 38th Division had fought in the wood, in their first bloody battle of the war.

Bad weather on 26 August made the deployment difficult but it started through Bazentin woods at 4 am on the right. Twenty-year-old Lance Corporal Henry Weale was advancing with the 14th Welsh Fusiliers when he saw the 13th Welsh Fusiliers were held up by machine-gun fire. His Lewis gun jammed as he put down suppressive fire, so he ran forward and killed one man while the rest of the crew fled. Weale's actions allowed the 13th Welsh Fusiliers to take Bazentin-le-Grand; he was awarded the Victoria Cross.

The 17th Welsh Fusiliers and 10th SWB bypassed High Wood before mopping up in the mass of tree stumps. The 14th Welsh Fusiliers had reached Longueval on the right but a counter-attack from Delville Wood forced them back to Bazentin-le-Grand. The 38th Division had discovered where the Germans planned to make their next stand.

Fourth Army

The French relieved 4th Canadian Division on the Santerre plateau over the nights of 24 and 25 August, as part of the Canadian Corps' transfer north to First Army. They also relieved part of the 4th Australian Division, moving Fourth Army's boundary as far north as Lihons. But the rest of Rawlinson's men still had to get clear of the 1916 battlefield, an area of many obstacles and few roads.

III Corps

Lieutenant General Richard Butler's left would secure the ridge east of Albert while his right supported the Australian Corps. His divisional commanders were to be prepared to organise mixed advanced guards if the Germans began to withdraw.

18th Division, 24 to 26 August, La Boisselle, High Wood and Montauban

The 8th Berkshires and 7th Queen's Own advanced behind a barrage across the Chapes spur during the early hours of 24 August. Captain Nicholson's company of the Berkshires were pinned down by machine-gun fire from Lochnagar crater (blown by the British on 1 July 1916) south of La Boisselle. Major Warr used Stokes mortars to pin the 250 men inside and they were taken prisoner in the charge that followed.

Major General Lee hoped to 'to secure as much ground as possible without becoming too heavily engaged' on 25 August. On the left, the 8th East Surrey and 7th Buffs were still waiting for their orders when Lee told them to get beyond Bécourt Wood as soon as possible. The Germans were also falling back in confusion in the fog, as the 2nd Bedfords and 6th Northants moved through Fricourt.

The 8th East Surreys, 7th Buffs and 11th Royal Fusiliers entered Mametz Wood and Caterpillar Valley at nightfall but rain soon stopped the advance. The Otago Mounted Rifles and Northumberland Hussars discovered that the Germans had withdrawn during the night but the three infantry battalions still faced a tough fight for the ridge east of the wood, the following morning. Lieutenant Colonel Minet's machine guns cut off the German line of retreat as Captain Whitmarsh's company of the Buffs cleared Montauban. A counter-attack from Bernafay Wood hit the 8th East Surreys on the left flank and the 7th Queen's were unable to secure the area.

12th Division, 24 to 26 August, Montauban and Carnoy

Major General Higginson pushed his flanks forward at 1 am on 24 August. The 7th Sussex captured Bécordel but the Germans spotted the 6th Queen's and 6th Queen's Own crossing Happy Valley in the bright moonlight and pinned them down. An artillery barrage failed to silence the German machine guns and three Whippets were disabled as they tried to go to the infantry's aid. Eventually 36 Brigade and 47th Division outflanked the main strongpoints and the Germans withdrew at dusk.

The advance through mist at 2.30 am on 25 August encountered little resistance. The 9th Royal Fusiliers, the 6th Queen's and 6th Buffs advanced south of Fricourt and Mametz after prisoners told them they had been abandoned. Major General Higginson ordered Brigadier General Beckwith to form an advanced guard and officers led 35 Brigade, Whippets and cavalry forward on compass bearings.

The cavalry found the Germans sheltering in the old trenches west of Montauban but the heavens opened as the 7th Norfolks and the 1/1st Cambridge Regiment worked their way along the ridge under machine-gun fire from Montauban. Sergeant Everitt of the Norfolks would lead the attack which eventually cleared Pommiers Redoubt during the night.

Higginson wanted to attack again at 4 am on 26 August but it took time to get the orders out and the battalions had to march across country in the rain and dark because the Germans were shelling the roads. The artillery had no idea where the front line was, so the supporting barrage landed far ahead and both the 7th Sussex and the 5th Berkshires suffered many casualties around Carnoy. A counter-attack cut off some of the Berkshires and they had

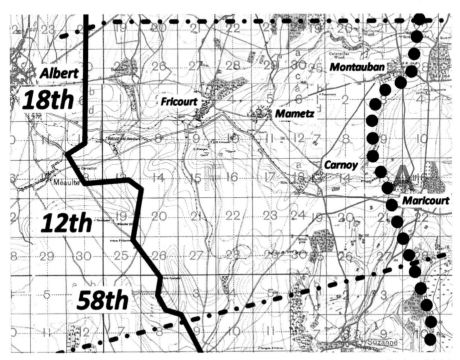

III Corps followed the withdrawal across the south part of the 1916 battlefield.

to be rescued by the 1/1st Cambridge Regiment. The Germans eventually withdrew when 18th Division finally cleared Montauban in the afternoon.

47th Division, 24 August, Happy Valley

Major General George Gorringe planned an advance across Happy Valley but Lieutenant Colonel Neely decided to stage a raid by the 18th London Regiment before zero hour. 'Silently working their way behind the German line of posts, they surrounded, captured and occupied them, without the enemy being aware of what happened.' Five tanks then accompanied 1/15th London Regiment as it advanced from the south end to the north of the valley at 1 am, taking over 300 prisoners in the dark. The British artillery then shelled the far side of the valley while the tanks waited for a counter-attack which never came. Eventually a tank helped the 1/15 and the 21st London Regiment clear the strongpoints around Pear Tree, securing the head of the valley. The 1/17th, 9th and 12th London Regiments could then secure the east slope.

58th Division, 25 and 26 August, Happy Valley to Maricourt

Fourth Army had run out of tanks by 25 August so Major General Frank Ramsay's infantry had to advance alone beyond Happy Valley. The tired men moved in silence into no man's land in the dark and then lay down to sleep while a thick mist formed. The Germans had withdrawn by the time 140 and 175 Brigades advanced at 5.45 am.

The 2/4th London Regiment came under fire from the low ridge west of Billon Wood and it was mid-afternoon by the time 2/2nd London Regiment cleared it. The hot day then ended with a thunderstorm while crossfire from Carnoy and Maricourt pinned down the Londoners. Brigadier General Maxwell received new orders to advance rather late, so his men had to advance hungry through Billon Wood in the pouring rain. A third advance before dawn on 26 August allowed the 3rd London Regiment and 2/4th London Regiment to get closer to Maricourt. The barrage overshot the German machine guns in Suzanne valley and they pinned down 8th and 7th London Regiment before more opened fire from the far slope at dawn. It was some time before the Australians had silenced them but Major General Ramsey was pleased to hear that his men had trapped the Germans on the Vaux spur by dusk.

The Australian Corps

3rd Australian Division, Bray and Suzanne, 24 to 26 August

Major General John Gellibrand faced the spurs and valleys north of the Somme. The 37th and 40th Australian Battalions crept towards Bray under an artillery barrage early on 24 August. A machine-gun barrage then hit the village while the assault troops advanced past the flanks and the rest of 40th Battalion cleared the ruins. Brigadier General McNicoll was pleased to hear that 200 prisoners and three trains loaded with supplies had been captured.

Guns south of the Somme fired a box barrage on the spur overlooking Suzanne at 2.30 am on 25 August while the 42nd, 39th and 37th Australian Battalions advanced through Ceylon Wood. The 40th Australian Battalion had to wear their masks as they cleared the area between Bray and Suzanne because the valley was full of gas.

Rawlinson's plan had been for III Corps to take Maricourt before the Australians advanced towards Vaux but there was a delay getting the order to 3rd Australian Division. It meant the mist was lifting by the time 11 Brigade was moving and Brigadier General Cannan's men were pinned down by fire from the copses around Maricourt and Suzanne. Both 44th and 43rd Australian Battalions advanced during a rainy night as 10 Brigade moved past Suzanne.

Orders were late and heavy rain delayed the deployment so it was light by the time 39th Battalion moved along trenches towards Suzanne on 26 August. Gellibrand was told to be 'quiescent' until 58th Division took Maricourt, so it was the early hours by the time 43rd and 44th Battalions were closing in on Maricourt and Vaux. Lance Corporal Bernard Gordon captured sixty men and six machine guns ahead of 41st Battalion and would be awarded the Victoria Cross.

Both the 37th and 38th Battalions had been 'sneaking in small groups along banks, old trenches and sunken roads' across the Vaux peninsula and 'several hundred Germans bolted across the open to Vaux Wood' as Lieutenant Le Freve's men entered the main trench. The Australians turned captured machine guns on the gun limbers which galloped after them. Later that evening, 40th Battalion pushed the flank along the river towards Frise.

1st Australian Division, 24 to 26 August, Cappy and Chuignes

Major General William Glasgow heard the Germans were retiring north of the Somme on 25 August, but his own patrols discovered they were intent on holding the woods between Cappy and Chuignes. As 9th Battalion moved along the river bank, 12th Battalion cleared Olympia Wood. At the same time 3rd Battalion cleared Canard Wood and 4th Battalion moved through Lapin Wood, but 2 Brigade made little progress astride the St Quentin road. The German artillery then fired off all their spare ammunition during the night while patrols discovered that the infantry had withdrawn. Brigadier General Bennett gave his men orders to reorganise and they started the pursuit when the morning mist lifted. By the early afternoon they were close to Dompierre while 1 Brigade was beyond Fontaine-les-Cappy. While things were going well on the corps' left, 2 Brigade and the 32nd Division were too weak to force the Germans back around Foucaucourt. Instead they had to endure endless gas barrages.

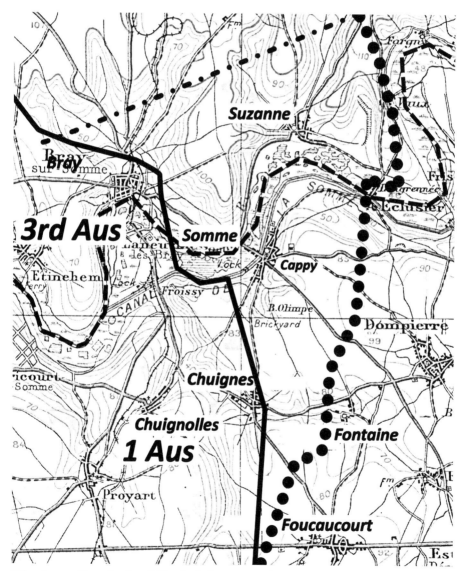

The Australians had a difficult fight across the spurs and valleys around the Somme.

The Germans

Ludendorff had assured the Kaiser that the German armies would not withdraw without a fight but repeated attacks were forcing his troops into awkward defensive positions which cost unnecessary casualties to hold. After meeting his generals, Ludendorff decided it was time to withdraw from the 1916 Somme battlefield to a better position.

OHL issued orders to Seventeenth, Eighteenth and Second Armies on 26 August to begin the first stage of the withdrawal the following evening. It was a daunting proposition because the Germans had had many months to plan the previous retirement in the spring of 1917; this time they only had a few days to carry it out and the Allies would no doubt be attacking at many points. It meant the troops facing Fourth Army would end up behind the River Somme south of Péronne, while those opposite Third Army had to abandon Bapaume. Despite the difficulties, the withdrawal was carried out without interference and everyone was in their new position before dawn on 27 August.

One of over 400 tanks deployed during Fourth Army's breakthrough on 8 August.

Rapid advances and well-practised tactics meant that many Germans were caught sheltering in their dugouts.

The faster moving Whippets worked alongside the cavalry to exploit the successes made by the Mark V tanks and the infantry.

Armoured cars searched the roads, looking to cut off retreating artillery and supply wagons.

The cavalry were always present but the opportunity to develop rarely came after 8 August.

The presence of tanks was always a morale boost for the Allied troops while they gave plenty for the Germans to worry about.

The long advances made communications difficult and these men are looking for light signals to forward to the aerial observers.

The field artillery were always on the move so they could provide cover during advances, often working closely with the infantry.

Heavy artillery, like this American 155 mm howitzer, often targeted roads and villages in the absence of organised enemy defences.

Tank chassis were converted to carry supplies, machine-gun teams and howitzers.

The advance began at 12.30 pm on 28 August but 4 Brigade 'could only muster what amounted to a composite battalion from its four battalions; the reserve consisting mainly of headquarters details, batmen and cooks.' Brigadier General Rennie's men could not extend their foothold in the Rouvroy–Fresnes Line due to thick wire and machine-gun fire.

On the right, 5 Brigade tried to extend the Sensée bridgehead. The 24th and 22nd Battalions entered the German trench, only to be driven out after dusk, and they sought cover in shell holes in the darkness. Clark-Kennedy was badly wounded but he refused to be evacuated until 24th Battalion had secured their position east of the village; he would be awarded the Victoria Cross.

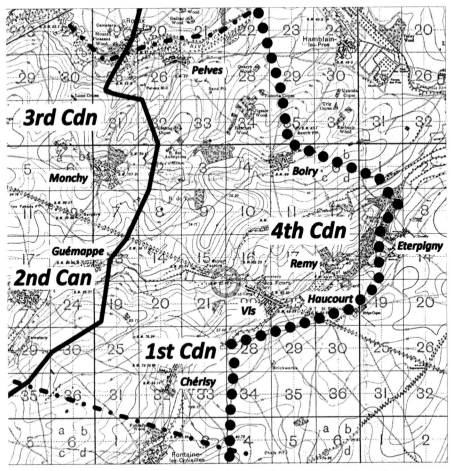

The Canadians advanced to the Sensée, astride the Cambrai road.

1st Canadian Division, Cojeul Stream, 29 August

Major General MacDonnell's men took over the line on the east bank of the Cojeul stream during the night. They did not attack on 29 August and instead prepared for the attack on the Drocourt–Quéant Line.

Third Army

General Byng's divisions were weak and tired but they had to keep up the pressure because prisoners were talking about an imminent withdrawal. His corps commanders were sure the German infantry had been told to hold on while the artillery was shooting all their surplus ammunition. General Georg von der Marwitz was indeed planning to withdraw his left to the Hindenburg Line around Croisilles and the rest of Second Army would follow once all the supplies had been evacuated from Bapaume.

XVII Corps

52nd Division, 27 August, Hénin Hill

Major General Hill waited to hear how the Canadian Corps' advance towards the Cojeul stream on his left went before attacking the Hindenburg Line north of Hénin hill. However, his order never reached Brigadier General Forbes-Robertson VC (awarded for leadership on the Lys in April 1918) and a gap was opening on his right flank, where 56th Division was advancing towards Croisilles.

Major Slater deployed the 4th Royal Scots well forward, so the German SOS barrage missed them, and then at 10 am they had 'to fan out as soon as they sprang over the parapets'. The 7th Royal Scots took nearly 250 prisoners along the Hindenburg trenches while the 4th Royal Scots took another 350 around Fontaine-lez-Croisilles.

On the right the 1/7th and 1/6th HLI advanced in a 'formation of blobs' which 'proved most suitable and elastic'. Lieutenant David MacIntyre led a party as they cut through the wire and then charged a machine-gun team. MacIntyre would be awarded the Victoria Cross for helping the 1/6th HLI to capture Hénin hill. Captain Fyfe was shot dead by a German prisoner after crossing the Cojeul stream, leaving the 1/5th HLI with no officers, so they dug in.

57th Division, 28 and 29 August, Hendecourt and Riencourt

Lieutenant General Fergusson set zero hour for 12.30 pm on 29 August, hoping to catch the Germans resting after their midday meal, but the attack did not start well. The 2/4th South Lancashires and 1/9th King's saw their contact plane blown out of the sky by a shell and then Lieutenant Colonel Lord and Major Bowring were hit as the King's entered Hendecourt. They found Londoners from 56th Division sheltering in the ruins but Lieutenant Williams decided it was safer to withdraw from the isolated position because he could not contact the troops to his flanks or rear.

Major General Reginald Barnes was unsure where 172 Brigade was, so the barrage landed 1,000 yards ahead of their jumping-off line and remained there until the infantry caught it up forty-five minutes later. It overshot several machine-gun posts and there were many casualties as the 2/4th Loyals cleared Greyhound Trench at Hendecourt and the 2/5th King's Own advanced to Riencourt. There were so many casualties that Brigadier Paynter had to withdraw his men when the Germans closed in.

56th Division, 27 to 29 August, Croisilles

Major General Hull's men were to advance to the Hindenburg Line as the Canadians moved behind it, but the Londoners had to capture Croisilles

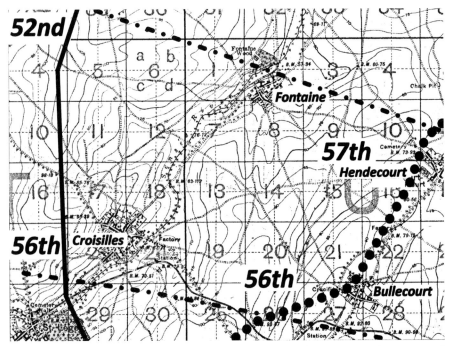

XVII Corps advanced astride the Hindenburg Line to Hendecourt and Bullecourt.

and cross the Sensée stream first. Lieutenant General Fergusson had to wait to hear how the Canadians were doing before issuing his orders, delaying 56th Division's attack until mid-morning.

The plan was for the 169 Brigade to push past Croisilles while the 1/13th London faced the village, but the 2nd and 5th London Regiments ran into uncut wire north of the ruins. The 2nd London Regiment eventually cleared enough of the outpost line along the Sensée stream, so Major General Hull could send 168 Brigade forward to join 169 Brigade in the fight for the Hindenburg Line.

The 1/8th Middlesex probed Croisilles throughout the night, and while an aerial observer reported it clear at dawn, there was still a fight for the ridge beyond. The 1/16th London Regiment faced a difficult deployment amongst the Hindenburg Line's wire entanglement and machine-gun fire then forced some of Lieutenant Colonel Savill's men out of the division's sector. The 2nd London Regiment helped them clear Hendecourt where they were joined by stragglers of 57th Division but they had to fall back to avoid being surrounded.

The rest of the 1/16th and 2nd London Regiment took all day to get through Bullecourt and all night to clear its 'hiding holes, underground ways and concrete emplacements'. The 1/4th and 1/13th London Regiment could not reach the railway to the south-west and it would be midday on 29 August before the division could reorganise. Patrols found the Germans had withdrawn from the Bullecourt area but the 200 survivors of the 5th London Regiment still struggled to clear Station Redoubt north of the village. The 1/14th and 1/13th London Regiment would finally mop up the Bullecourt area, clearing an important strongpoint on the Hindenburg Line.

VI Corps

Lieutenant General Haldane instructed his heavy artillery to shell Écoust, Vaulx and Vraucourt before his troops attacked.

The Guards Division, 27 to 29 August, St Leger and Écoust

There were concerns that prisoners taken from 56th Division would give away zero hour, so it was postponed from 7 am to 9.30 am. Unfortunately 1 Guards Brigade did not hear in time, so Major General Feilding had to let it go as planned, knowing its left flank would be exposed.

The 2nd Coldstream Guards were delayed moving through St Léger Wood, so they lost the barrage and then came under enfilade fire from Croisilles, where 56th Division should have been. They captured many prisoners along a sunken lane but the 1st Irish Guards had to help them stop a counter-attack. The 2nd Grenadier Guards' left was pinned down but the right cleared Banks Trench. Fire from the support trench diverted the guardsmen along a mile long stretch of Mory Switch. But it left them isolated and they had to withdraw with their 200 prisoners.

During the advance, Lieutenant Colonel Vickery's 'field guns came over the crest and into the valley… in full view, affording magnificent support to the infantry, both moral and material.' Machine-gun and artillery fire was turned on them but the gunners returned fire while the horse teams escaped. Banks Trench had not been cleared but 'the 1 Guards Brigade had never fought more gallantly.' The Germans would withdraw a short distance towards Écoust-Saint-Menin during the night.

62nd Division, 27 August, Vaulx-Vraucourt

At 7 am on 27 August, the 2/4th KOYLIs and the 5th KOYLIs advanced behind a 'practically perfect' barrage only to be pinned down by machine-gun fire from L'Homme Mort (The Dead Man) on their left flank. Captain Skirrew was killed as 187 Brigade's line inched towards Vaulx-Vraucourt while 186 Brigade's patrols made even less progress towards Vraucourt. The Yorkshire men might have taken 230 prisoners but it was clear that the Germans were intent on holding the two villages.

There was a lull in the fighting the following morning as the 8th West Yorkshires occupied an evacuated Banks Trench in front of Vaulx-Vraucourt. The division said goodbye to General Braithwaite, a man of 'humane sympathy and a never-failing cheerfulness', as he left to take command of XXII Corps. Major General Sir Robert Whigham immediately prepared to capture Vaulx-Vraucourt by having the 1/5th Devons and the 2/4th Hampshires clear posts in front of them on the afternoon of 29 August.

The 5th Duke of Wellington's were instructed to stop the Germans enfilading 5th Division's advance, so Captain Ellis's company bombed along two trenches. They used flares to keep in touch, while Lewis gun teams moved over the top to keep the Germans below ground. Sections were left behind to man captured trenches while a support company followed up to clear the isolated strongpoints between the trenches.

IV Corps

Lieutenant General Sir Montague Harper's left flank was 1½ miles ahead of his right because the Germans were intent on clearing Bapaume of stores.

5th Division, 27 to 29 August, Beugny and Frémicourt

The Germans abandoned Bapaume late on 28 August, leaving behind rearguards to delay Major General Ponsonby's men. The 1st Devons crossed Hill 140 and could not hold Beugny because the Germans were still holding Vaulx-Vraucourt to the north. The 1st DCLI came under heavy fire from Frémicourt to the south but they held onto Hill 120.

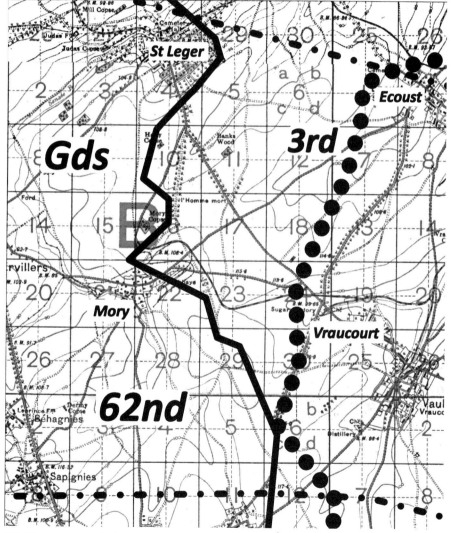

VI Corps struggled to make progress towards Écoust and Vraucourt.

   Two officers distinguished themselves during the advance. Captain Mayne's battery came 'galloping up through a heavy barrage in full view of the enemy, coming into action not 700 yards from them'. Meanwhile, Lieutenant Cecil Sewell was in command of the four Whippets of 3rd Tank Battalion which had accompanied the advance. He left his tank to rescue a trapped crew but was then mortally wounded attending to a wounded man. Sewell was posthumously awarded the Victoria Cross.

New Zealand Division, 27 to 29 August, Bapaume

'It was no part of the High Command's purpose to ram their heads against a brick wall,' so the New Zealanders waited and watched the smoke rising above Bapaume as the Germans burnt the stores they could not remove.

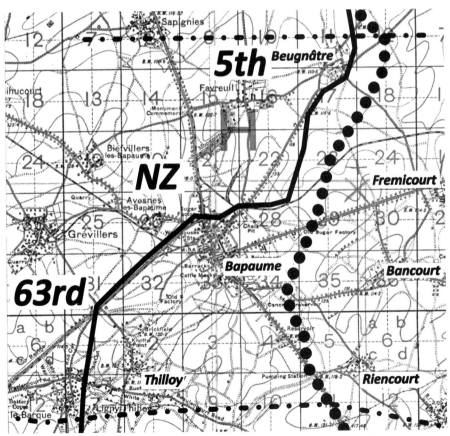

The Germans withdrew in front of IV Corps after clearing their stores from Bapaume.

The Germans withdraw late on 28 August and Captain Meilke's company entered the north side the following morning, earning the 3rd Rifle Brigade 'a flag bearing the word Bapaume' from Major General Russell. The 1st Wellingtons cleared the rest of the ruins as soon as the artillery ceased firing. The rest of the day was spent reorganising east of the town.

63rd Division, 27 and 28 August, Thilloy

The Germans held onto Thilloy while Bapaume was being cleared of stores. They withdrew late on 28 August as 42nd Division was taking over the line.

42nd Division, 29 August, Riencourt

Major General Solly-Flood followed up the German withdrawal and the 5th, 6th and 7th Manchesters had advanced south of Bapaume before the New Zealand Division squeezed 127 Brigade out of the line. Brigadier General Wedgwood was to keep 126 Brigade pushing east but the 5th East Lancashires were unable to make any progress while the 8th and 10th Manchesters found the Germans waiting for them in Riencourt.

V Corps

Lieutenant General Shute wanted a limited advance onto the Morval ridge and he let his divisional commanders decide the best time to advance. The plan was to rotate the brigades every two days to keep the men 'fighting fit', but the Germans were waiting for them. It meant all three divisions had to spend 28 August preparing for a formal attack at 5.30 am the following morning.

21st Division, 27 to 29 August, Beaulencourt

Major General Campbell thought there was only a rearguard delaying his men but 63rd Division's patrols soon found that the Germans intended to stay around Ligny-Thilloy. Staff officers had to run back to tell Lieutenant Colonel Holroyd-Smyth and Brigadier General Cumming to cancel the planned attack. The Germans eventually withdrew late on 28 August and Major General Campbell instructed Brigadier General Cumming to get moving the following morning after hearing that Delville Wood had been abandoned, but 110 Brigade found the Germans waiting from them around Beaulencourt.

17th Division, 27 to 29 August, Flers and Gueudecourt

The 7th East Yorkshires, the 6th Dorsets and the 10th West Yorkshires advanced at 1 am on 27 August, taking 200 prisoners around Flers. But the

East Yorkshires came under attack from Ligny-Thilloy, to the north, and they had to fall back taking the rest of 50 Brigade with them. The division spent 28 August reorganising while aerial observers 'brought reports of fires lit behind the German front' as their supply dumps went up in flames.

On 29 August, Major General Robertson had orders to wait until 38th Division cleared Delville Wood on his right flank but it transpired that the Germans had withdrawn during the night. It meant 51 Brigade could move through an abandoned Flers and Gueudecourt towards Lesboeufs. The 7th Border Regiment went as far as Le Transloy before it had to withdraw due to a lack of support.

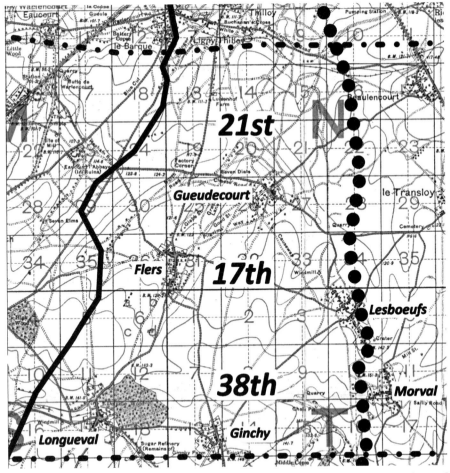

V Corps followed up the withdrawal, coordinated with the evacuation of Bapaume.

38th Division, Delville Wood to Lesboeufs and Morval, 27 to 29 August

Major General Cubitt's men advanced at 4 am on 27 August straight into machine-gun and artillery fire from Longueval and Delville Wood. A brigade of artillery had to canter forward by sections, to give the Welshmen support, and many gunners were hit firing over open sights during a counter-attack.

The Germans abandoned Longueval during the night and then left Delville Wood the following evening. As 115 Brigade moved past the north side of the wood and 113 Brigade moved around the south, 114 Brigade searched the maze of stumps and trenches. By dusk, Lieutenant Colonel Harvey's 10th SWBs and Lieutenant Colonel Norman's 17th Welsh Fusiliers had occupied Lesboeufs but the 14th and 16th Welsh Fusiliers found that the Germans planned to hold Morval for a little while longer.

Fourth Army, 27 to 29 August

General Oskar von Hutier planned to pull Eighteenth Army's right back in line with Second German Army but he wanted a longer withdrawal on his left, back to where the Somme ran north from Ham to Péronne. Both British Fourth Army and the First French Army's left began advancing on 27 August but Rawlinson's divisions were tired and weak. General John Pershing agreed to let two American divisions (the equivalent of four British divisions) stay with the BEF for another two weeks to help. Foch also sent the following encouraging message to Haig: 'I well know that your troops are continuing to advance with determination and that the enemy is retiring in disorder. Keep the same attitude and continue your pursuit.'

III Corps

Lieutenant General Godley had orders to advance towards Guillemont and Hardecourt-aux-Bois, starting at 4.55 am on 27 August.

18th Division, Bernafay Wood and Combles, 27 to 29 August

Machine-gun fire around Delville Wood showed that the Germans were 'all gay and chirpy' while the 8th Berkshires were pinned down in Trônes Wood. A counter-attack drove the 7th Queen's Own out of Bernafay Wood but Captain Wykes and Nicholson made sure the Berkshires were 'still hanging on to the edge of Trônes Wood and soon succeeded in getting a firm grip of it.' The Germans then 'worked forward energetically towards the weakly-held line. The countless communication trenches and shell-holes gave him good cover for this purpose.' Major Fraser brought two field guns forward to silence the machine guns in Delville Wood, so the 8th Berkshires and the 10th Essex could finish clearing Trônes Wood while the 7th Queen's Own covered the gap between the woods.

Major General Richard Lee renewed the advance after hearing 38th Division was advancing on 29 August, sending the 7th Bedfords through an abandoned Guillemont. Brigadier General Tyler heard that they had taken 200 prisoners in Leuze Wood, but it was too dangerous to enter Combles. The Germans were covering the ravine around the village and the 6th Northants had to abandon the ground they had taken to the south.

12th Division, 27 to 29 August, Favière Wood and Hardecourt

Major General Higginson arranged a special barrage on the Bricqueterie at the south end of Bernafay Wood but 36 Brigade still came under crossfire from the complex as well as from Favière Wood and Maltzhorn Farm when it advanced at 4.45 am. The 6th Queen's Own eventually took the brickworks

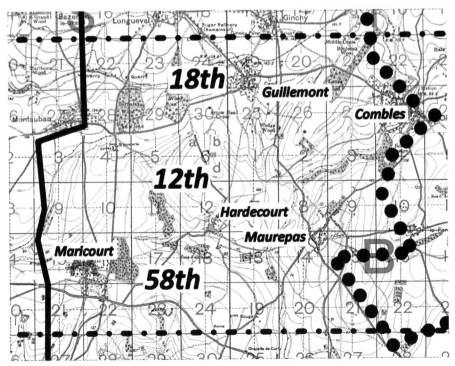

V Corps continued to follow up the withdrawal across the old Somme battlefield.

but reinforcements had to be sent forward after the 6th Buffs were driven back on the right.

Captain Hollis distinguished himself as the 9th Essex captured one hundred prisoners around Maltzhorn Farm early on 28 August but Lieutenant Colonel Saint was mortally wounded as the 1/1st Cambridge Regiment consolidated their position. It was nearly midday before the 9th Royal Fusiliers cleared Favière Wood and Hardecourt but it was a remarkable achievement considering Lieutenant Colonel Van Somerson had 'just received 350 recruits whose ages varied from eighteen and a half to nineteen and a half'.

The firing died down as the Germans withdrew during the hours of darkness and patrols had reached Maurepas by the time the 6th Queen's and the 6th Buffs passed through the following afternoon. Brigadier General Incledon-Webber's men soon found the new German line between Savernake Wood and Le Forest, south of Combles. Early on 30 August 47th Division passed through 12th Division; Higginson's men had advanced 8½ miles over the past week.

58th Division, 27 to 29 August, Maricourt

Brigadier General Corkran's men fought their way through Maricourt village and the wood beyond but the Germans stopped 173 Brigade advancing any further. Brigadier General Maxwell's 174 Brigade would clear Fargny Wood, next to the Somme, during the evening. The two brigades followed up the German withdrawal along the river bank the following day, only encountering resistance in Bois d'en Haut, south of Hardecourt-aux-Bois. Brigadier General Cobham's 175 Brigade took over the pursuit on 29 August only to find the Germans waiting for them north of Curlu.

The Australian Corps

3rd Australian Division, 27 to 29 August, North of the Somme

The 41st and 44th Battalions had crept forward in silence to Vaux Wood during the night, cutting off the spur where the Somme looped to the south. Then 41st Battalion advanced towards Curlu at dawn, to cover 58th Division's right flank. The move left the Australians in an exposed position until Lance Corporal Bernard Gordon shot the machine-gunner. He then entered Fargny Wood several times, taking sixty prisoners, and would be awarded the Victoria Cross.

Lieutenant Colonel White's 35th Battalion advanced beyond Curlu early the following morning, only to become pinned down by machine guns on the high ground around Cléry. Although 38th Battalion found bridges over the Somme at Curlu, the Germans were covering them until Lieutenant Poole seized the village. But the Germans were withdrawing and all day observers had watched their 'transport and guns being cleared, often at the gallop and the heavy artillery accordingly pounded the narrow valley at Cléry through which they must pass.'

The 35th Battalion pushed patrols through Summit Copse and then 34th Battalion used old trenches to outflank Hill 110 during the afternoon. They killed forty and took around seventy-five prisoners who came from the fifteen different regiments holding the area north of the Somme. A tired 38th Battalion got beyond Hem and Major General John Gellibrand was so anxious to keep up with the troops south of the river, he made it move through Howitzer Wood to Cléry.

2nd Australian Division, 28 August, South of the Somme

Captain Moss's company of the 23rd Battalion cleared Frise south of the River Somme and then Captain Galwer's and Captain Sullivan's companies of the 21st Battalion cleared the trenches across the base of the spur. Machine-gun fire from Herbécourt stopped 22nd Battalion getting beyond Dompierre until it was dark. Meanwhile machine-gun teams in Assevillers pinned down Lieutenant Colonel James's 24th Battalion until 32nd Battalion had cleared the village for the 5th Australian Division. The rapid advance was making it difficult to arrange bombardments at short notice, so forward observers were attached to the infantry companies while battery commanders spoke directly to the battalion commanders.

Lieutenant General Monash had instructed Major General Rosenthal to keep pushing, so 18th and 23rd Battalions went as far as Feuillères and Herbécourt by midnight on 28 August. Parties of the 18th Battalion cleared Mereaucourt Wood during the night, with patrols 'making a noise' to keep in touch, and the Germans then pulled out of Feuillères. Early on 29 August both 5 and 6 Brigades advanced in 'numerous files of weak platoons in artillery formation, with patrols ahead crossing the undulating moorland.' The 7 Brigade passed through only for 28th and 26th Battalions to come under machine-gun fire from the river bank until they were outflanked. One by one the rearguards fired off their ammunition before making a run for the bridges before the engineers blew them up.

Troops reached Biaches mid-morning but they came under a lot of fire from across the river and all but one of the bridges were down. The engineers had wired up the railway bridge south of Péronne but it was deemed too dangerous for anyone to stay behind and fire the charges. Instead observers kept watch until the Australians approached and then signalled the artillery to shell the area. The bombardment detonated the explosives and dropped the bridge into the river. All Brigadier General Wisdom could do was to tell 7 Brigade to establish posts along the canal bank.

There was no way forward for 2nd Australian Division, so General Monash told General Rosenthal to start moving his troops north across the

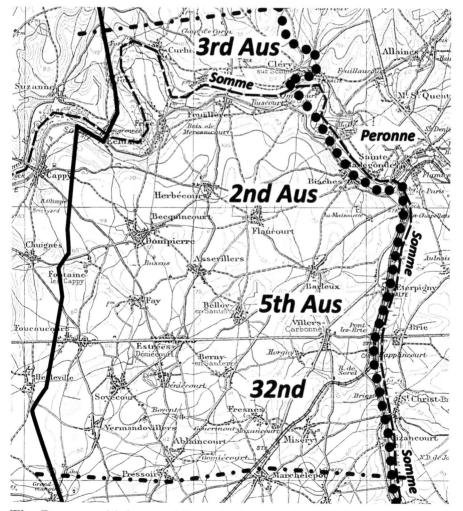

The Germans withdrew rapidly to the Somme ahead of the Australians.

Somme. He wanted to cross the Canal du Nord between Feuillaucourt and Halle and capture the high ground around Mont St Quentin. This would force the Germans to abandon Péronne, outflanking the Somme where it ran north to south.

The 18th Battalion found a bridge across the Somme Canal at the base of the Ommiécourt spur and three companies had crossed before they came under 'machine-gun fire from Cléry and the semicircle of heights beyond'. It meant the only way of getting 2nd Australian Division across the Somme was to wait for Captain Steele's engineers to repair the Feuillères bridge, 2 miles downstream.

5th Australian Division, 27 to 29 August, Advance towards the Somme

Lieutenant Colonels Street and Davies coordinated the advances of 32nd and 30th Battalions as they closed in on Foucaucourt. There was a lot of shell fire as the German artillery emptied their dumps while machine-gun fire forced the Australians to advance below ground. Monash had hoped to rush the Somme canal but German cyclists armed with machine guns made sure the Australians advanced with care on 28 August. As 32nd Battalion passed through Fay and Assevillers, 30th Battalion followed the St Quentin road through Estrées, en route to Belloy-en-Santerre.

Brigadier General Tivey's 8 Brigade advanced early into Villers Carbonnel, driving the rearguards before it. The few prisoners taken reported that their comrades were already at the Somme, holding bridgeheads, until everyone had crossed. The 29th Battalion came under fire from around Barleux so Captain Read's men advanced in small groups in 'a very fine piece of work'. The German engineers blew La Maisonette bridge prematurely and many men were hit as they ran to another crossing south of the village. Troops holding Éterpigny withdrew and the bridge was blown, leaving 29th Battalion looking for a way across the Somme. The best option was the demolished bridge at Brie and 15 Brigade was about to take over the line when Monash told Brigadier General Elliot he was changing his plan.

32nd Division, 27 to 29 August, Herleville to the Somme

Before dawn on 27 August, Major General Lambert heard that the 2nd Manchesters had discovered that the Germans had abandoned the trenches south of Herleville. Brigadier General Evans VC (awarded in the Third Ypres campaign) could not get the rest of 14 Brigade to advance until the enemy heavy artillery stopped shelling the area. Brigadier General Girdwood could not get 96 Brigade to advance because the French would not move until the morning mist had lifted. Rearguards holding Soyecourt, Starry Wood and Vermandovillers made sure they only advanced 1 mile.

The advance resumed against 'trifling opposition' early on 28 August. First the 5/6th Royal Scots and then the 15th HLI moved through Soyecourt, Déniécourt and Berny-en-Santerre, in what was little more than a procession across 14 Brigade's front. It was the same for 96 Brigade as it advanced 3 miles through Ablaincourt and Génermont to Marchelepot but it found the rearguards around Horgny and Misery.

The early morning patrols again found the Germans had withdrawn during the night. A battery of guns and their cavalry guards were seen galloping across the river at Cizancourt and then the last bridge was blown. All Major General Lambert could do was to establish a line close to the canal and wait until the river had been crossed around Péronne.

Summary

By the end of 28 August, the German soldiers were worn out after a long week of fighting. As much weaponry, equipment and stores as possible had been evacuated but the advancing British and Australian troops still found dozens of abandoned field guns and piles of abandoned supplies and ammunition. Indeed the situation was, for a short time, so fluid that Rawlinson believed open warfare had begun. The following day Haig met Foch on 29 August to discuss the future of the advance towards the Hindenburg Line.

The First French Army widened its attack front and General Fayolle was anxious to 'to follow up the enemy without giving him breathing space but not to play his game; that is to say, avoid useless losses'. The French cavalry soon found the Germans waiting for them along the Somme, south of British Fourth Army. Their new line then followed the Canal du Nord as it ran south between Nesle and Noyon. The French infantry were closing up to the waterways by 29 August.

Chapter 9

Indeed a Magnificent Performance

30 August to 1 September

First Army

General Henry Horne was to approach the Drocourt–Quéant Line, ready to break it between the River Scarpe and the Hindenburg Line. The Cavalry Corps could then pass through the gap and move east and towards Cambrai.

Canadian Corps

Lieutenant General Arthur Currie had to get close to the Drocourt–Quéant Line (D-Q Line), ready to assault it between Étaing and Riencourt on 2 September. Horne and Byng had already agreed 'not to attack it until we are ready and then to go all out'.

4th British Division, 30 August, Éterpigny

Captains Greetham and Malet were wounded leading the 1st Somersets through Éterpigny Wood while the 1st Rifle Brigade cleared the village during the afternoon of 30 August. At the same time, the 1st Warwicks cleared the high ground to the south while the 2nd Duke's had a tough fight for St Servin's Farm. Second Lieutenant James Huffam silenced two machine-gun posts around the farm but the exposed position had to be evacuated during the night. Huffam would be awarded the Victoria Cross. Brutinel's Force then waded across the Sensée stream, on the left flank, during the night. The following day, the 2nd Seaforths and 2nd Duke's pushed forward 4th Division's right around St Servin's Farm.

4th Canadian Division, 31 August, South of Éterpigny

Major General David Watson's men took over 4th (British) Division's right sector and then attacked after dusk on 31 August. The German position south of Éterpigny was strong and 12 Canadian Brigade was engaged in a see-saw battle for the low ridge throughout the day.

1st Canadian Division, 30 August, Vis-en-Artois Switch

Major General Archibald Macdonell arranged for a two-pronged attack while twelve artillery brigades fired 'an ingenious barrage that rolled from right to left across the divisional front.' Low flying planes swooped low over the Vis-en-Artois Switch at 4.40 am as the 3rd Battalion used old communication trenches to enter the north end of the position while the 2nd and 1st Battalions moved through Third Army's area to the south.

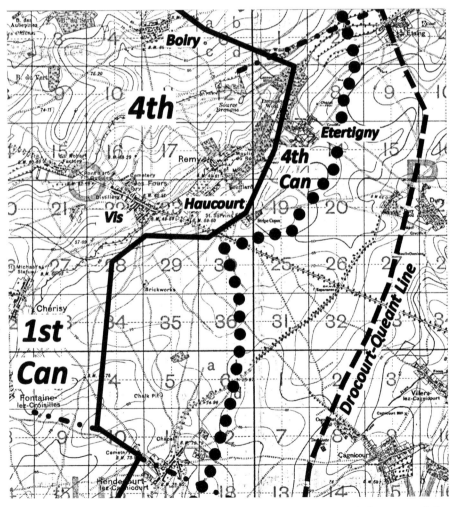

The Canadians had to fight hard to get within jumping off distance of the Drocourt-Quéant Line.

The plan had been made on the incorrect assumption that 57th Division was holding Hendecourt. It meant the Germans could fire on 1st Canadian Battalion but the attack was still a complete success. Brigadier General Griesbach then moved up 4th Battalion to face Hendecourt. The advance had straightened out the line, wiping out the two battalions in the Vis-en-Artois Switch. In a dawn attack on 31 August, the 8th Canadian Battalion finished off what it had started by clearing the trenches east of Vis-en-Artois and Ocean Work, a strongpoint south of Haucourt. The Canadian Corps was close to the D-Q Line and its heavy guns started cutting its wire entanglements.

The 5th Canadian Battalion bombed south-east along the Vis-en-Artois Switch at 4.50 am on 1 September and it took 200 prisoners while fighting off three counter-attacks. The 14th Canadian Battalion also captured the Crow's Nest, a strongpoint overlooking a large part of the D-Q Line.

XVII Corps

Lieutenant General Charles Fergusson faced the south end of the Drocourt–Quéant Line, where a triangle of trenches joined the Hindenburg Line. He also had to clear Hendecourt, Riencourt and Bullecourt before he could get to the main line of trenches but the Germans struck first.

57th Division, Hendecourt and Riencourt, 30 August to 2 September

The 2/4th Loyals stopped three attacks from Hendecourt during the afternoon but Brigadier General Boyd still had to withdraw his men during the night. The 8th King's captured Hendecourt before dawn on 1 September and the 2/6th King's then cleared the trenches to the east while the 2/7th King's advanced towards Riencourt-lez-Cagnicourt. Brigadier General Longbourne made sure the village was taken during the evening, bringing 171 Brigade close to the south end of the D-Q Line.

56th Division, Bullecourt, 30 and 31 August

The main attack was going to be made by VI Corps on XVII Corps' right flank but Major General Hull was to advance along Hindenburg Line if the opportunity arose. The Londoners had just taken over the Bullecourt sector when the Germans attacked at dawn on 30 August. The 7th Middlesex were forced back north of the village while the 1st London were driven from the ruins.

The 7th Middlesex failed to retake the factory to the north at dawn on 31 August while 4th London Regiment could not clear the village.

The only success was the capture of Station Redoubt by the 1/14th London Regiment. The 1/13th London Regiment had taken the factory and most of the village by the time 52nd Division took over the sector.

52nd Division, Bullecourt, 1 September

It took the 1/4th KOSBs and the 4th Scot Fusiliers most of 1 September to clear Bullecourt of 'lurkers'. The two battalions could not keep up with the barrage fired at 5.55 pm but they still reached Tank Avenue, east of the village. But there was a large gap on the right flank, where the Guards had been unable to capture Écoust-Saint-Menin, and the KOSBs suffered nearly 150 casualties trying to hold it. A company of the 5th Scots Fusiliers eventually secured the exposed flank facing the village.

Third Army

General Julian Byng was to push Third Army's left to the Hindenburg Line, where it followed the Canal du Nord. His centre was to clear Havrincourt Wood while his right was to reach Gouzeaucourt and Villers Guislain.

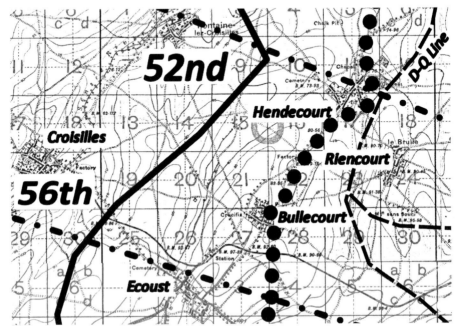

XVII Corps cleared more of the Hindenburg Line to get close to its junction with the D–Q Line.

VI Corps

Lieutenant General Haldane's men faced five fortified villages along the Hirondelle stream and the Germans intended to hold them all.

3rd Division, Écoust, 30 and 31 August, Longatte and Noreuil

The 2nd Suffolks and 1st Gordons advanced at 5 am. The Suffolks cleared Écoust-Saint-Menin only to come under attack from three sides, after 56th Division was forced out of Bullecourt. Lieutenant Colonel Stubbs' battalion had suffered 200 casualties by the time it fell back six hours later. Company Sergeant Major Jones and Private Roberts stayed behind disrupting German attempts to counter-attack, before returning to the battalion several hours

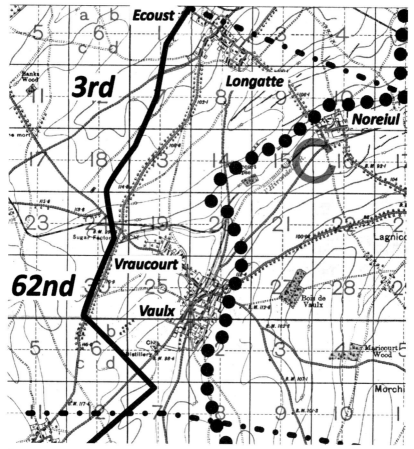

VI Corps had a struggle to cross the Hirondelle stream between Noreuil and Vaulx.

later. The 1st Northumberland Fusiliers discovered that the Germans had
abandoned Longatte Trench during the evening, so Brigadier General Potter
ordered the 4th Royal Fusiliers to move up to the Hirondelle stream.

62nd Division, 30 and 31 August, Vaulx-Vraucourt

Eight tanks joined the advance at 5 am on 30 August. The 8th West Yorkshires
cleared Banks Trench while the 2/20th London Regiment had a tough fight
for Vaulx. The 2/4th Duke's and a company of the 2/5th Duke's faced little
opposition as they took over one hundred prisoners around Vraucourt.
Lieutenant Colonel Warde-Aldam's Londoners came under machine-gun

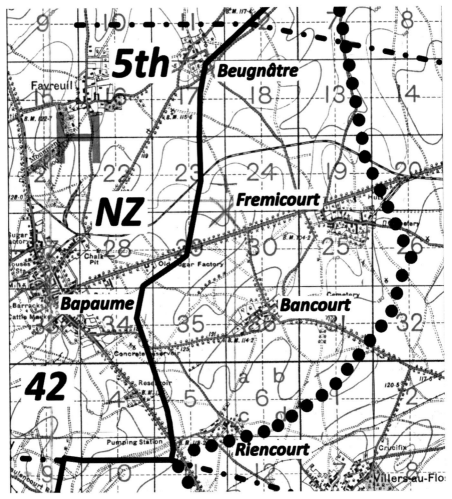

IV Corps found the Germans waiting for them east of Bapaume.

fire beyond the village and were forced to fall back, separating them from Lieutenant Colonel Wilson's Duke's. It had been a difficult day for the Londoners and the Devonshires because it was their first Western Front battle after prolonged service in Egypt and Palestine. There had been no time for reconnaissance, they had never faced masses of barbed wire and trenches before and it was the first time they had seen a tank.

The 2/20th London advanced north of Vaulx-Vraucourt at 6 am on 31 August but it was the first time the 5th Devons had worked with tanks and three went ahead into the village. Unfortunately Lieutenant Colonel Bastow had insufficient men to clear all the cellars and they were soon driven out of the village. Then it was the turn of the 8th West Yorkshires and this time the artillery had made the village 'a veritable death trap and even the deep dugouts and cellars were blocked by fallen debris and rendered quite untenable.'

IV Corps

Lieutenant General Montague Harper was to clear Frémicourt, Bancourt and Riencourt, east of Bapaume. General Byng told him to watch for signs of a German withdrawal to the Canal du Nord.

5th Division, 30 and 31 August, Beugny

Brigadier General Norton's men had a difficult time before zero hour on 30 August. The 16th Warwicks suffered eighty casualties when a German plane bombed them en route to the front line. Then the earlier attack by V Corps alerted the German artillery resulting in 95 Brigade's area being hit by a bombardment.

The artillery had pushed their guns as forward as they dared while seven tanks led the 5.15 am advance. The 1st Cheshires faced a tough fight in Beugny, and while the 1st Norfolks captured 250 prisoners to the south, heavy fire forced Major Walker to evacuate the village. Norton's men spent the following day stopping counter-attacks from Beugny with the help of Major Evans's battery. His 'guns did prodigious damage, causing the Germans to bolt in confusion over a ridge, throwing away their rifles and equipment.'

New Zealand Division, Frémicourt and Bancourt, 30 August to 1 September

Four tanks joined the 5 am attack east of Bapaume but 'it was clear that the operation was to be no walk over from the outset.' Heavy guns shelled

Frémicourt as Lieutenant Colonel Austin's 1st Rifle Brigade followed a tank to a railway cutting. The support wave cleared the ruins and Corporal Sheldrake's small group accounted for dozens of the 400 prisoners taken.

Major Turnbull's 1st Wellington Battalion advanced on 1 New Zealand Brigade's left while two tanks helped Major Sinel's 2nd Auckland Battalion clear Bancourt. The Aucklanders then came under fire from the south, and they could not advance any further until 42nd Division cleared Riencourt.

A barrage hit the New Zealanders the following morning and then tanks led the German infantry through the mist. It was some time before the SOS signals were seen, but two tanks were disabled by machine guns firing armour-piercing bullets while Major Wilding's battery forced the rest to turn back. Two parties penetrated 1st Rifle

V Corps' left reached Rocquigny but the right faced a tough fight around Sailly Saillisel.

Brigade's line, and while one was wiped out, the other was captured by Sergeant Cunningham. Sergeant John Grant charged several machine-gun posts as the Wellington Battalion retook the lost ground; he would be awarded the Victoria Cross. The Auckland Battalion even advanced a short distance before machine-gun fire from Villers-au-Flos forced it to withdraw.

42nd Division, 30 August, Riencourt

The mist had cleared when the 1/5th East Lancashires advanced just before 6 am. The plan was to use old trenches to enter Riencourt from the north but 'intense machine-gun fire raged from the village itself and the coppices round it.' It was early on 31 August before the 1/10th Manchester had cleared the ruins. Captain Thomas then pushed beyond the village and the success led to the battalion becoming known as the Night Jars. One stretcher bearer returned with a group of prisoners armed with nothing more than a broken beer bottle.

V Corps

Lieutenant General Cameron Shute's men wanted to get beyond the 1916 Somme battlefield but the Germans were determined to hold onto Beaulencourt, Le Transloy and Morval.

21st Division, Beaulencourt, 30 and 31 August

Patrols discovered that Beaulencourt 'presented a glacis-like slope with no cover'. So Major General David Campbell made arrangements to move through 42nd Division's sector to the north before dawn on 31 August. The 1st Wiltshires and 6th Leicesters followed a creeping barrage from Riencourt, 'taking the enemy by surprise and after some very heavy fighting, in which good use was made of Lewis guns and trench mortars,' they captured 130 prisoners, including inmates of a field hospital. A company of the 7th Leicesters failed to attack the sugar factory south of the village because they could not find their forming-up line in the dark.

17th Division, 30 August, Le Transloy

Crossfire prevented 51 Brigade from reaching Le Transloy on 30 August, so an attack by 52 Brigade was planned for midnight. One company of the 10th Lancashire Fusiliers became disorientated in the dark and failed to capture the cemetery south-west of the village, so the rest of Lieutenant

Colonel Cotton's men had to fall back. Brigadier General Allason organised another attempt for 4.20 am but gas shells made the men sneeze and they were spotted before zero hour.

Major General Robertson planned a third attempt to bypass the village at 5.40 am but 51 Brigade's brigade-major was hit while reconnoitring the position. Brigadier General Dudgeon stayed with him, so 52 Brigade's jumping-off line was placed too close to the Germans. The 12th Manchesters, 10th Lancashire Fusiliers and the 9th Duke's were all pinned down before they had gone far. The same happened the following day because the German position around Le Transloy was too strong.

38th Division, Morval and Sailly Saillisel, 30 August to 1 September

Brigadier General Hulke was wounded as 115 Brigade waited east of Lesboeufs on 30 August. Meanwhile Brigadier General Rhys Price launched a pre-dawn attack without a barrage but the 14th and 16th Welsh Fusiliers were unable to take Morval. 'Patrols trying to enter the ruins the next day found them strongly held; it was even thought the enemy had reinforced the position.'

Brigadier General Rhys Price repeated the attack at 4.45 am the following day and 114 Brigade was successful this time. At 6 am the 2nd and 17th Welsh Fusiliers advanced south-east from 115 Brigade's sector around Lesboeufs only to find the enemy dug in around Sailly Saillisel. A counter-attack from the direction of Le Transloy overran part of the 2nd Welsh Fusiliers while the rest of Lieutenant Colonel de Miremont's men fell back towards Morval. The 10th SWBs countered, returning 'with a good bag of prisoners and the menace was over'.

Major General Cubitt ordered Brigadier General Rhys Price to coordinate an attack with 113 Brigade and 18th Division against Sailly Saillisel but the lull in the fighting gave the Germans time to withdraw. The 13th and 16th Welsh Fusiliers would enter the ruins at dusk.

Fourth Army

General Rawlinson would keep advancing towards the Hindenburg Line, where it ran close to the St Quentin Canal.

III Corps

Lieutenant General Godley faced Combles, 'an extensive village which lies low, and it was under vigorous protection not only from the high ground to the south but also from the German positions on Morval Ridge to the north.' V Corps had to clear Morval to the north before there was any hope of clearing the deep valley surrounding Combles.

18th Division, Combles, 30 August to 1 September

Major General Richard Lee was supposed to push 54 Brigade forward, to support 47th Division's advance on his right early on 30 August. The 11th Royal Fusiliers were stopped by machine-gun fire from Priez Farm as they advanced through the mist south of Combles, so Lieutenant Steele wheeled 'a sniping gun' forward to engage targets pointed out by the infantry. Captain Currie would do the same with his entire battery the following day as the division waited for V Corps to clear Morval.

Godley planned a thirty minute barrage followed by an advance behind a creeping barrage, starting at 5.30 am on 1 September. He had also wanted V Corps to lay a smoke screen along Brigadier General Wood's north flank as 55 Brigade left Combles ravine.

Lieutenant Colonel Irwin's 8th East Surreys skirted the north side of Rancourt before heading for St Pierre Vaast Wood. Captain Gaywood's company of the 8th East Surreys eventually captured Priez Farm on the right flank in a ferocious battle 'testified by the number of dead in the

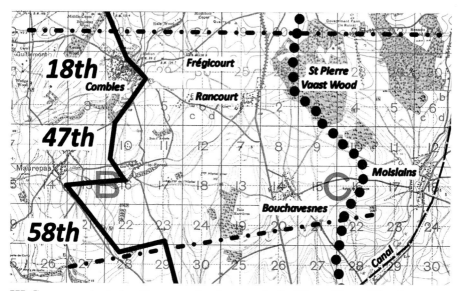

III Corps pushed the Germans back towards St Pierre Vaast Wood and the Canal du Nord.

vicinity'. Captain Strong's company of the 7th Buffs took one hundred prisoners along the west side of the wood, as the East Surreys cleared the undergrowth. At the same time the 7th Queen's mopped up Haie Wood and Frégicourt, bringing the total number of prisoners to over 700.

With his own objective secure, General Lee agreed to help 38th Division clear Sailly-Saillisel on his left flank. Captain MacDonald's company of the 7th Queen's Own helped the Welshmen secure the village during the evening.

47th Division, 30 August to 1 September, Rancourt

Major General Gorringe had been supposed to relieve 12th Division during the night but the Germans were retiring towards the Canal du Nord. It meant that Brigadier General McDouall sent 142 Brigade in pursuit mid-morning instead. The 1/22nd London were pinned down by fire from Priez Farm and Rancourt, but the 1/24th London found only rearguards in front of them.

The delays on 30 August meant that Major General Gorringe had to catch up with 58th Division on his right. 'Peaceful penetration' during the night took some ground while the plan was to wheel his right flank forward across Hill 145. The creeping barrage began at 5.30 am but the garrison of Priez Farm again delayed 1/23rd London Regiment. Meanwhile 141 Brigade advanced quickly, taking over 180 prisoners, resulting in a gap opening in the centre of the division. A counter-attack from Rancourt drove the 18th London Regiment back until the 19th London Regiment reinforced the line. On 1 September 140 Brigade advanced through Rancourt, en route to St Pierre Vaast Wood. The 23rd London Regiment captured Priez Farm behind a Stokes mortar bombardment and Captain Blofeld took eighty prisoners. Meanwhile, 141 Brigade advanced to the west side of Moislain Wood.

58th Division, 30 August to 1 September, Marrières Wood and Bouchavesnes

The 175 Brigade advanced early to catch up with the Australians by mid-morning. Around one hundred prisoners were taken on Hill 150 and the Londoners could look down over Marrières Wood. The 8th and 6th London Regiments advanced through the wood at 5.10 am on 31 August and Captain Cooke's men rounded up around 400 prisoners. Brigadier General Corkran was told to take 173 Brigade forward and his men took another 325 prisoners near Bouchavesnes. The Germans were obviously withdrawing across the Canal du Nord but it was too dangerous to move down the open slope to Moislains in daylight.

The Australian Corps

All the bridges west of Péronne were down and the engineers were kept busy looking for ways across the Somme. The girders of the demolished bridges opposite Péronne could be negotiated but machine guns were trained on them all. There was a footbridge at La Chapellette, a damaged bridge north of Éterpigny and a light railway bridge at Brie but none showed much promise. After hearing that Bapaume had been abandoned, Lieutenant General Monash discussed how to capture Mont St Quentin and Péronne with his divisional commanders, and outflanking the Somme position.

Rawlinson might have 'laughed at Monash's cheek' but he agreed to let him try. As the generals discussed their plans, Lieutenant Colonel West deployed the 5th Royal Horse Artillery Brigade on the heights opposite Péronne. His gunners 'enjoyed the best shooting they had ever had against targets of every description' both north and east of the river.

3rd Australian Division, Cléry and the Canal du Nord, 30 August to 1 September

Major General Gellibrand's command was deployed around Cléry but 58th Division had to advance on his left flank while 5 Australian Brigade still had to cross the Somme on his right. The plan was to clear the ridge between Bouchavesnes and Cléry but each battalion was only 300 rifles strong and the men were 'almost dazed for lack of sleep'. The brigadiers were shocked when they were told about the attack and said, 'it will fail; the men and the officers are too knocked out.' The senior commanders did not know the weak 10 and 9 Australian Brigades faced two divisions. They would have changed their plans if they had.

There had been no time to arrange any barrages, so the field guns moved close behind the infantry as they advanced before dawn on 30 August. Captains Macdonald and Beaver were hit when the machine guns in Road Wood opened fire and 34th Battalion was pinned down. However, Lieutenant Cox and Captain Towl took dozens of prisoners as 37th Battalion advanced past Cléry Copse.

Captain McIntyre then cleared Cléry on the river bank for 40th Battalion, allowing Lieutenant Game to clear the enemy trenches near the Canal du Nord. Prisoners taken during a counter-attack suggested that the Germans were about to withdraw, so Gellibrand made plans to renew the advance the following morning.

Early on 31 August, both 10 and 9 Australian Brigades came under fire as they advanced up the slope. Private George Cartwright ran forward to silence the machine guns holding up 33rd Battalion in front of Road Wood; he would be awarded the Victoria Cross. Attempts to cross the crest were stopped by heavier fire and then a counter-attack from the direction of Allaines pushed 10 Brigade back.

The 11 Australian Brigade advanced over the top and along trenches through the rain and mist early on 1 September. The 42nd and 41st Battalions found around 400 prisoners hiding in their dugouts as they advanced towards the Canal du Nord. But machine guns around Allaines stopped 43rd Battalion clearing the adjacent spur.

2nd Australian Division, Mont St Quentin, 30 August to 1 September

Major General Rosenthal's men held a 2 mile length of the Somme between Ommiécourt and Biaches. The 18th Battalion could not cross the Ommiécourt causeway and 19th Battalion found Halle causeway impassable. So Major General Rosenthal had to tell Brigadier General Martin to march 5 Australian Brigade downstream to Feuillères.

Lieutenant Colonel Forbes's men crossed the temporary bridge but the artillery could not get over so 20th Battalion used Lewis guns and rifle grenades as they followed a trench into Cléry. Captain Barlow's men took 'the risk of hopping from shell-hole to shell-hole' as they silenced the enemy machine-gun posts but Major McDonald advised against attacking the exposed 1916 Knoll just yet.

The advance forced the Germans to abandon Ommiécourt, so the engineers could repair the causeway for 17th Australian Battalion to cross the river. The engineers then built two bridges 'with pontoons, cork, floats, trestles and other bridging gear' around Biaches during the night. A company of the 26th Australian Battalion crossed the canal at dawn only to find a lagoon blocking their way, so Captain Cooper's men had to turn back.

Brigadier General Martin's plan was for 20th Australian Battalion to advance to the road between Feuillaucourt and Mont St Quentin while 17th Australian Battalion seized the village on the summit. Around 2,000 men advanced towards the summit of Mont St Quentin at 5 am and Captains McDonald and Barlow saw most of the 'Germans threw down their arms and ran forward to be captured. This raised our spirits considerably.' On the right, Captain Allan's company captured 'a tremendous lot' of Germans near the river before 17th Battalion were stopped by machine-gun fire from St

Denis and Anvil Wood. However, up ahead the Germans were abandoning the high ground:

'Ahead along the whole face of the Mount, Germans were running back, making for its northern and southern shoulders. The Australians, who had expected heavy fighting, hurried, with minds now carefree, half running, trying to catch them and taking occasional shots. As each new group of Germans broke from the trenches ahead the Lewis gunners would throw themselves down for a minute to fire.'

Lieutenant Croft and Captain Manefield cleared the village of Mont St Quentin as 19th Battalion moved up on the right flank.

A dawn counter-attack would drive 17th Battalion back and 20th Battalion would have to withdraw from Feuillaucourt on the left later in the day.

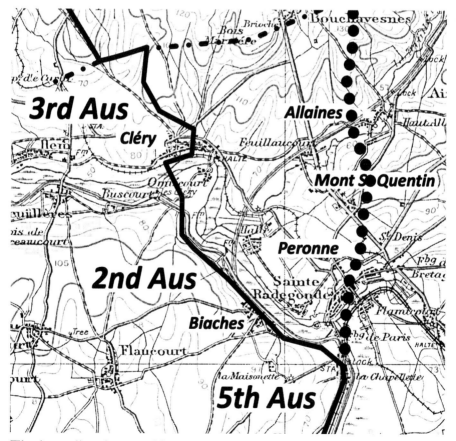

The Australians kept pushing north of the Somme to clear Mont St Quentin and Péronne.

However, eight weak companies, numbering only 550, had captured over 700 prisoners around Mont St Quentin. As luck had it, they had attacked during a relief; 'it all happened like lightning and we were taken unawares before we had fired a shot.' Commanders, from battalion headquarters right up to army headquarters, were astonished by the success and Rawlinson thought it was 'indeed a magnificent performance'.

Upon hearing the news, Monash ordered Brigadier General Paton to move 6 Australian Brigade across the Somme. The 23rd Battalion cleared Florina Trench while Lieutenant Holland's company advanced along the river bank to St Radégonde before they were forced to retire.

Lieutenant General John Monash's plan for 1 September was to clear the ground south of Mont St Quentin, so he could tackle Péronne. As 6 Australian Brigade reinforced 5 Australian Brigade, 14 Australian Brigade moved up from 5th Australian Division, ready to advance into the town.

Brigadier General Paton had no idea where 6 Australian Brigade's front line was, so he was unable to organise a barrage. Instead he ran from shell hole to shell hole as they closed in on the enemy outposts south of Mont St Quentin.

On the left, Lieutenant Colonel James's 24th Battalion moved through Feuillaucourt and along the Canal du Nord towards Allaines. Lieutenant Edgar Towner of 2nd Australian Machine Gun Battalion silenced one machine-gun team with his revolver and then turned the weapon on the Germans. He then directed his Vickers machine guns to stop a counter-attack and took twenty-five men prisoner. Towner was wounded when advance resumed but he still retrieved a machine gun after all its crew were hit and 'continued to engage the enemy whenever they appeared'. He stopped a second counter-attack before he was evacuated with exhaustion and would be awarded the Victoria Cross.

Lieutenant Colonel Brazenor's men were pinned down in Florina Trench, so Private Bob Mactier climbed out and killed three machine-gun teams before forcing another forty men to surrender. Mactier was killed approaching a fourth machine-gun team (he would be awarded Victoria Cross posthumously) but his actions allowed the rest of 23rd Battalion to approach Mont St Quentin from the south-west. They found the survivors of 17th, 19th and 20th Battalion holding out, surrounded by their dead comrades, and then went on to secure the village.

The 21st Battalion then advanced beyond Mont St Quentin only to come under fire from a crater in St Quentin Wood. Sergeant Alby Lowerson led a small party of men forward as he 'threw bomb after bomb into the crowded enemy'. Lowerson was wounded but his comrades were able to secure the line east of the village; he would be awarded the Victoria Cross.

5th Australian Division, 30 August and 1 September, Péronne

Major General Talbot Hobbs was holding the 2 mile stretch of the Somme upstream from Biaches but Brigadier General Tivey's men had again been unable to cross the river. Monash had 32nd Division relieve the division as far north as La Chapellette, allowing both 8 and 15 Australian Brigades to withdraw into reserve.

The following morning, 14 Australian Brigade crossed the Somme at Feuillères, marched in single file along the north bank and then crossed a tree trunk over the Tortille stream in single file. Brigadier General Stewart assembled his men in the valley east of Cléry, ready to attack Péronne through mist and drizzle. Meanwhile Brigadier General Elliott's 15 Australian Brigade remained south of the Somme, in case the Germans abandoned Péronne.

Major Murray's company of the 53rd Battalion advanced toward St Denis Wood but Captain Evers' company was pinned down by fire from Anvil Wood until Captain Smith's men found a gap in the wire. Private William Currey killed the crew of a field gun and then turned it on the machine guns in the area. He would later silence a strongpoint and then carry orders forward to an isolated company under heavy fire. Currey would be awarded the Victoria Cross. But 53rd Battalion then came under fire from Péronne's ramparts, stopping any further advance.

The 54th Battalion cleared St Radégonde next to the Somme, only to find the bridge across the town moat had been blown up. Corporal Alexander Buckley led the charge, silencing a machine-gun post, only to be killed scrambling across the rubble. Private Arthur Hall dealt with another machine-gun team, so his comrades could enter the town, 'advancing at a half run, as fast as they could go… shooting from the shoulder and giving the [Germans] no time to stop'. Both Buckley and Hall would be awarded the Victoria Cross.

The rest of 14 Australian Brigade spread out along the streets, clearing the enemy and civilians from houses and cellars. By the end of the day, Brigadier General Stewart's men had taken all but the north-east suburbs and Major General Hobbs told him to consolidate his position until his flanks were secure. Brigadier General Elliott had already led 59th Australian Battalion across the Somme by the ruined railway bridge. It meant that 57th and 58th Australian Battalions could deploy close to the moat, ready to advance south of Péronne.

32nd Division, 30 August to 1 September, Along the Somme

Major General Lambert's men had found the Germans waiting along the Somme between Brie and Cizancourt on 29 August. The obstacle included the canal, which had firm banks and was narrow, and the river beyond, which had meandering water channels, lagoons and marshes. On 30 August the 5/6th Royal Scots found a bridge but it just led into a maze of mud, water and reed beds covered by machine-gun teams and snipers.

The engineers built three bridges over the canal during the night but the dawn patrols came under fire from across the river and had to withdraw. There was no easy way forward so Monash made 32nd Division relieve 5th Australian Division to within 2 miles of Péronne. Lambert was then told to bridge the Somme ready for when the Germans abandoned the river line.

Summary

On 1 September, Haig was considering the difficult days ahead. First Army faced the Drocourt–Quéant Line while Third Army had to clear the area between Vaulx-Vraucourt, Frémicourt and Le Transloy. Fourth Army had to cross the Canal du Nord and push beyond Mont St Quentin and Péronne. To make matters worse, he received a warning telegram from the Chief of the Imperial General Staff, General Sir Henry Wilson:

'Just a word of caution in regard to incurring heavy losses in attacks on the Hindenburg Line as opposed to losses when driving the enemy back to that line. I do not mean to say that you have incurred such losses, but I know the War Cabinet would become anxious if we received heavy punishment in attacking the Hindenburg Line without success.'

Heavy casualties during the next couple of weeks would make the War Cabinet question the chances of the BEF breaking through the Hindenburg Line. But Haig did not change his plans and he did not pass on Wilson's concerns to his army commanders.

German casualties had been high and there were too few replacements, so ten divisions had to be disbanded to provide them. At the same time, battalions were being reduced from four to three companies. Morale was suffering, as demonstrated by the thousands of men who had surrendered. The message came no clearer to Crown Prince Rupprecht than when he was returning to the front from sick leave. His train passed a railway carriage with the message 'Slaughter Cattle for Wilhelm and Sons' chalked on the side; they were referring to the Kaiser and his soldiers.

Chapter 10

The Hardest Fighting During the Whole Advance

2 and 3 September

First Army

First Army faced the Drocourt–Quéant Line (the D-Q Line), 'one of the most powerful and well organized German defence systems', south of the River Scarpe. The Buissy Switch connected the south end of the D-Q Line to the Hindenburg Support Line. Thick wire entanglements would push assault troops into the path of the many concrete machine-gun posts while the infantry had plenty of shelters to hide in.

General Henry Horne's plan was for XXII Corps to cover the flank north of the Scarpe, while the Canadian Corps made the main attack against the D-Q Line at 5 am on 2 September. He wanted any success to be 'exploited by pushing forward rapidly to seize the crossings over the Canal du Nord.' The XVII Corps could then clear the south end of the D-Q Line. Lieutenant General Arthur Currie was given all the tanks III Brigade had while Lieutenant General Charles Kavanagh put the Cavalry Corps on standby.

The Canadian Corps

Lieutenant General Arthur Currie had given each division two companies of Mark V tanks, and aircraft flew over the assembly area before zero hour to drown out the engine noise. The tanks deployed in the centre would return after the two Canadian divisions had taken the D-Q Line, ready to attack again. At 5 am the guns opened fire and the three divisions of the Canadian Corps advanced.

4th (British) Division, 2 September, Éterpigny

Two anti-tank guns covered the only crossing over the marshy Sensée stream so the nine tanks supposed to help the 1st King's Own and 2nd Essex were delayed. They struggled through the D-Q trenches alone until Lieutenant

Colonel Kirby's 2nd Lancashire Fusiliers moved up and Second Lieutenant McIntosh and Private Currie silenced the guns. The tanks crossed the stream but machine-gun fire from Étaing Wood stopped the infantry reaching the village.

Lieutenant Colonel Earle's 1st Hampshires were pinned down by enfilade fire until the 1st King's Own captured Prospect Farm on their left flank. They then joined Lieutenant Colonel Majendie's Somersets as they cleared the D-Q Line. 'As each post was located, it was at once engaged by rifle and Lewis gun fire, under cover of which [men] then started to work around to a flank.' The Germans withdrew as soon as they saw their escape route was threatened.

A second attack timed for 5 am on 3 September was cancelled with just minutes to go. Patrols had discovered that the Germans had withdrawn, so the batteries were told to cease fire. On the left, 12 Brigade drove the rearguard out of Étaing and moved to the Sensée around Lécluse. Meanwhile, 11 Brigade advanced to the River Scarpe under fire from across the river.

4th Canadian Division, 2 September, Dury

Major General Sir David Watson's men had to clear the D-Q Line north of the Cambrai road before advancing across the 'long, exposed crest of Mont Dury'. They did not know that the Germans had deployed most of their machine guns and artillery beyond the summit, out of range of the British guns.

Eleven tanks led 50th and 47th Battalions through the D-Q Line around Éterpigny and men of 46th Battalion mopped up the remaining machine-gun posts by engaging them with fire while manoeuvring around their flanks. The tanks then did an about turn and took Dury from the rear as 46th Battalion attacked from the front. 'There was particularly vicious fighting for the village' but the capture of 120 prisoners in the ruins secured 10 Brigade's front.

The twenty-two tanks earmarked to support 12 Brigade were late, so Brigadier General MacBrien had to tell his battalion commanders to advance without them. Machine-gun fire delayed the deployment, so they were late as the creeping barrage crossed the 'heavily wired and strongly garrisoned' D-Q Line north of the Cambrai road. Fortunately the Germans facing 85th and 38th Battalion were eager to surrender, even more so when the tanks eventually caught up. But a few were determined to fight 78th Battalion along the Cambrai road.

The Canadians crossed the valley beyond the D-Q trenches only to come under heavy fire from the sunken road south of Dury. The Germans in

Villers-lez-Cagnicourt were also firing into 78th Battalion's flank. No one could get any further and MacBrien's men had to dig in before the counter-attacks started. Private Claude Nunney had made sure 38th Battalion reached its objective and then, for a second day running, he encouraged his comrades to fight off a counter-attack; he would be awarded the Victoria Cross.

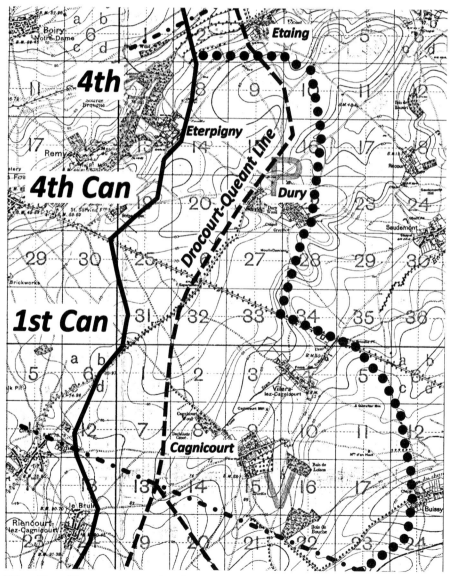

The Canadians overran the Drocourt–Quéant Line around Dury on 2 September.

Brigadier General Odlum's four battalions were hit by artillery fire as they advanced towards Dury. There was no creeping barrage, no tanks, no smoke and the Germans were waiting for them. The 54th and 75th Battalions could not advance north of the village and neither could 44th Battalion on their left flank. It was the same south of the village, where 87th and 78th Battalions faced a tough fight for a sunken road; 78th Battalion could not make any progress along the Cambrai road either.

Two men would be awarded the Victoria Cross for rescuing the wounded between Éterpigny and Dury. Captain Bellenden Hutcheson, a member of the Royal Canadian Army Medical Corps, made sure every wounded man of 75th Battalion was rescued. He then attended a seriously injured officer and a sergeant under heavy fire. Private John Young was a stretcher-bearer who rescued a dozen wounded men of 87th Battalion, returning for more dressings when he ran out.

1st Canadian Division, 2 September, Villers-lez-Cagnicourt

Major General Archibald Macdonell's men faced the D-Q Line south of the Cambrai road but they also had to clear the Buissy Switch, which ran parallel to their line of advance. The 5th Battalion was still fighting for the jumping-off line as four tanks led 7th Battalion forward, 'knocking out one enemy post after another'. Another seven tanks crushed the wire south of the Cambrai road as Private Walter Rayfield bayoneted two men and took ten prisoners in one trench. He then captured another thirty men before rescuing a wounded man under fire; he would be awarded the Victoria Cross. Many more Germans would surrender in the D-Q support trenches and in the north end of the Buissy Switch.

The 10th Battalion then took over, only to see all but two of the tanks knocked out on the slope leading down to Villers-lez-Cagnicourt. Brigadier General Loomis sent a field battery forward to help and the gunners used captured German guns while the infantry bypassed the village.

Sergeant Arthur Knight silenced several machine-gun and trench mortar teams before directing a Lewis gun onto the retreating enemy. He then killed three Germans hiding in a tunnel before another twenty surrendered. Knight was mortally wounded soon afterwards; he would be posthumously awarded the Victoria Cross.

Loomis sent the 8th Battalion forward to form a flank along the Cambrai road, while arranging a new barrage to hit the Buissy Switch south of Villers-lez-Cagnicourt. The 10th Battalion fought well into the night as it worked its way along the trenches towards Buissy.

Eight tanks led 13th and 16th Battalions through the wire, spraying smoke to cover the infantry who were close behind. The Canadians charged and the Germans in the first pair of D-Q trenches surrendered. The tanks were then recalled, leaving 13th Battalion to take the support trenches. Then 14th Battalion took over the advance, moving forward in platoon and section rushes. They pushed through Cagnicourt, where they 'surprised and captured enough Germans in the village cellars to make a full battalion'. They also cleared Bois de Loison advancing towards the Buissy Switch.

The right flank suffered from enfilade fire directed from Hendecourt and Riencourt. Lieutenant Colonel Cyrus Peck saw that part of 16th Battalion was held up so he 'went forward through bursting shells and withering machine-gun fire to make a personal reconnaissance and compel roaming tanks to protect his open flank'. Peck then led his battalion towards Cagnicourt; he would be awarded the Victoria Cross. Lance Corporal William Metcalf, an American serving with the Canadian Expeditionary Force, guided a tank along the trench, pointing out the strongpoints firing at 16th Battalion. He was wounded but carried on fighting until he was ordered to go back and have his wounds dressed. Metcalf would also be awarded the Victoria Cross.

The enfilade fire from the right continued to pin 16th Battalion down until Lieutenant Colonel Peck gathered together all the machine guns he could find, so his men could clear the rest of the D-Q trenches in front of Lagnicourt. The 15th Battalion then passed through and cleared Bois de Bouche. In places the 1st Canadian Division had advanced over 4 miles.

The Pursuit to the Canal du Nord

The plan to attack the following morning was issued but 'air patrols flying over the enemy lines on the morning of 3 September saw no Germans between the Cagnicourt-Dury Ridge and the Canal du Nord.' Third Army to the south had also discovered that the Hindenburg Line around Quéant and Pronville had been abandoned.

The advance towards the Canal du Nord began at 8 am on 4th Canadian Division's front. Both 46th and 44th Battalions wheeled north to face the Sensée, finding all the bridges between Récourt and Écourt St Quentin had been demolished. At the same time 87th, 54th and 102nd Battalions moved slowly east, finding the Germans waiting along the Canal du Nord around Sauchy-Cauchy. Again, the bridges were down but a party of the 102nd Battalion crossed the broken railway bridge, west of Sauchy-Lestrée. South of the Cambria road, the 1st Canadian Division was only 1 mile from the

Canal du Nord, so it waited until midday. The four battalions of 1 and 2 Brigades came under fire as they approached Marquion, losing many before they had established a new line along the west bank.

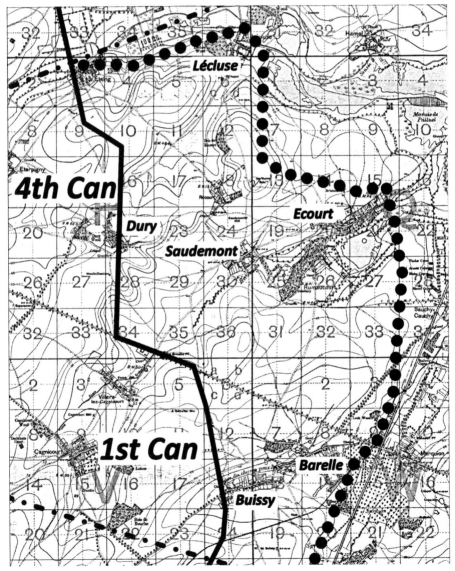

The Canadians followed up the withdrawal to the River Sensée and the Canal du Nord.

Third Army

General Julian Byng's left had to advance astride the Hindenburg Line around Pronville and Inchy, to support First Army's attack on the D-Q Line. Meanwhile his centre faced the new German line east of Bapaume while his right was looking to escape the 1916 battlefield.

XVII Corps

Lieutenant General Sir Charles Fergusson had no tanks available, so he did not dare to make a frontal attack. Instead 57th Division would follow the Canadian Corps through the D-Q Line before turning south to bomb down it. The 52nd Division could then tackle the Hindenburg Line west of Quéant. The artillery started by supporting the Canadian Corps' attack before switching to the D-Q Line, eighty-four minutes before zero hour, which was set for 5 am.

57th Division, 2 and 3 September, Riencourt

The barrage switched to the area east of Riencourt in front of 172 Brigade before lifting at 7.15 am. Then the 1st Munsters and 2/4th South Lancashires 'fought their way with bayonet and bomb' down the south end of the D-Q front system. Company Sergeant Major Martin Doyle took command of his company of the Munsters after all his officers were hit. He then went on a one man crusade, rescuing comrades and carrying back a wounded officer to safety. He then helped save a tank crew in difficulties, silenced a machine gun, took several prisoners and brought in a wounded man under fire. He finally made sure a counter-attack was stopped. Doyle would be awarded the Victoria Cross.

63rd Division, 2 and 3 September, Pronville

Major General Cyril Blacklock had just replaced Major General Laurie and he immediately had to plan a difficult manoeuvre for 188 Brigade. On hearing of the Canadian success, Blacklock gave the code word 'Move' and 188 Brigade marched east through Calling Card Wood before wheeling south behind the south end of the Drocourt–Quéant Line. All the artillery was busy supporting 57th Division, so the Drake Battalion, 1st Royal Marines and 2nd Irish Regiment relied on their rifles and machine guns for firepower. Chief Petty Officer George Prowse captured one strongpoint as the Drake Battalion cleared the Hindenburg Support Line. Sub Lieutenant Simmonds cleared another machine-gun nest and captured an artillery convoy trying to escape the Quéant area. The Marines and the Irish Regiment were then pinned down until the Anson Battalion helped them get closer to the railway.

It was late afternoon before the Hood and Hawke Battalions reached the railway in front of Inchy on 189 Brigade's front. The Drake Battalion had been left to fight on alone and Prowse had silenced another two machine-gun posts. Unfortunately he would be killed on 27 September and was posthumously awarded the Victoria Cross.

The Germans abandoned Quéant and Pronville during the night, allowing the Hood and Hawke Battalions to clear the Hindenburg Support Line en route to Inchy. The Drake Battalion cleared Pronville and Tadpole Copse on the right flank before stopping in front of Moeuvres. Brigadier General Curling's men eventually found the Germans holding the west bank of the Canal du Nord.

52nd Division, 2 September, Quéant

As soon as Brigadier General Leggett reported 57th Division's success around Riencourt, Major General Hill gave the order to advance. Lieutenant Colonel Mitchell's 1/4th Royal Scots outflanked the Germans at the south end of the D-Q line, so the 1/7th Scottish Rifles could begin clearing the Hindenburg Front Line. The 1/4th Scots Fusiliers cleared the Hindenburg

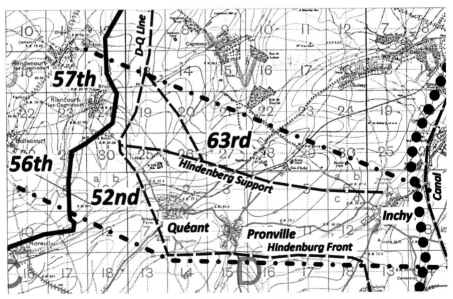

XVII Corps advanced astride the Hindenburg Line to the Canal du Nord.

Front Line on the east bank of the Hirondelle stream but they could not contact the 3rd Division on their right flank.

Brigadier General Forbes-Robertson heard that Quéant had been evacuated during the afternoon while the 1/7th Royal Scots discovered the Germans had abandoned the Hindenburg Support Line, north of Quéant, during the night. The following morning, 157 Brigade cleared Quéant and Pronville while 155 Brigade mopped up the Hindenburg Front Line. The converging advances of 63rd Division and VI Corps squeezed 52nd Division out of the line.

VI Corps

Lieutenant General Sir Haldane's men had to cross sunken roads and old trenches to reach Lagnicourt and Morchies. Both 3rd and 62nd Divisions had been given a company of tanks but the late issuing of orders meant there had been no time to discuss any plans for an early morning advance through the mist.

3rd Division, 2 September, Noreuil

The early start by XVII Corps meant Major General Deverell's troops had to endure a bombardment before they advanced at 5.30 am. Brigadier General Fisher's men failed to cooperate with the tanks and four were soon knocked out as they crossed the Hirondelle stream. It was getting light by the time 1st Scots Fusiliers and 2nd Royal Scots crossed the valley and many were pinned down along a railway line. Captain Gordon had cleared Noreuil but Lieutenant Colonel Henderson needed help to take Macaulay Avenue and Lagnicourt Trench. A company of the Suffolks helped his men take over 300 prisoners.

The 1st Shropshires lost all their officers after 62nd Division were driven from Vaulx-Vraucourt, so Lieutenant Colonel Richard West led two Whippet tanks forward on horseback. He then rode back and forth encouraging the Shropshires until he was killed. West was posthumously awarded the Victoria Cross. Major General Deverell sent the 2nd Suffolks forward to reinforce the threatened flank and Captain Nagle's company rounded up 400 prisoners in the trenches and sunken roads.

2nd Division, 3 September, Morchies, Beaumetz and Lagnicourt

The German guns ceased firing around midnight, as the crews limbered up and headed for the Canal du Nord. The British barrage began as the gunners 'fed their own guns without fear of rebuke from higher commands' at 5.20 am 'because the days of a shortage of shells had passed for ever'.

The 1st KRRC and 23rd Royal Fusiliers 'only encountered slight opposition' en route to Morchies and Beaumetz. Meanwhile, the 17th Royal Fusiliers and 2nd Staffords were accompanied by three tanks as they moved past an abandoned Maricourt Wood en route to Lagnicourt. Major General Pereira gave Brigadier General Willan permission to advance to Hermies and Demicourt, but his men discovered the Germans were holding the Hindenburg Line west of the Canal du Nord.

62nd Division, 2 September, Vaulx-Vraucourt

The German guns responded to IV Corps' early attack against Beugny, leaving 187 Brigade 'only too anxious to leave this barrage and get under our own'. They rapidly overran the German machine-gun teams but anti-tank rifles knocked out six of the eight tanks supporting the Yorkshire men. Lieutenant Colonel Hart's 2/4th York and Lancasters overran a battery of field guns

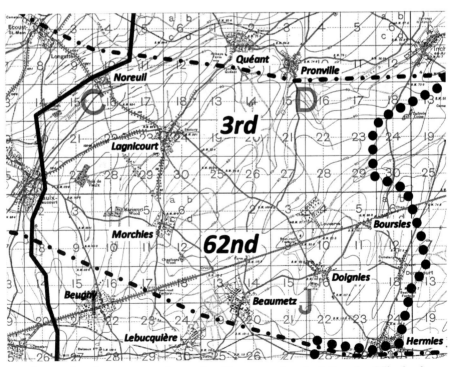

VI Corps fought rearguards as the Germans headed for the Hindenburg Line.

beyond Vaulx Trench but they then had to throw back a flank because 3rd Division was struggling. Enfilade fire pinned down the 5th KOYLIs' right around Vaulx Trench while a counter-attack threatened to cut Lieutenant Colonel Peter's men off. Lieutenant Colonel Chaytor's 2/4th KOYLIs were embroiled in a bitter fight for Vaulx Wood until the 9th Durhams (Pioneers) arrived. After a shaky start, Brigadier General Reddie summarised that the Durhams' attack 'concluded a most satisfactory day's fighting'.

Guards Division, 3 September, Advance to Inchy and Moeuvres

Two Mark IV tanks and three Whippets joined the early morning advance across the Lagnicourt–Morchies ridge but the Germans had withdrawn to the Canal du Nord. 'The Guards had the pleasurable experience of being able to march steadily onward without having to fight for every foot of ground.' As the 3 Guards Brigade moved along the spur beyond Pronville, 2 Guards Brigade went beyond Lagnicourt. 'So strange and novel indeed was the sensation caused amongst the officers and men by the unwonted absence of hostile machine-gun fire and the comparative silence of the enemy guns, that the troops at first advanced with an unnecessary caution, suspecting some cleverly concealed trap.'

The 2nd Scots Guards and the 1st Welsh Guards soon reached Inchy while the 1st Scots Guards and the 3rd Grenadier Guards cleared the old British trenches west of Moeuvres. Abandoned dumps burned up ahead and 'not a machine gun broke the stupefying stillness. No distant guns opened. The advance became a route march, a Sunday walk out, edged with tense suspicion.'

IV Corps

Lieutenant General Sir Harper had to break the position east of Bapaume, in the expectation that the Germans would retire to the Canal du Nord, some 4 miles to the south-east. The canal ran through a 4 mile long tunnel in front of IV Corps, making it an ideal place for tanks to operate.

5th Division, Beugny, 1 and 2 September

An SOS barrage hit 15 Brigade before zero hour but four tanks helped Major Walker's 1st Cheshires clear Beugny while a fifth helped the 1st Norfolks capture Delsaux Farm. The Cheshires had to abandon Beugny because it was a shell trap while Brigadier General Oldman had to send the 1st Bedfords forward to help the Norfolks stop a counter-attack.

The following day, the 16th Warwicks and Bedfords approached an abandoned Beugny and then passed through Lebucquière and Vélu, to establish outposts along the canal, north of Ruyaulcourt. Major General Ponsonby's men were relieved by 37th Division during the night. They had advanced 14 miles in twelve days but it had cost the division 4,275 casualties.

New Zealand Division, east of Frémicourt and Bancourt, 2 September

The 2 Brigade took over the front facing Haplincourt, ready to advance at 5.15 am on 2 September. Part of the 1st Canterbury Battalion occupied their objective but some were pinned down by two disabled German tanks until Corporal Putman silenced all the machine guns in the area. The 2nd Otago Battalion found the Germans in a trench close to their line after the barrage moved on, and while a charge took fifty prisoners, Sergeant Brown's men were cut off until reinforcements arrived.

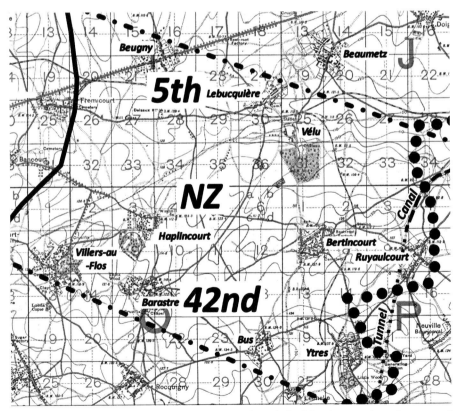

IV Corps followed the retirement to the Canal du Nord, crossing the tunnel at Ruyaulcourt.

The firing died down at dawn on 3 September while plumes of smoke along the horizon showed the Germans were burning their dumps. Patrols discovered that Haplincourt and its wood had been abandoned so 2 Brigade advanced towards the Canal du Nord. The 2nd Dragoons reported Bertincourt was clear and the New Zealanders crossed the canal tunnel and clear Ruyaulcourt during the night.

42nd Division, Villers-au-Flos, 2 and 3 September

Brigadier General Henley's 127 Brigade was due to attack Villers-au-Flos but two tanks broke down and the other two were late. The barrage started 400 yards in front of 127 Brigade, rather than the usual 200 yards, because the New Zealand Division was ahead on the left flank. The artillery had to open fire nine minutes before zero, to cover the infantry as they moved up, but it alerted the German artillery, inviting counter-barrages right along the line.

The 1/6th Manchester came under enfilade fire from the north end of Villers-au-Flos while the 1/5th Manchester were hit as they moved to the south. Two field guns engaged the enemy over open sights while a low-flying plane strafed their line and the village was taken with 300 prisoners. Brigadier General Henley thought Manchester 'may well be proud of her sons as [he] was of commanding such soldiers'.

Both the 8th Lancashire Fusiliers and 7th Manchesters reported that Barastre was empty the following morning so they were told to advance to the railway east of Ytres and check out the Canal du Nord tunnel. It was 'a most exhilarating advance, reminding one of a field day on Salisbury Plain.' The infantry 'grinned and waved' as the Scots Greys cantered forward during 125 Brigade's march through Ytres.

V Corps

Lieutenant General Cameron Shute's divisions had been fighting their way across the 1916 battlefield for ten days. All his battalions were well below strength and the ninety survivors of the 2nd Welsh Fusiliers of 38th Division had to organise into a company.

21st Division, North of Le Transloy, 2 September

The 7th Leicesters fought all night to clear the Sugar Factory north of Le Transloy while the 1st East Yorkshires cleared Lubda Copse. In the meantime, the convergent advances of 42nd Division and 17th Division through Villers-au-Flos and Le Transloy squeezed 21st Division out of the line.

17th Division, Le Transloy and Rocquigny, 2 September

News that 21st Division had cleared Beaulencourt meant that Major General Philip Robertson could launch a pincer attack against Le Transloy. The 10th West Yorkshires cleared a sunken road north-west of the village while the 12th Manchester and 9th Duke's moved around the south side of the village before dawn. The plan was for a company of the 7th East Yorkshires to move around the north side at first light but the garrison had withdrawn and the 6th Dorsets only found two men in the ruins.

At 8 pm, 50 Brigade advanced through Rocquigny towards the Wotan Line, bringing the day's total of prisoners to 160. Brigadier General Allason had also moved 52 Brigade forward to cover the south flank where 38th Division was struggling to reach Le Mesnil. While Robertson was pleased with progress, he was concerned that he was out of touch with the divisions on both flanks. Both moved up early in the morning and 50 Brigade found the Germans waiting along the Canal du Nord tunnel north of Étricourt.

38th Division, Sailly Saillisel, 2 and 3 September

Major General Cubitt waited until Le Transloy had been taken before giving the order to advance. Sailly Saillisel was shelled before zero hour but the

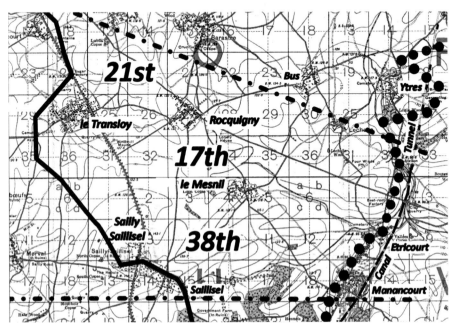

V Corps followed up the German withdrawal to the Canal du Nord.

creeping barrage landed too far ahead and the 14th Welsh Fusiliers were pinned down in front of Loon Copse. Both the 10th SWBs and the 2nd Welsh Fusiliers were hit as they left their jumping off line and it would take well into the night to clear the ruins.

Patrols noticed that the enemy trenches were empty early on 3 September, so the 6th Dragoon Guards went exploring. They came under fire from Étricourt and Manancourt so an advanced guard of infantry, artillery and engineers pushed 'battle patrols' down to the Canal du Nord.

Fourth Army

III Corps, 2 September

Lieutenant General Alexander Godley had just been given the 74th Division, and while it was inexperienced, having recently arrived from Palestine, it was at full strength and the men were fresh. He wanted to get across the Canal du Nord around Moislains before the Germans could dig in, meaning the Australian Corps would have to keep advancing north of Péronne. Lieutenant General Monash would have preferred another day to move his artillery across the canal.

18th Division, North Half of St Pierre Vaast Wood, 2 and 3 September

The 7th Queen's Own followed a creeping barrage past the north end of St Pierre Wood, starting at 5.50 am on 2 September. The 10th Essex negotiated the tree stumps and undergrowth but they could not take the 'heap of broken bricks and shattered timbers' that had once been Government Farm. The 8th Berkshires also worked their way through the narrow northern section of the wood before sending patrols down the east side, outflanking the machine-gun teams waiting for a frontal attack. Nearly one hundred prisoners were taken but it still needed help from the heavy artillery and the 4th Welsh Fusiliers to clear the vast wood.

'Three great glares in the sky' showed that the Germans were again burning their dumps before withdrawing across the Canal du Nord. The following morning 'sniping 18-pounders' accompanied 53 Brigade through an abandoned Vaux Wood. They found the Germans waiting in Riverside Wood across the canal.

47th Division, South Half of St Pierre Vaast Wood, 2 and 3 September

The 1/24th London Regiment cut off sixty Germans sheltering in dugouts at the south-west corner of St Pierre Vaast Wood and the rest ran, taking many more with them. The 1/22nd London Regiment captured a battery of field guns but Captain Oakley was killed leading his men to Sorrowitz Trench north-east of Moislains. Private Jack Harvey silenced the machine-gun post pinning down his company before taking thirty-seven prisoners in a dugout; he would be awarded the Victoria Cross. The 1/4th Welsh Fusiliers (Pioneers) would mop up the south half of St Pierre Vaast Wood while 142 Brigade formed a defensive flank from Lonely Copse to Monastir Trench at the south-west corner of Vaux Wood.

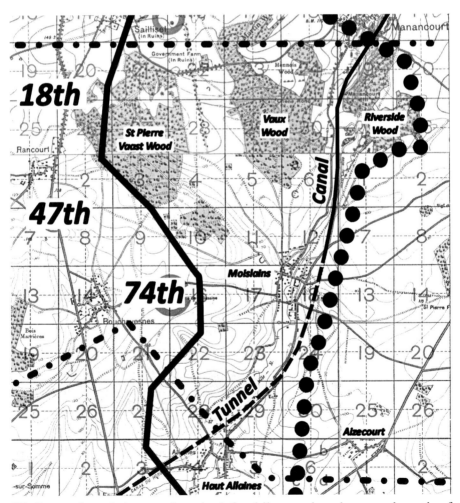

III Corps cleared the wood on its left while crossing the tunnel south of Moislains.

All three of 140 Brigade's battalions came under fire as they passed through Moislains Wood. 'This was indeed some of the hardest fighting during the whole advance.' Lieutenant Colonel Fielding's 1/15th London Regiment suffered many casualties when it came under attack from Lonely Copse behind their left rear and from Vaux Wood. The 1/17th London Regiment also lost many reaching Moislains Trench and Lieutenant Colonel Dawes' men then had to fight off a counter-attack.

Brigadier General Kennedy lost touch with 74th Division because all his runners were hit and some of his men withdrew when 229 Brigade fell back on their right flank. The Londoners eventually exhausted their supply of bombs fighting off attacks from Vaux Wood and Moislains and they needed help from the 18th London Regiment.

General Gorringe was forced to withdraw the battered 140 and 141 Brigades, and 142 Brigade and 74th Division took their place. The following day patrols checked out the canal, finding it was dry below the lock, north-east of Moislains.

74th Division, Moislains, 2 September

The division had arrived in France in May 1918, having served in Palestine for the past twelve months. It had spent the summer training in Western Front tactics and then spent several weeks holding a quiet sector in Flanders before joining Fourth Army.

Major General Eric Girdwood had been told he faced a weak German division across the Canal du Nord but his men actually faced the elite Alpine Corps. There 'had been no time to reconnoitre the ground ahead and the information available proved highly inaccurate'. Many guides were hit en route to the front while the enemy were found to be holding their jumping off trenches. Scutari and Broussa Trenches had to be cleared with the help of 47th Division, making 229 Brigade late, and Brigadier General Hoare's men then came under machine-gun fire as they tried to catch up with the creeping barrage.

The 12th Somersets came under enfilade fire as they crossed the Canal du Nord because the Australians were not due to clear Haut Allaines until later. They took seventy prisoners in the village before resuming their advance north-east. The 14th Black Watch had been told Moislains was unoccupied but they were pinned down and Captain Muntz was hit when the 16th Devons tried to enter the ruins. The Alpine Corps counter-attacked mid-morning, pushing all three battalions back to the canal and they took some of the men of the 47th Division with them.

Late in the afternoon the 15th Suffolk and 16th Sussex contacted the Australians on the right. Major General Girdwood then instructed 230 and 229 Brigades to advance their outpost line towards the canal at dusk so the line could be straightened out.

The Australian Corps, 2 September

Lieutenant General Monash had wanted to give 2nd Australian Division a day's rest after the capture of Mont St Quentin but Lieutenant General Godley was anxious to keep pushing the Germans back. Monash's chief of staff, Brigadier General Thomas Blamey, thought it was an ambitious plan and was worried about having insufficient time to prepare the orders, but the Australian Corps would keep moving.

2nd Australian Division, 2 September, Haut Allaines

Major General Charles Rosenthal received the order to attack at 9.30 pm but it was 2 am by the time the instructions reached the battalions. The plan was to advance north-east of Mont St Quentin at 5.30 am but 'neither the men nor the NCO's of the British company on their flank had any notion where they were going or what they had to do'.

Both 27th Battalion and Major Mitchell's two companies of the 28th Battalion came under 'staggering' machine-gun fire as they cleared Allaines. Both Major Page and Captain Cross were wounded as the 25th Battalion came under 'terrific fire' crossing Hill 115 and the situation looked bleak until 27th Battalion turned the German flank, taking one hundred prisoners. Those in front of the 25th then fled, 'throwing away machine guns, packs and other kit'.

The 26th Battalion was hit by machine-gun fire as soon as it moved but Lieutenant Monteith's men still advanced over 1 mile along trenches. Lieutenant Colonel Robinson had to hold the rest of his battalion back until 5th Australian Division was ready. The German artillery opened fire as soon as the attack started and his men had to endure half an hour of shelling before they could advance.

The Germans abandoned their next position at first light and 7 Brigade was able to take most of its objective along with 200 prisoners. Only 27th Battalion had a problem on its left, where 74th Division had fallen back from the Canal du Nord. It meant that Brigadier General Wisdom's men were left in an exposed salient around Haut Allaines.

At dusk 43rd Australian (from 3rd Australian Division) was pinned down along the canal around Allaines, but it had covered the north flank. Lance

Corporal Lawrence Weathers located the enemy and then returned for three comrades to help him take prisoners. He clambered onto the parapet and lobbed bombs down until 180 men surrendered. Weathers came back 'festooned like a Christmas tree' with German binoculars and pistols; he was mortally wounded on 29 September but was posthumously awarded the Victoria Cross. The 2nd Australian Division was relieved the following day.

5th Australian Division, North-East Péronne, 2 September
The late issuing of orders meant that Major General Talbot Hobbs had to attack St Denis Wood, north-east of Péronne at 6 am. Brigadier General

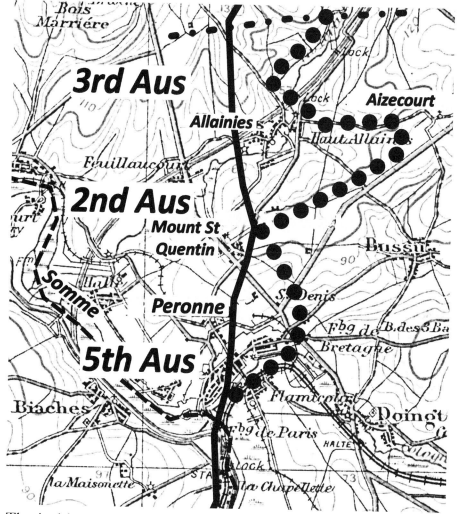

The tired Australians kept probing beyond Mount St Quentin and Péronne.

Elliott rode a horse around his battalion commanders but he forgot to tell them they would advance thirty minutes after 2nd Australian Division. It meant his men did not take precautions against the German SOS barrage fired in response to the attack north of Péronne.

The late zero hour meant 'it was daylight, the mist was rising, and the machine-gun crews were visible along the ramparts.' The 54th Battalion was hit hard as it waited for 56th Battalion to pass through but Lieutenant Colonel Marshall's men were able to advance past the north side of Péronne while the Australian artillery hammered the ramparts. Lieutenant Colonel Sproule's 58th Battalion was also caught by the German artillery before it cleared the north-east suburbs of Péronne. Two companies of 55th Battalion then turned south behind the hill south of Flamicourt but the marshes along the Cologne stream prevented further progress eastward. All together the two Australian Divisions had captured 2,600 prisoners but it had cost them 3,000 casualties.

32nd Division, 2 and 3 September; River Somme

Patrols were unable to cross the River Somme but the engineers continued erecting bridges across the canal at night. Rawlinson was considering a feint attack by the Australians north of Péronne, to draw reserves north. It would mean there would be hardly any troops to counter the advance across the Somme at Brie and St Christ.

Summary

The Canadian Corps had broken the Drocourt–Quéant Line across a 7 mile wide front, and while General Horne wanted to pursue the Germans, the Canadian Corps was asking for time to reorganise. In Third Army's area, Byng ordered his corps commanders to pursue to Canal du Nord with 'properly constituted advanced guards of all arms'.

Ludendorff had issued instructions for a general retirement as soon as he had heard the D-Q Line had been broken. He also knew that the Australian Corps had taken Mont St Quentin, outflanking the River Somme position south of Péronne. The plan was for Seventeenth Army to complete its withdrawal back to Canal du Nord. Second Army would follow late on 3 September and then Eighteenth Army late on 5 September. Finally, Ninth Army would fall back from the River Somme opposite Fourth Army at the same time. They would all stop after withdrawing some 8 miles, abandoning the last of the area captured during the March offensive.

Ludendorff thought the retirement would 'shorten his line, economise troops, and give them at least a short rest'. He also announced a plan to evacuate the Lys area captured by Fourth and Sixth Armies during Operation Georgette in April 1918. But the Germans were not the only ones reaching the end of their endurance. The Australians were particularly suffering after four weeks of constant fighting: 'Battalions are going into some of these fights 150 strong; 300 or 350 seems to be a big number in the fighting line nowadays. They are not as done as they were after Pozières, but they certainly are feeling that they have had more than their share of fighting.'

Chapter 11

Germany is Defeated and the Sooner We Recognise it the Better

4 to 11 September

First Army

Canadian Corps

By dawn on 4 September, Lieutenant General Currie's men were covering all the crossings over the Sensée stream and the Canal du Nord, making 12 miles of front safe. The Canadians would not have to attack for the next two weeks but their preparations made the Germans think they were planning to.

Third Army

XVII Corps

63rd Division, 4 September, Canal du Nord

Lieutenant Colonel Sandilands' Marines helped the Hawke and Hood Battalions clear the west bank of the Canal du Nord. Sub Lieutenant Harris crossed near Inchy but his men were soon forced back. The fighting for the canal eventually died down and the division was relieved by 57th Division on 8 September.

57th Division, 11 to 15 September, Moeuvres

Major General Barnes wanted to cross the Canal du Nord around Moeuvres. Both the 2/4th Loyals and 1/5th Loyals attacked late on 11 September but after four days and nights, Brigadier General Longbourne reported his men had secured the village but they had been unable to cross the waterway.

VI Corps

Lieutenant General Sir Haldane's men advanced to the Hindenburg Line where it ran next to the Canal du Nord south of Moeuvres; the whole area was a crater field. The engineers found the roads 'were usually covered with

2 to 3 feet of debris but they were quickly cleared by working parties.' The pioneers then repaired them ready for traffic.

Guard Division, 4 to 12 September, Moeuvres

The 2nd Scots Guards and 1st Welsh Guards failed to clear the trenches west of the canal before dawn on 4 September. The 2nd Scots Guards bombed closer to Moeuvres during the evening and cleared Goat Trench the following day. First the 2 Guards Brigade and then 1 Guards Brigade held the area facing the Hindenburg Line but both suffered from the machine-gun fire across the canal. The 1st Irish Guards finally made some progress towards Moeuvres on 8 September.

2nd Division, 4 to 11 September, Canal du Nord

Major General Pereira gave 6 Brigade instructions 'to discover the enemy's main line of resistance… push forward patrols on the east of the canal. The crossings over the canal will be occupied…' The 1st King's were 'worried by machine-gun fire' close to the Hindenburg Line. A night raid failed to capture the Spoil Heap (spoil from the canal excavations) because 'enemy machine-gun fire and rifle fire came from all round and both sides of the canal.'

The German infantry abandoned the Spoil Heap during the night, and while the 1st Berkshires occupied the summit during the morning, it was a death trap. Instead the mound was covered by machine guns while 99 Brigade bombed along the west bank of the canal for four days and nights. The 2nd Ox and Bucks and 2nd HLI made a night attack along the Canal du Nord late on the 11th. 'The ground was thick with mud and slippery and the enemy's guns put down a terrific barrage' but the position was secured.

IV Corps

Lieutenant General Harper's men could cross the Canal du Nord tunnel but they then faced Havrincourt Wood and Gouzeaucourt Wood en route to the Hindenburg Line.

37th Division, 4 September, Havrincourt Wood

The 13th Royal Fusiliers moved around the north edge of Havrincourt Wood while the 1st Hertfords edged through it. A policy 'of persistent penetration' meant 112 Brigade had cleared most of the wood before Brigadier General Challenor's 63 Brigade tackled the north-east corner.

New Zealand Division, 4 to 9 September, Havrincourt Wood

On 2 Brigade's front, a misunderstanding as 2nd Canterbury Battalion approached Havrincourt Wood meant there were unnecessary casualties. 'A large number of Germans came forward over the valley with their hands up but an untimely activity on the part of our own guns, misapprehending

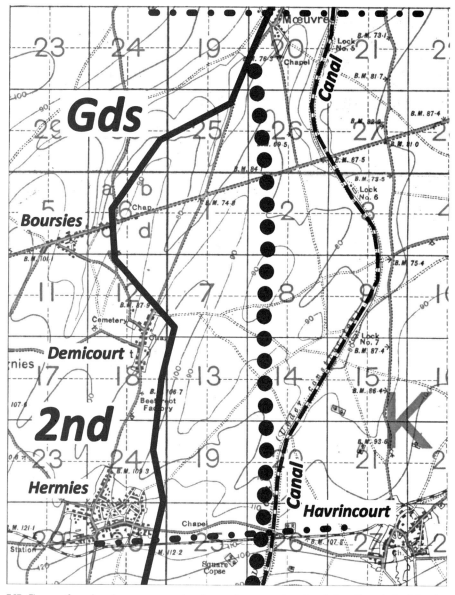

VI Corps fought the rearguards along the west bank of the Canal du Nord.

their intention, drove them back.' Major Wilson's men then came under machine-gun fire from the edge of the wood.

Major Hargest's 1st Otago Battalion eventually cleared Neuville late on 5 September as heavy artillery hit Havrincourt Wood. Major General Russell wanted to avoid a frontal attack so the Otago Battalion advanced through Metz-en-Couture, south of it, before the Otago Mounted Rifles came under fire from Gouzeaucourt. The move unsettled the Germans in the wood and an aerial observer noticed they were withdrawing, so the 2nd Canterbury Battalion advanced cautiously through the north half of the undergrowth during the night. The 3 New Zealand Brigade faced a difficult fight for the rest of the wood on 8 September so they pulled back until the artillery convinced the Germans to leave.

The attack on Trescault Ridge began at 4 am on 9 September but the New Zealanders ran into stiff resistance. Fortunately the German machine guns fired high while the artillery overshot the assembly areas in the dark. The 4th Rifles cleared the rest of Havrincourt Wood but it was a different story around Gouzeaucourt Wood. The 2nd Rifles reached Dead Man's Corner only to come under enfilade fire from Gouzeaucourt. Lieutenant Kennedy's

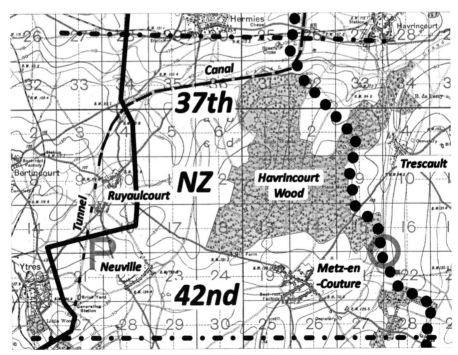

IV Corps exploited the Canal du Nord tunnel to enter Havrincourt Wood.

company drove off many counter-attacks over the next twenty-four hours and the Germans wore British helmets during their final one late on 10 September. They failed to take any ground and Kennedy's men took nearly 150 prisoners.

42nd Division, 4 and 5 September, Neuville Bourjonval

Lieutenant Colonel Castle's 1/5th Lancashire Fusiliers were stopped by machine-gun fire from Neuville Bourjonval but Captains Hartley and Haywood's men still crossed the Canal du Nord tunnel. Second Lieutenant Riley's men cleared the north end of the village, Lieutenant Colonel Brewis sent a company of the 1/7th Lancashire Fusiliers forward to help, and Lieutenants Pearson and Worden cleared the rest of the village. The division was relieved by the New Zealand Division late on 5 September.

V Corps

Lieutenant General Cameron Shute's men faced the Canal du Nord. His left faced the tunnel around Ytres but his centre and right had to clear Étricourt and Manancourt before crossing the waterway.

17th Division, Équancourt to Gouzeaucourt, 4 to 10 September

Brigadier General Gwyn-Thomas sent the 10th West Yorkshires through Vallulart Wood and across the canal tunnel at 6 am. The 7th East Yorkshires then crossed the canal, expanding 50 Brigade's frontage, but neither battalion could reach Équancourt. Brigadier General Dudgeon's 51 Brigade was given the wrong trench to hold during the night and it turned out to be too far south. The 7th Lincolns came under fire from the north-east as they attacked the canal tunnel the following morning. But the 7th Border Regiment found the trenches around Équancourt had been abandoned when they advanced at dusk. The withdrawal continued the following day but Robertson was told to 'husband resources' as he drove the rearguards out of Équancourt and Fins.

Heudicourt was cleared on 7 September and then Revelon Farm the following day but 52 Brigade discovered that the Germans intended to hold Chapel Ridge. The 12th Manchesters and 10th Lancashire Fusiliers took 120 prisoners in the Heather system of trenches with the help of the 9th Duke's.

In blinding rain, inky darkness and a driving gale, 50 Brigade tried to deploy in muddy craters early on 9 September. Brigadier General Saunders had the attack postponed but the conditions were so bad it was eventually called off.

38th Division, Étricourt and Manancourt, 4 September

Patrols believed the German machine-gun teams could not see the canal bottom where it ran through a cutting. A platoon of the 13th Welsh ran forward to a trench on the canal bank and then followed a ditch down to the water. Some of Major Hobbs' men suppressed the machine gun overlooking the demolished Étricourt bridge while the rest crawled across the rubble. They 'then leapt up and bayoneted the gunners; they were quickly joined by the remainder of the platoon and a bridgehead was formed.' Captain Beecham led the rest of the battalion across. Meanwhile, Major Daniel led his company of the 14th Welsh across the canal at Manancourt. Brigadier General Price was soon able to report that the two battalions were half a mile beyond the waterway.

21st Division, 6 to 11 September, Canal du Nord to Chapel Hill

Major General Campbell's men took over the east bank of the Canal du Nord on 6 September, only to find the Germans had withdrawn through Fins and Sorel-le-Grand. Dessart Wood and Heudicourt were cleared over the next

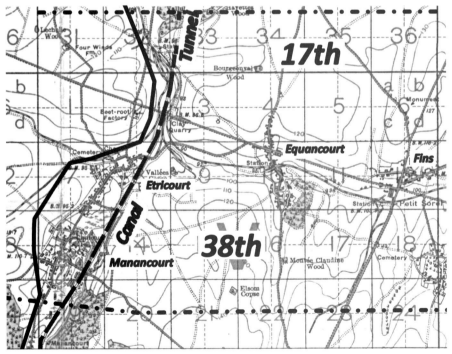

After crossing the Canal du Nord, V Corps followed up the German withdrawal.

two days. Brigadier General Edwards was supposed to capture Chapel Hill on 9 September but 64 Brigade was driven back to Lowland Trench, near Revelon Farm. Early on 11 September the 7th Leicesters captured fifty prisoners on the hill but it would take until the following night before the 6th Leicesters drove back the group of Germans east of Peizières.

Third Army Summary

By 10 September the Germans had retired towards the Hindenburg Line along the Canal du Nord opposite VI Corps. They were holding old British trenches which followed a low ridge running west of Trescault, Gouzeaucourt and Villers Guislain. A couple of days earlier, Foch had told Haig he wanted to attack before the Germans dug in, so Haig had asked his army commanders what they thought. Byng was convinced they would hold on to the old British trenches for as long as possible, to give their tired divisions time to occupy the Hindenburg Position.

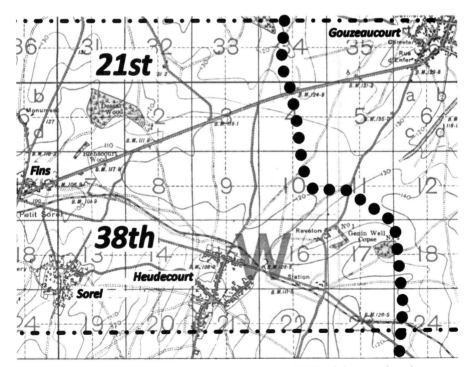

V Corps found the Germans waiting in the old British trenches between Gouzeaucourt and Peizières.

Fourth Army

Late on 4 September, Rawlinson learnt that the Germans were withdrawing opposite Third Army and the First French Army. Haig wanted Fourth Army to make a steady pursuit but Rawlinson wanted to move fast, to stop the Germans destroying the roads and railways he needed. The problem was his battalions were weak and his troops were tired.

The Australian Corps had been in action for four weeks and there was a crisis looming. Several battalions had less than 350 men and the nation's no–conscription policy meant there was a lack of reinforcements. Some of the men had not had any home leave for over three years and a few were Gallipoli veterans. The Australian Prime Minister, Billy Hughes, was visiting London when he heard and he asked to be personally informed before the corps were used again. Immediate arrangements were put in place to give the veterans of the Australian Imperial Force home leave. It would leave the corps even shorter of men.

The Australian Corps' frontage had doubled while it was along the Somme but it now needed help 'to press the pursuit as rapidly and vigorously as possible and give the enemy's rear guards no respite'. Lieutenant General Sir Walter Braithwaite's IX Corps headquarters took over its right sector, facing Vermand and Holnon Wood, as it approached the old British trenches in front of the Hindenburg Line.

III Corps

Lieutenant General Godley's three divisions prepared to cross to the Canal du Nord as the Germans withdrew rapidly towards the Hindenburg Line. As III Corps' machine guns targeted the canal crossings, its artillery shelled the ridge beyond, interfering with the rearward movement.

18th Division, 4 September, Riverside Wood

Both 53 and 55 Brigades drove the rearguards out of Riverside Wood only to find the enemy waiting for them on the Nurlu ridge.

12th Division, 5 September, Nurlu

Major General Harold Higginson's men took over the east bank of the Canal du Nord as gas shells rained down during a dark night. The attack still started at 6.45 am, and while the 9th Essex captured the forward trench, they could not reach Nurlu. The 7th Norfolks were stopped by wire until Private Johnson cut a gap through. Lieutenant Nock then led a company of the 1/1st Cambridge Regiment forward but they were all killed or wounded. Both the 9th Royal Fusiliers and 7th Sussex were delayed by the wire but enough men cut through to capture the trench beyond.

Brigadier Generals Owen and Beckwith organised a second attack by the 7th Norfolks, 1/1st Cambridge Regiment and 7th Sussex at dusk but they still could not reach Nurlu and a counter-attack drove the Essex back after dark. The 9th Essex, the 1/1st Cambridge Regiment and 5th Berkshires eventually captured Nurlu the following morning, triggering a general retreat. Patrols from the Northumberland Hussars and XXII Corps Cyclist Battalion encountered machine-gun teams and snipers en route to Sorel Wood and Liéramont but the Germans continued their withdrawal on 7 September. The 6th Queen's Own drove one rearguard back towards Peizières while Major Kindersley's guns drove another rearguard out of Guyencourt for the 6th Buffs. Brigadier General Incledon-Webber was then told to halt until 21st Division had cleared Heudicourt, on his left.

Major General Harold Higginson's men were relieved by 58th Division during the night. They had made seventeen attacks in four weeks, capturing over 1,000 prisoners, 200 machine guns and 100 mortars during a 17 mile advance. Despite their exertions, they would be back in the line a few days later.

58th Division, 8 to 10 September, Peizières and Epéhy

Peizières and Epéhy had been fortified by the British the previous winter and the 8th and 7th London Regiment could not clear them on 8 September. Patrols then probed the German positions, looking for targets for the artillery before the next attack at first light on 10 September. The 2/4th London Regiment entered Peizières while the 2/2nd London Regiment forced their way into Epéhy but they were both driven out. Stokes mortars then covered the 3rd London Regiment as they bombed along the trenches south-east of Epéhy.

47th Division, 4 September, Aizecourt-le-Bas and Liéramont

The Germans abandoned Moislains early on 4 September, allowing 142 Brigade's patrols to cross the canal and advance onto the ridge beyond. Major General George Gorringe wanted to make sure the east bank was clear, so Brigadier General McDouall withdrew his patrols while the area was shelled. But some of Londoners preferred to wait in the German dugouts as the barrage passed over, joining 141 Brigade when it advanced at dawn.

Brigadier General Mildren's men found the Germans waiting along the Nurlu–Aizecourt road and there was heavy fighting around Ville Wood, Cat

Copse and Save Wood. Mildren was ahead of the divisions on his flanks, so he had to wait for Brigadier General Kennedy to deploy 140 Brigade on the east bank. The two brigades then reached the Nurlu–Aizecourt road in a violent thunderstorm.

Patrols of the Northumberland Hussars and the XXII Corps Cyclist Battalion led the two brigades forward at 8 am on 6 September. They encountered rearguards around Curlu Wood but the 'forward sections of guns had good targets as the enemy withdrew' through Aizecourt-le-Bas and Liéramont.

74th Division, Aizecourt-la-Haut, 5 to 10 September

Brigadier General Kennedy instructed the 10th Buffs, 15th Suffolks and the 16th Sussex to advance towards Templeux-la-Fosse after hearing 47th Division was advancing on 5 September. Meanwhile Brigadier General Heathcote made the 24th Welsh and 10th Shropshires advance through Aizecourt-la-Haut, while the 25th Welsh Fusiliers took over the Australian trenches around Bussu. Patrols from the Northumberland Hussars and XXII Corps Cyclist Battalion encountered rearguards en route to Longavesnes on 6 September. The 25th Welsh Fusiliers then formed a flank because the Australians were held up around Tincourt.

The 24th Welsh and 10th Shropshire occupied Villers Faucon and advanced toward Sainte Emilie on 7 September. The following morning the

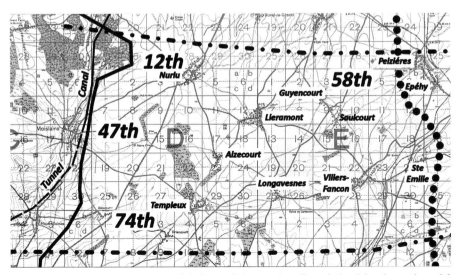

III Corps followed up the withdrawal from the Canal du Nord to the old British trenches around Peizières, Epéhy and Sainte Emilie.

Welsh came under machine-gun fire as they approached Epéhy while the rest of 231 Brigade failed to reach Ronssoy Wood and Templeux-le-Guerard. Stormy weather then stopped operations for forty-eight hours.

Late on 10 September, the 25th Welsh Fusiliers, 14th Black Watch and 16th Devons cleared the two spurs which ran south-west towards Templeux Wood and Sainte Emilie. But 58th Division had failed to take Epéhy to the north and German bombers drove the Devons back.

The Australian Corps

3rd Australian Division, Advance east of the Somme, 5 to 10 September

Major General John Gellibrand's men took over the front east of Péronne on 5 September. Patrols from the 13th Australian Light Horse and the Corps Cyclist Battalion led the 42nd Battalion and the 3rd Pioneer Battalion along the Cologne stream but they rarely saw the enemy. Lieutenant Colonel Sanday's pioneers had no experience of 'peaceful penetration' and they were soon too far ahead. The Australians saw 'the horizon ahead of Fourth Army was lurid with burning villages' as they stopped around Tincourt for the night.

On 7 September, 41st Battalion bypassed Roisel, so the artillery could shell the rearguard in it. Both 44th and 41st Battalions had 'to outflank one machine-gun post after another' en route to Hervilly and they discovered the Germans were holding Hesbécourt the following day. Major General Gellibrand's men spent 10 September probing the enemy line before 1st Australian Division took over.

5th Australian Division, Advance east of the Somme, 5 to 11 September

The 8 Australian Brigade was weary after 'the heaviest and weariest work the battalions have done', so Major General Lambert let it rest while his own 14 Brigade continued the advance. The 13th Light Horse and the Corps Cyclist Battalion located rearguards around Bouvincourt on 6 September. Overnight, 8 Brigade took over from 32nd Division and the 29th and 31st Battalions advanced through Vraignes to Bernes and Flechin. Major General Hobbs' men then probed the new German line around Jeancourt and Vendelles until they were relieved by 4th Australian Division late on 9 September.

32nd Division, Advance east of the Somme, 4 to 11 September

None saw the Germans withdraw from the River Somme late on 4 September but Lieutenant Hepburn crossed south of Éterpigny early the following morning and found no one on the far bank. Before long the rest of the 15th

HLI were holding the high ground north–east of Brie. Two companies of the 5/6th Royal Scots used a footbridge or waded across the river around Brie, joining up with the HLI on the east bank. The 1/5th Border Regiment reinforced the Brie bridgehead before contacting the 2nd KOYLIs who were

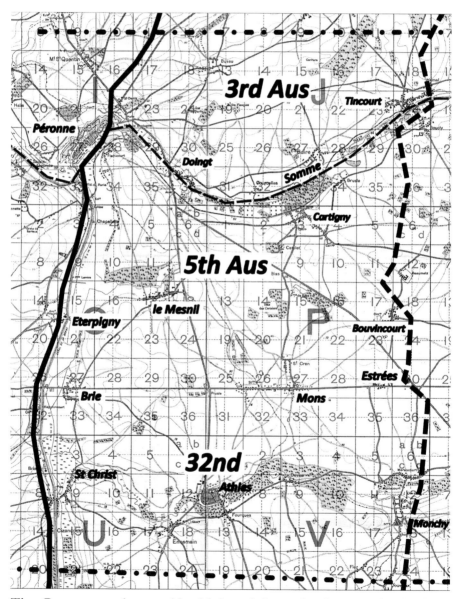

The Germans made a rapid withdrawal from the Somme ahead of the Australian Corps.

crossing at St Christ and Cizancourt. The Germans were falling back so Brigadier General Evans instructed the 1st Dorsets to occupy Mons-en-Chaussée on the St Quentin road.

Brigadier General Minshull-Ford's men discovered the Germans waiting in Martenville and Holnon Wood on 9 September. The creeping barrage the

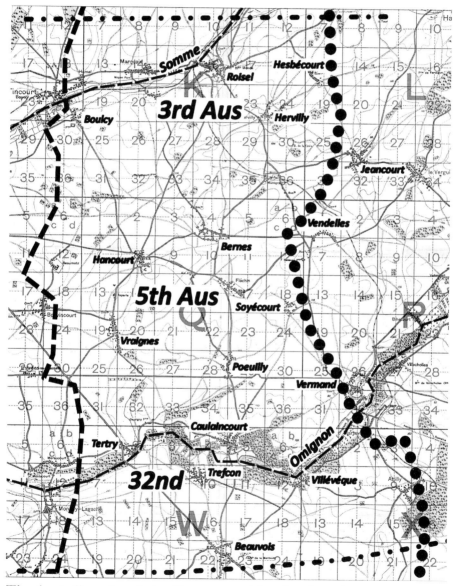

The Australians found the Germans waiting for them in the old British trenches.

following morning straddled 97 Brigade, hindering 2nd KOYLIs' advance, but the 10th Argylls entered Attilly as the Germans withdrew into Holnon Wood. The division was relieved as the Australian Corps handed over the area south of the St Quentin road to IX Corps on 11 September.

Fourth Army Summary

The weather took a turn for the worse and the roads became rutted and thick with mud. The area had been the Allied rear area in 1917 and early 1918, so most landmarks had been obliterated, making navigation difficult. But the Germans were suffering more, as summed up by one prisoner:

'Passing back under escort I saw things that I could scarcely believe; such transport, such horses, such men and these masses of artillery. I compared them with our wretched iron-wheeled transport, skidding all over the place and blocking the roads in wet weather, our scanty and badly-fed horses, and those boys pretending to be Guards. We still have a certain amount of artillery but you must have five guns to our one, and we are not well off for shells, whilst you seem to have an endless supply. No, Germany is defeated and the sooner we recognise it the better, but you will admit we have put up a good fight. No nation could have done more.'

Chapter 12

They Went Over Like
a Pack of Hounds

The Lys Salient, 5 August to 7 September

The attacks being carried out by the British Fourth and Third Armies had a knock-on effect across the Flanders area to the north. The German Sixth Army had been left holding a salient facing Hazebrouck after the Lys offensive at the end of April 1918. General Ferdinand von Quast had been told to prepare to attack again after the attack on the Aisne which started on 15 July. However, the Allied counter-attack on the Aisne three days later meant that Ludendorff had to move reserves south and Operation Hagen was cancelled. Ludendorff also had to tell Crown Prince Rupprecht to prepare to evacuate the Flanders salient so he could increase the size of his reserve.

General Sir Herbert Plumer's Second Army held the line covering Ypres and Hazebrouck while General Sir William Birdwood's Fifth Army defended Béthune. All of their divisions had been mauled during the German spring offensives but they had been rebuilt and were alert to any activity from the Fourth and Sixth German Armies. Plumer and Birdwood both knew the Germans were preparing to attack but they were relieved to hear that divisions were being sent south to the Aisne.

Birdwood was told Sixth Army could be planning a withdrawal north of Béthune at the end of July, so his Fifth Army stepped up its patrols and raids. Battalion and company commanders were told to exploit any withdrawals without waiting for permission from their superior headquarters. Plans were also circulated to all arms so they knew how to respond in the event of a pursuit.

The first withdrawal began opposite XIII Corps late on 4 August. Early the following morning, 4th Division's patrols discovered that Pacaut Wood, near the La Bassée Canal, had been abandoned. The following day, 61st Division's patrols saw German troops withdrawing astride the Clarence stream opposite XI Corps. So Birdwood gave instructions to probe the enemy lines, warning everyone to beware of booby traps and ambushes. It soon became clear that Sixth Army had withdrawn across an 8 mile front but the Tommies were often reluctant to follow because 'nearly everybody seemed to have forgotten how to use a rifle'.

Sixth Army withdrew 2 miles astride the River Lys on 9 August and IX Corps followed up; XIII Corps discovered similar retirement north of Béthune. Little happened over the following week, with only localised withdrawals around Vieux Berquin, Merville and Pacaut.

XV Corps Outtersteene Ridge, 18 and 19 August

Outtersteene Ridge was a problem because the Germans could see across XV Corps' area from the low summit. On 10 August, Lieutenant General Beaurevoir de Lisle issued plans to attack the ridge. One brigade of 9th Division would advance past the bend in the Meteren Becque stream to Hoegenacker Mill and Belle Croix Farm. A small party of 29th Division would then clear the stream banks so the rest of the division could clear Outtersteene.

De Lisle's plan was to attack at 11 am on 18 August, a later than usual time to catch the Germans out. The men would enter the trenches before dawn and then wait behind screens made of cocoa matting, painted with dark bands to simulate shadows. A captured document said the Germans thought smoke had been the key to success at Meteren, so the assault troops were told to count to ten as soon as the first shells exploded, to allow a screen to form, and then run as fast as they could.

9th Division, Hoegenacker Mill

After spending a hot morning in the trenches, Major General Tudor's men 'went over like a pack of hounds and were consequently difficult to stop.' The 9th Scottish Rifles and 11th Royal Scots surprised the Germans and then formed a defensive flank on the left. At the same time, the 6th KOSBs fought along the east bank of the Meteren Becque stream to the Hoegenacker Mill, 'the key of the position'. The results were reported by firing blue smoke rifle grenades for the ground observers and red flares for the aerial observers.

Lieutenant Colonel Smyth's 1st KOSBs 'went over the top as one man' and took 350 prisoners and sixty machine guns on the far side of the Meteren Becque. Patrols then found that the Germans had abandoned Outtersteene,

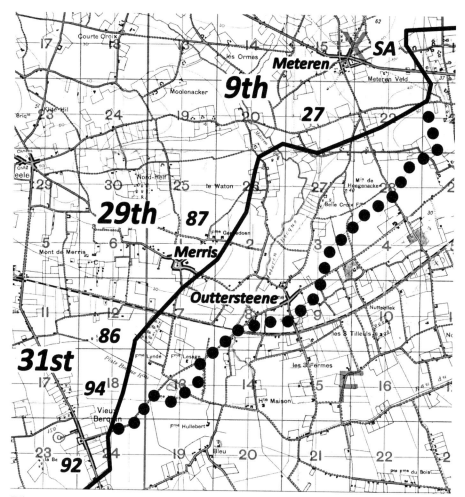

The capture of Outtersteene Ridge on 18 and 19 August.

allowing the 1st KOSBs to extend their line. Part of the 1st Border Regiment and the 2nd SWBs of 87 Brigade could also move east from Merris.

29th Division, Vieux Berquin

Brigadier General Cheape cancelled a simultaneous an attempt to advance between the Armentières railway and Vieux Berquin on 18 August. He had no artillery support, while the trench mortars had been unable to silence the German machine guns hidden in railway trucks. The following evening, 12th Norfolk and the 2nd Royal Fusiliers cleared 86 Brigade's objectives while the 12 Norfolks of 31st Division moved up on the right.

The Withdrawal from the Lys Salient

The loss of Outtersteene forced the Fourth German Army to abandon the area south of the ridge and Sixth German Army conformed, abandoning the Merville salient. The withdrawal continued across an 18 mile front between Mont Kemmel and the La Bassée Canal on 30 August. Fourth Army's retirement also allowed Second Army to occupy the Bailleul area.

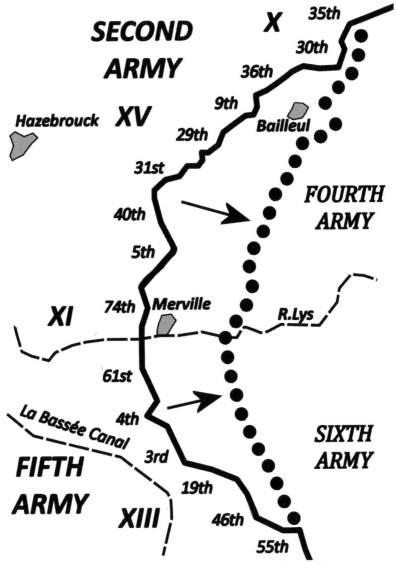

The first part of the German withdrawal, between 20 and 31 August.

On Second Army's left, 6th Division moved through Vierstraat while 41st Division advanced over Kemmel Hill and to the foot of the ridge topped by Wytschaete. The 35th and 30th Divisions moved through Dranoutre to the bottom of the slope leading up the Messines while 36th Division reached Hill 63 overlooking Ploegsteert Wood. On Second Army's right, 9th, 29th, 31st and 40th Divisions moved side-by-side to the old front line between Ploegsteert and the River Lys at Erquinghem. The withdrawal was equally fast opposite Fifth Army and 5th, 74th and 61st Divisions withdrew astride the River Lys back to the old front line. Meanwhile, 4th, 3rd, 19th and 46th Divisions moved north of Béthune as far as the Neuve Chapelle area.

The withdrawal from the Lys salient unsettled the men of the German Fourth and Sixth Armies because they were never told why they were retiring. But it had encouraged Foch and he told Haig and Lieutenant General Cyriaque Gillain, the Belgian Army's Chief of the General Staff, to prepare to attack on 2 September. Three days later, Second Army was given instructions to seize the high ground east of Ypres. But General Plumer wanted to widen the attack and he asked Haig to request help from the Belgians.

By 7 September the front lines were back to the April line where they had been before the Lys Offensive. The line ran along the west slope of the Messines Ridge, past Armentières and then behind the Lys. It meant that most of the ground captured during the April offensive had been abandoned. Foch visited Plumer's headquarters on 9 September with news that he would now be taking orders from the King of the Belgians and report to General Jean Degoutte as his Chief of the Staff.

One of the last acts of the withdrawal occurred on 12 September when Lance Corporal Alfred Wilcox tackled a machine-gun team pinning down the 2/4th Ox and Bucks near Laventie. He then used a pile of German bombs to silence three more weapons. Wilcox would be awarded the Victoria Cross.

The withdrawal across the Lys plain had triggered further movement opposite First Army across the old Loos battlefield. The Germans withdrew towards Auchy-lez-La-Bassée and Cité Ste Elie, so 16th and 15th Divisions could advance on 11 September. Both Auchy and Fosse 8 colliery were abandoned two days later. They then withdrew in two stages towards La Bassée, so 55th Division could advance north of the canal on 14 and 17 September.

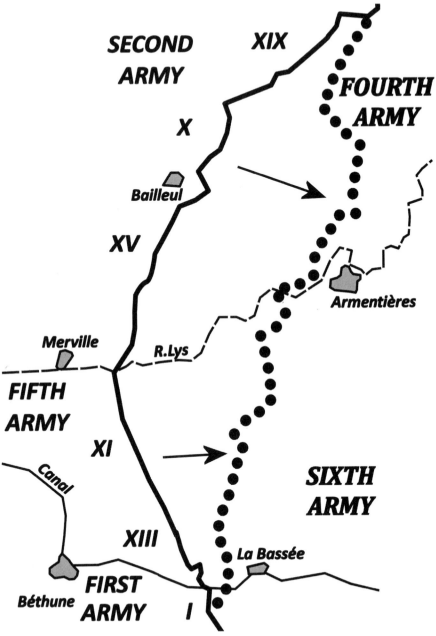

The second part of the German withdrawal, between 1 and 7 September.

Conclusions

The Marne Counter-Offensive

Operation Peace Storm was OHL's last attack after a costly three months. Foch correctly assumed the Germans would be tired after several days advancing towards the Marne. He made the right decision to strike back as planned, albeit from a different position to that expected. The French eventually found the Germans waiting behind the Vesle and the Aisne between Reims and Soissons. Pétain prepared for another attack on 8 August but the offensive astride the Somme would take its place.

Many say the Allied 'Advance to Victory', known as the 'Hundred Days Offensive' started on 8 August along the Somme. But, as we have seen, it started on 18 July astride the Marne. French, British and American troops played an important part in turning the tide of the war there, leaving Hindenburg and Ludendorff in no doubt that the German armies had to go on the defensive. The two divisions of XXII Corps alone suffered 7,000 casualties attacking the Marne salient; they had advanced 4 miles, taking over 1,000 prisoners and 30 guns. The battle for the Marne salient was over and the German reserve built up during the winter of 1917-18, following the collapse of the Russian front, had been exhausted. The German armies had suffered 1.5 million casualties in just four months.

The Black Day

Fourth Army suffered less than 9,000 casualties on 8 August 1918 but it took 12,400 prisoners (French First Army had captured another 3,350). The deployment plan had been masterful with tens of thousands of men and dozens of tanks moving into no man's land without being seen. The absence of a preliminary barrage and mist made sure the Germans knew nothing until the barrage opened at zero hour.

It was the biggest armoured attack of the war and the Tank Corps had learnt many lessons from Cambrai. But this time the tank crews and infantry platoons worked close together. Scouts pointed out enemy positions to tank commanders as the German machine-gunners fired blindly into the mist.

The Germans either surrendered or ran away as the huge vehicles approached. But the biggest surprise for the British and Empire troops was that there were 'practically no German defences; trenches or wire entanglement'.

Fourth Army made the mistake of deploying too many tanks (over 450 in all) and the big problem arose when the mist lifted. A single anti-tank gun could knock out several tanks; if the tank was the nemesis of the machine gun, the field gun was the tank's. Around half the tanks were knocked out or disabled and Fourth Army sorely missed them over the days that followed. The rest of the BEF would miss them over the following weeks.

The Royal Air Force also suffered many losses and it was a mistake to change the air plan to attack the Somme bridges. But German Second Army had lost many front line battalions and field batteries while the reserve battalions 'had either been thrown back or had not got into action at all'.

Continuing the Advance

Foch had wanted to 'go as far as you can the first day, go on again on the second, and again on the third, before the enemy can concentrate his reserves. After that you will certainly have to pause...' It turned out he was right because the Crown Prince rushed reserves to block the breach in Second Army's line. Both the Australian and Canadian Corps had advanced 8 miles on the first day, the 'Black Day' for the German Army, as Ludendorff later wrote. Changes in orders delayed the advance on the second day, and increasing resistance brought the advance to a halt over the next two days.

The decision to halt on the old Amiens Defence Line on the afternoon of 8 August stalled Fourth Army. Then the decision to let the three corps' commanders decide their start times the following day resulted in many lost hours. The two pauses had given the Germans an extra twenty-four hours to move thirteen divisions opposite Fourth Army and Haig concluded it was time to halt the advance for the time being.

Widening the Attack

Third Army attacked on 21 August and again the Germans were 'overwhelmed with a perfect hail of shell' across their position. The combined arms tactics were successful until the mist lifted and again the tanks became vulnerable to the German anti-tank guns. The tanks had to be used sparingly but the infantry knew how to fight with their 'bayonets, bombs and rifle butts' in hand-to-hand fighting which was often 'too bitter for taking prisoners'. 'Tanks had become more precious and they were not to be allowed to roam afterwards but must be sent back automatically half an hour after the main advance finished.'

By 26 August, many thought the mood of the battle had changed because 'it was now open warfare, with battalions moving in extended order while fog brought the compass into use.' But the battles were difficult to control. Staff officers and battalion commanders found it difficult to communicate in fast moving situations and had to resort to mounted messengers or despatch riders. Commanders also found it difficult to keep control of their men as they advanced.

The BEF's Tactics

By this stage of the war, battle hardened soldiers preferred to be commanded by a few efficient officers who had experience, while conscripts followed their older comrades. The German offensives of the spring had resulted in many British battalions being rebuilt with teenagers and there was some anxiety as to how they would perform in their first battle. They were disciplined, fit and eager but the BEF's quiet summer meant that the new arrivals had no chance to experience the new tactics. Both the Australian and Canadian divisions had missed most of the German offensives and GHQ took advantage of the fact they had a higher proportion of veterans.

Many times were tried for zero hour but pre-dawn was the favourite. The Germans relied heavily on machine guns and batteries to fight a deep defensive battle but the early mists blinded the machine-gunners and artillery observers.

The artillery had reached a high degree of efficiency by this stage of the war. Sophisticated surveying meant batteries could quickly deploy to a new position and be ready to fire accurately at a target. Ground observers were attached to infantry units while aerial observers had various ways to pass on information. Guns were calibrated individually, weather conditions were checked and complicated mathematics were worked out so targets could be hit the first time.

A main feature of the bombardments was flexibility. The Germans rarely used linear defensive systems so it made no sense to use pre-set barrages. Creeping barrages protected the infantry to the maximum range of the field guns and smoke shells were fired if there was no mist. And surprise night attacks, with no creeping barrage, were often used. Around a third of the heavy artillery focused on defensive points; another third hit assembly areas and roads; the remaining third waited for counter-battery work.

Tanks

The introduction of the new Mark V at the battle of Le Hamel on 4 July was a leap forward for the tank. Its engine was more powerful and its steering system was better than the Mark IV. A raised cabin allowed the crew to release the ditching beam without leaving the tank; an extra machine gun at the back of the hull gave the vehicle all-round defence.

Tanks were still vulnerable to anti-tank weapons but the rolling Somme countryside was ideal in the dry summer months. Supply tanks reduced the amount of manpower needed to carry ammunition and supplies forward by a huge amount. They were also used, with limited success, to carry machine-gun teams forward. Mobile howitzers were also tried for the first time.

A standard tactic was for heavy artillery to target villages and woods while the infantry outflanked the enemy behind the field artillery's creeping barrage. They then spread out beyond the held area to cut the Germans' escape route. Tanks and machine-gun teams had been pouring fire into the held area from the flanks until the moppers-up moved in.

Reconnaissance and Exploitation

There was hope that the Cavalry Corps could exploit a break-in, using the faster moving Whippet tanks to provide fire support. As early as 8 August it had been realised that horse and machine moved at different speeds and were unable to work together efficiently. The main use for the cavalry was still reconnaissance and regiments were often used to find the new German positions following a withdrawal.

German Tactics

The German commanders found it difficult to defend in the open. Reinforcements were being 'thrown piecemeal into the fight and into the mix-up of the units' because there was no time to deploy properly. 'The infantry of some divisions had had to go into action straight off lorries, while their artillery had been sent to some other part of the line. Units were very badly mixed up.'

Ludendorff recognised that open warfare meant the German soldier had to come up with 'well thought out defensive measures... The enemy has naturally the intention of destroying our reserves. We only can escape this by accepting the attack solely where the ground offers favourable conditions for defence. When this condition is not present, we must retire sector by sector according to a definite plan.'

Once in open terrain, there were few trenches to defend. Villages and woods turned out to be shell traps, leaving the German soldier hiding in shell craters or under camouflage. The fast moving battles meant their artillery could only fire on map targets with confidence. They had few tanks of their own, so they had to rely on semi-static anti-tank guns and mobile anti-tank rifle teams to tackle the British ones.

The backbone of the German defence turned out to be the machine-gun team and they were deployed in a 'pepper pot' formation. Many were deployed ahead of the main line of resistance, to avoid the British barrages. They would lie in wait under camouflage until the tanks had passed and then target the infantry who were following.

Often parties of infantry 'equipped with machine guns, trench mortars, demolition charges, smoke producers, rifle-grenades and bombs' had to work their way around the machine-gunners before they could silence them. But usually the riflemen fled or surrendered as soon as their nearest machine gun had been silenced.

The Germans withdrew 7 miles back towards the Drocourt–Quéant Line opposite First Army between 30 August and 1 September. On one day alone they retired 5 miles towards the Canal du Nord opposite Third Army. Fourth Army had also moved forward 8 miles to the River Somme in just three days. The rapid advances were encouraging but they also put enormous strains on the lorries and horses hauling ammunition and supplies from the railheads to the British forward dumps. 'Although enormous strides had been made to rebuild the railways, they were still many miles behind and completed work was frequently destroyed by delayed-action mines… The roads had suffered considerably, both from shell fire and neglect, and with the enormous lorry traffic upon them were, in most cases, nothing but broken track with a rough stone surface.'

The Canadian Corps then had to break the Drocourt–Quéant Line. Lieutenant General Arthur Currie wrote, 'It is a question of whether our victory of 8 August is the greatest, but I am inclined to think that yesterday's was.' He believed it 'one of the finest performances in all the war'. (No mention of Vimy Ridge).

The Canadians broke the vital hinge which connected the defensive system north of Arras and the Hindenburg Line on 2 September. It forced Ludendorff to order the withdrawal to the Canal du Nord, just 'one of the disagreeable decisions forced upon the High Command in the first week of September.'

It made strategic sense for Prince Rupprecht's Army Group to retire, but pulling back such huge distances posed many tactical problems. The Germans had taken several months to plan and execute the last long withdrawal during the winter of 1916-17 but this time they only had a matter of days to organise it.

The Germans were very short of lorries by this stage of the war, so they were reliant on horses to haul guns and ammunition to the rear. Their engineers blocked the roads with mine craters, booby traps and felled trees as soon as the last wagon had passed. They also ripped up the railway lines to stop the Allies using them. All the time Byng's and Rawlinson's men were probing the German line, so the tired German soldiers could not rest:

> 'The enemy tried every method to work forward close to the front, especially by night, and there were some stiff bomb fights. Even if one's own front was quiet, that of one's neighbour was seething. Consequently we were everlastingly on the *qui vive* and in a perpetual state of being alarmed and standing to. Nearly all the available effectives were required for reconnaissance and outpost duties. Company commanders had to exercise much skill to give their men the sleep that was necessary for them. Every morning it could be seen that the enemy had got closer. Losses weakened the already small companies.'

The Hindenburg Line

Rawlinson thought Fourth Army faced six lines of defence. The first three had been built by Fifth Army over the winter of 1917-18 and while the trenches were looking the wrong way, they would slow his troops down. But Rawlinson's biggest concern were the three trenches of the Hindenburg Line. The Outpost Line, the Main Line and the Reserve Line based around the St Quentin Canal between Vendhuille, Bellicourt and Bellenglise. He wanted to 'hustle' the Germans from the British trenches but he also needed to conserve as many men, guns and tanks as possible for the attack on the Hindenburg Line.

Rearguards kept the Allied troops at bay between 4 and 7 September while their comrades fell back to find the Hindenburg Line. But it was very different to the one built over the winter of 1916-17 because it now incorporated the old British trench lines. They also found that the original Hindenburg Line had 'been reconditioned' and that 'a great quantity of artillery' was ready. Allied patrols discovered German outposts in the old British reserve trench around Jeancourt, Maissemy and Holnon. The First Line of Resistance, or *Haupt Widerstands Leitung 1* (HWL1), was based on the main British trench around 1 mile behind. The British outpost line was the HWL2 line, while the Hindenburg outpost line was the HWL3.

Hindenburg and Ludendorff met the chiefs of the general staffs of the three army groups on 6 September to outline the gravity of the situation and express their dissatisfaction with the troops on the defensive. They all agreed a new defensive position was required in case the Hindenburg Line was breached. The *Hermann Line* would be 20 miles behind Prince Rupprecht's Army Group. It would run from the Dutch frontier, east of Bruges, down the Eeklo Canal, south to the Lys, then upstream east of Courtrai, before following the Scheldt to south-west of Valenciennes. The *Hunding-Brunhild Line* would run in a south-east direction from Laon to Verdun behind the Boehm army group and the Crown Prince's army group. Major General Fritz von Lossberg, chief of staff of Boehn's army group, suggested building it along a straighter line which ran north-west between Antwerp and the River Meuse. It would reduce the front line by 45 miles but it increased the withdrawal to 80 miles. Ludendorff rejected the idea out of hand.

The problem was, it would require tens of thousands of labourers to build a new defensive line measuring some 175 miles from end to end and the German army did not have them. Instead Ludendorff had to agree that infantry battalions could disband one of their companies to provide reinforcements for the other three.

By 9 September, Lieutenant Colonel Wilhelm Wetzell, chief of OHL's Operations Section, had had enough of Ludendorff's interfering ways. He was supposed to be advising on strategy but his ideas were often ignored. Major Walter Bronsart von Schellendorf was given the difficult task of advising Ludendorff during the final weeks of the war.

Index

Ablaincourt, 133
Ablainzevelle, 79
Achiet-le-Grand, 80–1, 100
Achiet-le-Petit, 78–9, 81
Aisne, River, 8, 18–19, 21, 23, 189, 195
Aizecourt-le-Bas, 183–4
Aizecourt-la-Haut, 184
Albert, 26, 68, 73, 85–6, 104, 109
Albert, King of the Belgians, 72
American Expeditionary Force, 70
Amiens, 1, 21–3, 26
Amiens Defence Line, 34–6, 40–2, 44,
    46–8, 51–2, 54–5, 58–60, 62, 65, 68, 196
Armentières, 191, 193
Arras, 25, 65–6, 68, 71–3, 94, 199
Arras-Albert railway, 73, 76, 78
Assevillers, 130, 132
Aubercourt, 42–3
Auchy-lez-La-Bassée, 193
Authuille Wood, 85, 107
Australian Expeditionary Force
Corps, 3–6, 21–2, 25, 33–41, 49, 51, 54–60,
    68, 72, 85, 89–92, 109, 111–14, 129–33,
    147–52, 167, 170–2, 182, 185–8, 188
Divisions,
    1st Australian, 36, 55, 58–60, 89–90,
        112–13, 185
    2nd Australian, 33–6, 55–9, 130–2,
        148–51, 170–2
    3rd Australian, 34–5, 55–6, 89, 111–12,
        129–30, 147–8, 170, 185
    4th Australian, 4, 36–8, 54–5, 108, 185
    5th Australian, 4, 36, 38–40, 55–6,
        58–60, 130, 132, 150–2, 170–2, 185
Battalions,
    1st, 90
    3rd, 112
    3rd Pioneer, 89, 185
    4th, 112
    5th, 60, 90
    6th, 60, 90

7th, 90
8th, 59–60, 90
9th, 60, 90
10th, 60
11th, 59–60
12th, 90, 112
13th, 37
14th, 37
15th, 5, 37, 58
16th, 5, 38
17th, 35, 58, 148, 150
18th, 35, 129, 132, 148
19th, 35, 58, 148, 150
20th, 35, 58, 148, 150
21st, 5, 129, 150
22nd, 129
23rd, 5, 129, 150
24th, 129, 150
25th, 58, 170
26th, 35, 58, 129, 148, 170
27th, 35, 58, 170
28th, 35, 58–9, 129, 170
29th, 58, 132, 185
30th, 39, 132
31st, 39, 185
32nd, 39, 129, 132
33rd, 89, 148
34th, 34, 129, 147
35th, 34, 89, 129
37th, 56, 111–12, 147
38th, 56, 112, 129
39th, 34, 112
40th, 56, 111–12, 147
41st, 34, 112, 129, 148, 185
42nd, 5, 34, 112, 148, 185
43rd, 5, 56, 112, 148, 170
44th, 5, 34, 112, 129, 185
45th, 37
46th, 37
48th, 38
49th, 55

50th, 55–6
51st, 55–6
53rd, 151
54th, 151, 172
55th, 172
56th, 172
57th, 39, 151
58th, 39, 59, 151, 172
59th, 39, 90, 151
60th, 59
Aveluy, 83, 85
Avesnes, 100–102, 146–7, 184
Avre, River, 21, 24, 47, 49
Ayette, 73, 75

Bailleul, 192
Bancourt, 141–2, 164
Bapaume, 68, 71, 93, 95, 100–105, 114, 119, 122–6, 140–1, 147, 159, 163
Barleux, 132
Barnes, Maj Gen Reginald, 120, 175
Bayonvillers, 36, 38–40
Bazentin-le-Grand, 108
Beaucourt, 71, 83
Beaucourt-en-Santerre, 45–7, 66, 71
Beaulencourt, 125, 143, 166
Beaumetz, 161–2
Bernafay Wood, 109, 127–8
Beugnâtre, 101–103
Beauregard Dovecot, 82–3
Bécordel, 87, 109
Bécourt, 86, 109
Béhagnies, 78, 99
Belgian Army, 72, 193
Belloy-en-Santerre, 132
Below, Gen Otto von 73
Bernes, 185
Berthelot, Gen Henri, 9–10
Béthune, 8, 21, 189–90, 193
Béthune coalfields, 8, 21
Beugneux, 17–18
Beugny, 123, 141, 162–4
Biaches, 131, 148, 151
Biefvillers, 81, 100–102
Bihucourt, 81
Birdwood, Gen Sir William, 189
Boehn, Gen Max von, 10, 201

Boiry Becquerelle, 74–5
Boiry Notre Dame, 116, 117
Bois d'Hartennes, 18
Bois de Courton, 11, 13–14
Bois de Reims, 13
Bois de Reugny, 17
Bois l'Abbé, 29
Borderland, Operation, 2
Bouchavesnes, 147, 147
Bouchoir, 65–6
Bouilly, 13
Boyelles, 75–6
Blacklock, Maj Gen Cyril, 159
Braches, 47
Bray-sur-Somme, 51, 54, 89
Brie, 132, 147, 152, 172, 186
Brioche, 39
British Expeditionary Force
Armies
    First, 1, 21–2, 26, 65, 69, 71–2, 93–5, 108, 115–19, 135–8, 152–9, 175, 193, 199
    Second, 7, 26, 189, 192–3
    Third, xi, 7, 22, 26, 68–9, 71–2, 73–85, 92–3, 95–108, 114, 119–27, 136, 138–44, 152, 157, 159–67, 172, 175–82, 196, 199
    Fourth, ix, 6–7, 22–7, 29–49, 51–69, 70–2, 85–93, 108–14, 127–33, 144–52, 167–72, 182–8, 195–6, 199–200
    Fifth, 189, 193, 200
Corps
    III, 22, 25, 29–33, 49, 51–5, 83, 85–9, 109–12, 127–9, 144–7, 167–70, 182–5
    IV, 73, 78–83, 95, 100–105, 122–6, 141–3, 162–55, 176–9
    V, 83–5, 95, 104–108, 125–8, 140, 143–4, 165–7, 179–81
    VI, 74–8, 95–100, 121–3, 137, 139–40, 161–3, 175–7, 181
    VII, 116
    VIII, 93, 115–16
    IX, 47, 69, 182, 188, 190
    XI, 1–3, 189
    XIII, 189–90
    XV, 6–7
    XVII, 95, 119–21, 137–8, 153,

159–61, 175
XXII, 10, 54, 115, 122, 153, 195
Cavalry, 21, 51, 135, 153, 198

Divisions
Guards, 74–5, 97–100, 121–2, 162
2nd, 75–6, 78, 97, 99, 161–2, 176
3rd, 35, 76–8, 139–40, 161, 163
5th 78, 79–82, 101, 123–4, 141, 163–4
6th, 193
8th, 115
9th, 6–7, 190–1
12th, 21, 38, 52, 109–11, 128–9, 146,
    182–3
15th, 15, 18–19
17th, 84–5, 105–107, 125–6, 143, 165–6,
    179
18th, 27–8, 31, 109, 111, 127–8, 143,
    145, 167, 182
21st, 83–4, 104–106, 125, 142–3, 165–6,
    180–1, 183
29th, 190–1
31st, 191
32nd, 41, 60, 66–7, 90–2, 113, 132–3,
    151–2, 172, 185–8
34th, 16–17, 18
36th, 193
37th, 79, 81, 100–101, 164, 176
38th, 105–108, 126–8, 143–4, 146,
    165–6, 180
41st, 193
42nd, 82–3, 104–105, 125, 141,
    165, 179
47th, 109, 111, 129, 146, 167–9, 183–4
51st, 11–13, 93, 115–16
52nd, 74, 96–7, 119, 138, 159–61
55th, 193
56th, 75, 96–7, 119–21, 137–9
57th, 119–21, 137, 159, 175
58th, 27, 30, 52–5, 111–12, 129, 146–7,
    183, 185
59th, 74
62nd, 13–14, 99–100, 122, 140–1, 161–3
63rd, 78–9, 103–104, 125, 159–61, 175
2nd Cavalry, 67, 95
3rd Cavalry, 47–8, 68

Infantry Battalions
Argylls,

5th, 17–18
1/7th, 11, 13, 115
10th, 66, 90, 188
Bedfords,
1st, 81, 163, 164
2nd, 27–8, 86, 109
7th, 128
Berkshires,
1st, 99, 176
5th, 32–3, 52, 75, 87, 110, 183
8th, 32, 109, 127–8, 167
Black Watch,
4/5th, 15
1/6th, 11, 13, 93, 115
1/7th, 11, 93, 115
8th, 7
14th, 169, 185
Border Regiment,
1st, 191
1/5th, 66, 91, 186
7th, 126, 179
Buffs,
6th, 52, 87, 110, 129, 183
7th, 32, 86, 109, 146
10th, 184
Cambridgeshire,
1/1st, 31, 52, 87, 110–11, 129, 183
Camerons,
5th, 7
6th, 15, 18
Cheshires,
1st, 79, 141, 163
1/4th, 18
7th, 17
Coldstream Guards,
1st, 74–5
2nd, 99, 121
Devons,
1st, 79, 82, 123
5th, 13–14, 122, 141
16th, 169, 185
Dorsets,
1st, 67, 187
6th, 85, 105, 125, 166
Duke of Wellington's,
2/4th, 140
2/5th, 140

Durhams,
  2nd, 135
  2/4th, 14, 100, 139
  5th, 13, 100, 122
  9th, 143, 166
East Lancashires,
  1/5th, 125, 143
  11th, 2
East Surreys,
  1st, 79–80, 82
  8th, 27–8, 86, 109, 145–6
East Yorkshires,
  1st, 83, 104, 165
  7th, 85, 105, 125, 166, 179
  10th, 2
  11th, 2
Essex,
  1st, 81
  2nd, 153
  9th, 31, 52, 87, 129, 182–3
  10th, 31–3, 86, 128, 167
Gloucesters,
  12th, 3, 80–2
Gordons,
  1st, 77, 139
  1/4th, 11, 115
  1/4th, 11
  1/5th, 15
  6th, 115
  1/7th, 11, 13, 115
Grenadier Guards,
  1st, 75, 97, 99
  2nd, 99, 122
  3rd, 74–5, 163
Hampshires,
  1st, 154
  2/4th, 14, 100, 122
Hertfords,
  1/1st, 17–18, 79, 81, 176
Highland Light Infantry (HLI),
  2nd, 78, 99, 176
  1/5th, 96, 119
  1/6th, 96, 119
  1/7th, 119
  15th, 67, 133, 186
Irish Guards,
  1st, 122, 176

Irish Regiment,
  2nd, 79, 103, 159–60
King's,
  1st, 78, 99, 176
  2/6th, 137
  2/7th, 137
  8th, 137
  1/9th, 120
  13th, 77
King's Own,
  1st 153–4
  2/5th, 120
  8th, 77
KOSBs,
  1st, 190–1
  2nd, 3, 101
  1/4th, 96, 138
  1/5th, 17, 18
  6th, 190
  7/8th, 15
KOYLIs,
  2nd, 67, 90–1, 186, 188
  2/4th, 13–14, 122, 163
  5th, 12, 14, 100, 122, 163
  9th, 104
King's Royal Rifle Corps (KRRC),
  1st, 78, 162
  13th, 81, 105
Lancashire Fusiliers,
  2nd, 154
  1/5th, 82, 179
  1/7th, 83, 179
  1/8th, 83, 165
  10th, 107, 143, 179
  15th, 66–7
  16th, 66–7, 92
Leicesters,
  6th, 83, 143, 181
  7th, 83, 143, 165, 181
Lincolns,
  1st, 105
  2nd, 105
  7th, 179
  8th, 100–101
London,
  1/1st, 96, 137
  2nd, 121

2/2nd, 33, 54, 97, 111, 183
3rd, 33, 54, 111, 183
1/4th, 75, 111, 137
2/4th, 33, 54, 111, 183
5th, 121
6th, 33, 53, 146
7th, 33, 53–4, 111, 183
8th, 27, 146, 183
9th, 33, 54, 111
2/10th, 33, 53
12th, 54, 111
1/13th, 75, 121, 138
1/14th, 75, 121, 138
1/15th, 111, 169
1/16th, 121
1/17th, 169
1/18th, 111, 146, 169
1/19th, 88, 146
1/20th, 88
2/20th, 140–1
1/21st, 111
1/22nd, 88, 146, 168
1/23rd, 88, 146
1/24th, 88, 146, 167
Loyals,
    1/5th, 175
    2nd, 17–18
    2/4th, 120, 137, 175
Manchesters,
    2nd, 67, 132
    1/5th, 104, 165
    1/6th, 104, 125, 165
    1/7th, 83, 104, 125, 165
    8th, 125
    1/10th, 83, 143
    12th, 107, 125, 143, 166, 179
Middlesex,
    4th, 101
    7th, 96, 137
    8th, 96–7, 121
Munsters,
    1st, 159
Norfolks,
    1st, 81, 141, 163
    7th, 31, 87, 110, 182, 183
    12th, 191
Northants,

6th, 27–8, 86, 109, 128
Northumberland Fusiliers,
    1st, 77, 140
    13th, 83, 105
Ox and Bucks,
    2nd, 99, 176
    2/4th, 193
Queen's,
    2/4th, 17–18
    6th, 52, 109–10, 129
    7th, 146
Queen's Own,
    1st, 3, 82
    6th, 52, 88, 109, 128, 183
    7th, 27, 31–2, 109, 127–8, 146, 167
Rifle Brigade,
    1st, 135, 142
    13th, 81, 101
Royal Fusiliers,
    2nd, 191
    4th, 77, 140
    9th, 31–2, 52, 87, 110, 129, 183
    10th, 81, 101
    11th, 28, 81, 86, 109, 145
    13th, 79, 81, 176
    17th, 162
    23rd, 73, 75, 99, 162
    24th, 78, 99
Royal Scots,
    1st, 77
    2nd, 77, 161
    1/4th, 74, 119, 160
    5/6th, 67, 133, 152, 186
    1/7th, 96, 119, 161
    9th, 18
    11th, 190
    13th, 18
Scots Fusiliers,
    1st, 77, 161
    2nd, 7
    4th, 160
    5th, 96, 138
Scots Guards,
    1st, 75
    2nd, 97, 99, 163, 176
Scottish Rifles
    1/7th, 74, 96, 160

1/8th, 17–18
9th, 190
10th, 15, 18
Seaforths,
    2nd, 135
    1/4th, 11
    1/5th, 11, 13
    6th, 13
    8th, 15
Shropshires,
    1st, 161
    7th, 77
    10th, 184
Somersets,
    1st, 135, 154
    2/4th, 17
    8th, 81, 101
    12th, 169
South Lancashires,
    2/4th, 120, 159
South Staffords,
    2nd, 78
South Wales Borderers,
    2nd, 191
    10th, 85, 107–108, 127, 143, 167
Suffolks,
    2nd, 77, 139, 161
    15th, 184
Sussex,
    4th, 17–18
    7th, 31, 52, 87, 109–10, 183
    16th, 170, 184
    XXII Corps Battalion, 183–4
Warwicks,
    1st, 135
    14th, 82
    15th, 3, 82
    16th, 79, 81, 141, 164
Welsh,
    13th, 180
    14th, 85, 107, 180
    15th, 85, 107
    24th, 184
Welsh Fusiliers,
    2nd, 85, 107–108, 143, 165, 167
    4th, 167–8
    13th, 85, 108, 144

14th, 85, 101, 108, 167
16th, 107–108, 127, 143–4
17th, 85, 107–108, 127, 143
25th, 184–5
Welsh Guards,
    1st, 79, 99, 163, 176
West Yorkshires,
    2/5th, 13–14
    8th, 11, 13–14, 122, 140–1
    10th, 85, 105, 107, 125, 166, 179
    17th, 2
Wiltshires,
    1st, 143
York and Lancasters,
    2/4th, 13–14, 100, 162
Cavalry Regiments
1/1st Northumberland Hussars, 88, 109,
    183–4
2nd Dragoon Guards (Queen's Bays),
    39–40
2nd Dragoons (Royal Scots Greys), 66, 165
5th Lancers, 63
7th Dragoon Guards, 48
9th Lancers, 61
13th Australian Light Horse, 185
15th Hussars, 42
16th Lancers, 62
19th Hussars, 42
17th Lancers, 48
Royal Canadian Dragoons, 48
Lord Strathcona's Horse, 48

Bruce-Williams, Maj Gen Hugh, 79,
    100–101
Brutinel's Independent Force, 45, 47–8,
    65, 138
Bucquoy, 69, 71, 79
Buissy Switch, 153, 156–7
Bullecourt, 95, 120–1, 137–9
Bussu, 184
Butler, Lt Gen Richard, 22, 29–31, 51,
    54, 109
Buzancy, 10, 15, 19
Byng, Gen Julian, 22, 69, 71–3, 81, 92–3,
    95, 104, 119, 135, 138, 141, 159, 172,
    181, 200

Campbell, Maj Gen David, 104, 125, 143, 180

Canadian Expeditionary Force, xiv, 21–2, 25–6, 34, 41–9, 60–9, 71, 93–5, 108, 116, 119, 135–7, 153–9, 172, 175, 196, 199

Divisions,
1st Canadian, 41–4, 61–5, 119, 136–7, 156–7
2nd Canadian, 41–2, 61, 95–6, 117–18
3rd Canadian, 41, 44–5, 47, 60, 64–6, 67, 94–5, 116–17
4th Canadian, 41, 44–6, 61, 63–6, 108, 135, 154–7

Battalions,
1st, 63, 136–7
2nd, 44, 63, 136
3rd, 44, 63, 136
4th, 44, 63, 137
5th, 62, 137, 156
6th, 63
7th, 44, 156
8th, 62–3, 137, 156
10th, 44, 156
13th, 42–3, 64, 156
14th, 42–3, 137, 156
16th, 43, 156
18th, 42, 117
19th, 41, 64
20th, 95
21st, 42, 95
22nd, 61, 117–18
24th, 42, 117–18
25th, 61
26th, 42, 117
27th, 61, 95
28th, 61, 95
29th, 42, 61
31st, 42, 61
38th, 46, 64, 155
42nd, 45, 64, 117
43rd, 45, 117
44th, 63, 156
46th, 63, 154
47th, 63, 154
49th, 45, 117
50th, 64, 154

52nd, 64, 116–17
54th, 47, 156
58th, 45, 116–17
72nd, 63
75th, 47, 65, 156
78th, 46, 63–4, 154–6
85th, 63
87th, 65, 156
102nd, 47
116th, 45, 64, 116–17
1st Mounted Rifles, 44, 66, 94
2nd Mounted Rifles, 44, 66
4th Mounted Rifles, 66, 94, 117
5th Mounted Rifles, 66, 94–5, 117
PPCLI, 64, 95, 117
Royal Canadian Regiment, 45, 95

Canal du Nord, 132–3, 138, 141, 145–8, 150, 152–3, 157–8, 160–7, 169–70, 172, 175–82, 184, 199
Cappy, 90, 112
Carnoy, 109–11
Carter-Campbell, Maj Gen George, 11, 93
Cayeux-en-Santerre, 44, 48
Châlons, 21
Channel ports, 1, 7, 21
Chapel Hill, 95, 180–1
Chaumuzy, 11, 13
Chaulnes, 22, 27, 51
Chaulnes railway, 34, 40–1
Chérisy, 95, 117
Chuignes, 89–90, 112
Chuignolles, 40, 54, 89–90
Cité Ste Elie, 193
Cizancourt, 133, 152, 187
Cérisy, 30, 33–5, 37, 39, 89
Chilly, 63–5
Chipilly, 33, 37, 54
Chipilly spur, 22, 32–3, 38–9, 51–2, 54–5
Cléry, 130, 132, 147–8, 151
Cojeul stream, 74, 95–6, 117, 119
Combles, 70, 125, 127, 129, 144–5
Courcelles, 44–5, 75–8
Courdoux, 17
Croisilles, 96–7, 119–21
Crown Prince Rupprecht, 1, 10, 23–5, 152, 189, 196, 200–201
Crown Prince, 15, 201

Currie, Lt Gen Arthur, 22, 29, 41, 51, 55, 60, 65, 67–8, 93–4, 135, 145, 153, 175, 199
Curlu, 129–30, 184

Damery, 64–8
Debeney, Gen Marie-Eugène, 21–2, 47, 49, 69, 71, 92
Degoutte, Gen Jean, 10, 193
Delville Wood, 108, 125–8
Démuin, 44–5
Dernancourt, 51, 86
Deutsche Luftstreitkräfte *see* German Air Force
Domart, 27, 44–5
Drocourt-Quéant Line, xi, 93, 119, 135–8, 152–7, 159–60, 172, 199
D-Q Line *see* Drocourt-Quéant Line
Dury, 154–7

Eastern Front, 21
Eaucourt l'Abbaye, 104–105, 107
Écoust-Saint-Menin, 122, 138–9
Équancourt, 179
Erquinghem, 193
Ervillers, 75–7
Espilly, 11
Estrées, 132
Étaing, 135, 154
Éterpigny, 132, 135, 147, 153, 154, 156, 185
Étinehem, 55–6
Étricourt, 166–7, 179–80

Favière Wood, 128–9
Favreuil, 99–102
Fay, 132
Feuillaucourt, 132, 148–50
Feuillères, 130, 132, 148, 151
Final Preparations, 8 August, 24–7
Fins, 179–80
Flechin, 185
Flers, 126, 143–4, 152, 165–6
Flixecourt, 22
Fontaine-les-Cappy, 113
Fontaine-lez-Croisilles, 119
Fouquescourt, 61, 63–4, 66–7
Framerville, 40, 56, 58

Fransart, 63–4
Frémicourt, 123, 141–2, 152, 164
French Army
Armies,
  First, 21, 27, 29, 49, 47, 68, 71, 92, 127, 133, 182, 195
  Third, 9, 22
  Fourth, 9
  Fifth, 9–10
  Ninth, 10
  Tenth, 10, 15, 65, 69, 72–3
Corps,
  X, 69
  XXXI, 21, 47
Fresnoy, 47–8, 65
Friedensturm, Operation *see* Peace Storm, Operation
Frise, 112, 130

Gavrelle, 93, 115
Gellibrand, Maj Gen John, 55, 89, 111–12, 130, 147, 185
Génermont, 133
George V, King, 72
German Armies
  First, 9
  Second, 24, 27, 68, 70, 127, 196
  Third, 9
  Fourth, 192
  Sixth, 189–90, 192
  Seventh, 9–10
  Ninth, 70, 172
  Seventeenth, 24, 68, 73, 172
  Eighteenth, 27–8, 49, 69–70, 127, 172
German Air Force, 27, 49
German reaction, 8 August, 49
German Supreme Army Command, 1, 21, 23–4, 70, 92, 114, 195, 201
Glasgow, Maj Gen William, 59–60, 63, 90, 112
Godley, Lt Gen Sir Alexander, 9–10, 54, 85, 127, 144–5, 167, 170, 182
Gomiécourt, 75–8
Gourard, Gen Henri, 9
Gouzeaucourt, 138, 176, 178–9, 181
Goyencourt, 65, 68
Grand Rozoy, 17–18

Grandcourt, 83, 104–105
Greenland Hill, 93, 115–16
Gressaire Wood, 31–3, 53–4
Grévillers, 81, 101, 103
Guémappe, 95
Gueudecourt, 125–6
Guillaucourt, 41–2

Haig, FM Sir Douglas, 1, 5, 7–8, 21–3,
    49, 54, 68–73, 77, 85, 92, 127, 133, 152,
    181–2, 193, 196
Hagen, Operation, 1, 10, 189
Haldane, Lt Ge Sir Aylmer, 74, 77, 95, 121,
    139, 161, 175
Halle, 132, 148
Hallu, 63–4
Ham, 127
Hamel, 71, 83
Hamelincourt, 74–5
Hangard Wood, 41–2
Happy Valley, 87–8, 109, 111
Harbonnières, 36–40, 59
Hardecourt-aux-Bois, 127–9
Harper, Lt Gen Montague, 78, 81, 100,
    104, 122, 141, 163, 176
Hartennes, 16
Haucourt, 117, 137
Haut Allaines, 169–70
Havrincourt Wood, 138, 176–8
Hazebrouck, 1, 7, 189
Hénin, 74, 95-8, 119
Hendecourt, 119–21, 137, 157
Herbécourt, 130
Herleville, 58, 90–1, 132
Hervilly, 185
Hesbécourt, 185
Heudicourt, 179–80, 183
Higginson, Maj Gen Harold, 52, 86,
    109–10, 128–9, 182–3
High Wood, 107–109
Hindenburg, FM Paul von, 1
Hintze, Adml Paul von, 10
Hobbs, Maj Gen Sir Talbot, 4, 38–40, 58,
    60, 151, 171, 180, 185
hole-boring, 94
Holnon Wood, 182, 187–8
Horgny, 133

Horne, Gen Sir Henry, 1, 71, 74, 93–4,
    135, 153, 172
Humbert, Gen Georges, 22
Hutier, Gen Oskar von Hutier, 28, 49, 127

Ignaucourt, 44–5, 48
Inchy, 159–60, 163, 175
Irles, 79–80, 82, 100

Jeancourt, 185, 201

Kaiser Wilhelm II, 70, 114, 152
Kavanagh, Lt Gen Charles, 153
Kuhl, Gen Hermann von, 23

La Bassée, 192
La Bassée Canal, 189
La Becque, 1–3, 190
La Boisselle, 85, 107, 109
La Chavatte, 64, 67
La Neuville, 47, 56
Lagnicourt, 157, 161–3
Lambert, Maj Gen Thomas, 66–7, 69,
    132–3, 152, 185
Lamotte-en-Santerre, 34–5
Lawrence, Lt Gen Sir Herbert, 7, 9, 71
Lawrie, Maj Gen Charles, 79, 103–104
Le Hamel, 3–6, 198
Le Transloy, 125, 144
Le Quesnel, xiv, 47–8, 65–6
Le Quesnoy, 65–6
Lesboeufs, 126–7, 144
Liéramont, 183–4
Ligny-Thilloy, 103, 107, 125, 127
Lihons, 57, 59–60, 63, 92, 108
Ligny-Thilloy, 103, 107, 125–6
Lisle, Lt Gen Beaurevoir de, 6, 190
Logeast Wood, 79
Longavesnes, 184
Longatte, 139–40
Lossberg, Maj Gen Fritz von, 20, 201
Luce steam, 22, 41, 43–5, 48, 61
Ludendorff, Gen Erich, 1, 10, 23–5, 152,
    189, 200–201
Lys, River, 6, 16, 24, 119, 173, 189–90,
    192–3, 201

Malard Wood, 33, 54
Mametz, 108, 110
Manancourt, 167, 179–80
Mangin, Gen Charles, 10, 15
Marchelepot, 133
Marcelcave, 35, 39, 41, 43
Marfaux, 11, 13
Maricourt, 111–12, 129, 162
Marwitz, Gen Georg von der, 24, 28, 49, 119
Matz, River, 1, 69
Marne, River, ix, xii–xiii, 1, 7, 9, 12, 16–17, 21–2, 195
Marne salient, 23, 47, 195
Marrières Wood, 146
Martenville, 187
Méaulte, 52, 86–7
Méharicourt, 61, 63
Mercatel, 74
Méricourt, 28, 30, 38, 56
Merville, 190, 192
Messines, 193
Meteren, 6–7, 190
Mézières, 44–5, 47
Milner, Lord Alfred, 92
Miraumont, 78, 80, 82–3, 100, 104–105
Misery, 133
Moeuvres, 160, 163, 175–6
Moislains, 146, 167–9, 183
Mons-en-Chaussée, 187
Monchy-le-Preux, 94–5, 114–16
Mont de Bligny, 11, 13–14
Mont Kemmel, 192
Mont St Quentin, 132, 147–52, 170, 172
Montauban, 109–11
Montdidier, 22, 69
Morchies, 161–3
Morcourt, 36–40
Moreuil, 45, 47
Morisel, 47
Morlancourt, 27, 30–1, 52–3, 87
Morval, 125, 127, 143–5
Mory, 75, 78, 97, 99–100, 122
Moyenneville, 74–5

Nancy, 21
Nesle, 35, 60–1, 67, 133
Neuve Chapelle, 193

Neuville Bourjonval, 179
Neuville Vitasse, 94–5
New Zealand Division, 80, 82–3, 101–103, 124–5, 141–3, 164–5, 177–9
New Zealand Infantry Battalions,
2nd Auckland, 101, 142–3
1st Canterbury, 164
2nd Canterbury, 177–8
1st Otago, 178
2nd Otago, 164
Otago Mounted Rifles, 178
1st Rifle Brigade, 142
2nd Rifle Brigade, 178
3rd Rifle Brigade, 82, 125
4th Rifle Brigade, 82, 178
1st Wellington, 101, 142–3
Nieppe Forest, 2–3
Noreuil, 139, 161
Noyon, 69–70, 133
Nurlu, 182–4

Oberste Heeresleitung (or OHL) *see* German Supreme Army Command
Ommiécourt, 132, 148
Oppy, 115
Oulchy-le-Château, 10
Outtersteene, 190–2
Ovillers, 106–108

Pacaut, 189–90
Parvillers, 64–7
Peace Storm, Operation, 8–10
Peaceful Penetration, 3, 146, 185
Peizières, 181, 183–4
Pelves, 117
Péronne, 27, 70–1, 114, 127, 131–3, 147, 149–52, 167, 171–2, 185
Planning, 8 August, 22–3
Ploegsteert Wood, 193
Plouvain, 116
Plumer, Gen Sir Herbert, 189, 193
Ponsonby, Maj Gen John, 80, 82, 123, 164
Pozières, 106–108, 173
Preliminaries, 8 August, 21–2
Pronville, 157, 159–61, 163
Proyart, 36, 38, 40, 56, 58, 92
Puisieux, 71, 82

Quéant, 157, 159–61

Ramsey, Maj Gen Frank, 33, 52, 54, 111
Rancourt, 145–6
Rainecourt, 40, 56, 58
Rawlinson, Gen Sir Henry, 3, 5, 21–4, 49,
    51, 55, 60, 64, 68, 71, 85, 89, 92, 108, 112,
    127, 133, 144, 147, 150, 172, 182, 200
Reed VC, Maj Gen Hamilton, 15, 18–19
Reims, 8–10, 13, 15, 195
Remy, 117
Riencourt, 119–20, 125, 135, 137, 141–3,
    157, 159–60
Rocquigny, 142, 166
Roeux, 93, 115
Rosières, 61
Rouvroy–Fresnes Line, 117–18
Roye, 22, 51, 68, 69
Roye road, 41–2, 44–5, 47–8, 67–8
Ruyaulcourt, 164–5

Sailly-Lorette, 30
Sailly Saillisel, 142, 144, 146, 166
St Christ, 172, 187
St Léger, 97–9, 121
St Martin, 74, 96
St Mihiel salient, 21, 70
St Pierre Vaast Wood, 145–6, 167–8
St Quentin, 35, 58, 112, 132, 187–8
St Quentin Canal, 144, 200
Sainte Emilie, 184, 185
Salmond, Maj Gen John, 48
Santerre plateau, 22
Sapignies, 78, 99, 101
Sauchy-Lestrée, 157
Scarpe, River, 93, 116, 135, 153–4
Sensée stream, 75, 97, 99, 117–18, 121,
    135, 153–4, 157–8, 175
Shute, Lt Gen Cameron, 83, 104–105, 107,
    125, 143, 165, 179
Sinclair-Maclagan, Maj Gen Ewen, 3, 37, 55
Smuts, Gen Jan, 8
Soissons, 15, 19, 72, 195
Somme, River, 3–4, 22, 32, 34, 48–9, 51,
    55, 70, 85, 88, 91, 114, 130, 172, 185, 199
Somme-Oise Canal, 70

Sorel-le-Grand, 180
South African composite battalion, 7
Stosstruppen, 1
Supreme War Council, xii, 7
Suzanne, 111–12

Thennes, 45
Thiepval ridge, 72, 83–4, 104–107
Thiepval wood, 85, 107
Thilloy, 102–104, 107, 125–6
Tigny, 19
Tincourt, 184–5
Trônes Wood, 127–8
Tudor, Maj Gen Hugh, 6, 190

Vauvillers, 39–40, 58–9
Vaux, 111
Vaux Wood, 112, 129, 167–9
Vaulx, 121, 138, 140, 163
Vaulx Vraucourt, 121, 123, 140, 152, 161–2
Vendelles, 185
Verdun, 70, 201
Vermandovillers, 133
Vesle, River, 18–19, 195
Vierstraat, 193
Vieux Berquin, 2, 190–1
Villemontoire, 18
Villers-au-Flos, 143, 165
Villers-aux-Érables, 45
Villers-lez-Cagnicourt, 155
Villers Bretonneux, 3, 28, 41
Villers Faucon, 184
Villers Guislain, 138, 181
Vis-en-Artois, 95, 117, 136–7
Vraignes, 185
Vraucourt, 121–2, 140
Vrély, 61–2

Wancourt, 95–6
War Cabinet, xii, 8, 24, 152
Warlencourt, Butte de, 105
Wilson, Gen Sir Henry, 152
Wiry-au-Mont, 23
Wotan Stellung, 93
Wytschaete, 193

Ytres, 165, 179